HOME OFFICE

NEW RELIGIOUS MOVEMENTS
A Practical Introduction

By
Eileen Barker
London School of Economics

LONDON: HMSO

For William Alexander Roxburgh
with love

HMSO publications are available from:

HMSO Publications Centre
(Mail, fax and telephone orders only)
PO Box 276, London, SW8 5DT
Telephone orders 071-873 9090
General enquiries 071-873 0011
(queuing system in operation for both numbers)
Fax orders 071-873 8200

HMSO Bookshops
49 High Holborn, London, WC1V 6HB
(counter service only)
071-873 0011 Fax 071-873 8200
258 Broad Street, Birmingham, B1 2HE
021-643 3740 Fax 021-643 6510
Southey House, 33 Wine Street, Bristol, BS1 2BQ
0272 264306 Fax 0272 294515
9-21 Princess Street, Manchester, M60 8AS
061-834 7201 Fax 061-833 0634
16 Arthur Street, Belfast, BT1 4GD
0232 238451 Fax 0232 235401
71 Lothian Road, Edinburgh, EH3 9AZ
031-228 4181 Fax 031-229 2734

HMSO's Accredited Agents
(see Yellow Pages)

and through good booksellers

Readers of this book are invited to respond by providing 'feed-back' through INFORM, Houghton Street, London WC2A 2AE. New religious movements are continually being formed, and those that have been around for some years are continually changing in character. Information needs constantly to be checked and up-dated – not only information about the beliefs and practices of the movements, but also information about the effects that their existence has on members of the society of which they are a part. All communications of a personal nature will, of course, be treated with utmost confidence.

Table of Contents

PART TWO
WHAT CAN BE DONE?

PREFACE

The impetus behind my writing this book is much the same as that behind my setting up of INFORM (the Information Network Focus on Religious Movements – see *Appendix I*). Both ventures came into being as the result of a conviction that a great deal of unnecessary suffering has resulted from ignorance of the nature and characteristics of the current wave of new religious movements (NRMs) in the West. This conviction is coupled with another – that there exists a considerable amount of information that could and should be made available to a wider audience. I hope the book will fill a gap by presenting information not readily available to the non-specialist in such a way that it can be of practical use.

Existing sources of information
Generally speaking, there are five sources of information about NRMs. First, there are the movements themselves. Information from this source is sometimes readily available and accurate, but there are numerous instances of its being unobtainable, selective or misleading.

Secondly, there is the extremely valuable information held by ex-members and the relatives and friends of members. This exhibits both the advantages and disadvantages of direct, personal knowledge, with one person's experiences not infrequently appearing to contradict the experiences of others. Such information is rarely accessible to those who might benefit from it. When it is more readily available, this is usually because the people concerned are prepared to talk to the media or have become involved in 'anti-cultist' activities; and the experiences of such people, although undoubtedly of value, have been shown by researchers to be atypical of the experiences of ex-members and relatives and friends in general.[1]

Thirdly, there are organisations that specialise in collecting information about NRMs. These vary enormously in the scope, the reliability and the accessibility of their information. Some, such as The Institute for the Study of American Religion,[2] the Graduate Theological Union Library

---

1. Beckford (1985); Lewis (n.d.); Shupe and Bromley (1980); Trudy Solomon "Integrating the 'Moonie' Experience: A Survey of Ex-Members of the Unification Church" in Robbins and Athony (ed) (1981); Wright (1987). See also Barker (1984), Chapter 6, for an account of the diversity of subjective reactions to a Unification 'workshop'.
2. P.O. Box 90709, Santa Barbara, CA 93190–0709, USA.

in Berkeley, California,[3] the Institut for Missionsteologi og Økumenisk Teologi at Aarhus University,[4] and the Centre for New Religions at King's College, London, are to be found in academic settings. Some of the organisations offer expertise in a special area: the Centre for New Religious Movements at the Selly Oak Colleges in Birmingham[5] has a unique collection of information about new religions in 'primal societies'; the Housetop Centre in London[6] can provide specialist counselling services; the Dialog Center in Denmark[7] places fundamental stress on Christian mission work.

There are several organisations that are concerned primarily to warn the public about the 'cults'. Much useful and accurate information can be obtained from such sources – from, for example, publications of an organisation such as the American Family Foundation.[8] But as, naturally enough, it is the more worrying aspects of the movements that such organisations are concerned about, this can sometimes result in a partisan and misleading picture being disseminated.

Associated with some 'cult-watching' groups are people who believe that it is their public duty 'to expose all cults as totally evil' and that any attempt to be objective or 'even-handed' is dangerous and irresponsible. Information emanating from such sources is, as a consequence, confined to that which will reinforce their position, with any contrary evidence being ignored or indignantly dismissed. Such people are paralleled by others who believe, with equal fervour, that all new religions should be welcomed and that any attack on their beliefs or practices must be dismissed as nothing but bigoted ignorance.

Fourthly, there are the media. Some excellent reporting has appeared in print, on radio and on television, but it is often difficult to have access to these reports. More accessible, partly because they are likely to be collected and distributed by the 'anti-cultists', are newspaper cuttings of a sensational nature, many of which are grossly distorted, and some of which are blatantly untrue.

Academics, who have by now done a considerable amount of research on numerous aspects of the NRMs, provide the fifth source of information.[9] Although much of this work is of a high standard, it is not readily available to the general public: it tends to be published in academic journals or scholarly books that are only rarely on sale in non-specialist bookshops, and it is often written in the kind of prose that

---

3. 2400 Ridge Road, Berkeley, CA 94709, USA.
4. Hovedbygningen Ndr. Ringgade, 8000 Aarhus C, Denmark.
5. Selly Oak Colleges, Birmingham B29 6LQ, UK.
6. 39 Homer Street, London W1H 1HL, UK.
7. Katrine bjergvej 46, DK–8200, Aarhus N, Denmark.
8. P.O.Box 336, Weston MA 02193, USA.
9. For overviews of the literature see Choquette (1985); Robbins (1988); Saliba (1987); and Eileen Barker "Religious Movements: Cult and Anticult since Jonestown", *Annual Review of Sociology*, vol. 12, 1986 pp. 329–46.

appears to be designed to put off all but the most persistent of readers. Furthermore, for a number of eminently respectable and sensible reasons, academics tend to fight shy of offering practical suggestions.

A personal statement

This is not an academic book in the commonly understood sense of the word. It is written as a *practical* introduction to the NRMs. Concrete suggestions are offered to the reader, and several statements reflecting my own beliefs about the rights and wrongs of certain actions are made quite explicitly on a number of points. None the less, it does draw heavily on academic research, and I am an academic. I do not feel the need to apologise for this fact. There are, however, people who appear determined to propagate the view that my academic practice should preclude me from expressing my views on the subject – there are even those who, while having no idea as to the contents of this book, have been campaigning to have it banned. In the light of misconceptions that have been expressed in public, it might be helpful to try to clarify one or two points. Those who are uninterested in this somewhat peripheral subject should skip the rest of this section.

Sometimes it is said that academics sit in their ivory towers and have very little contact with what goes on in 'the real world'. So far as research into NRMs is concerned, this simply is not true. Many of us have spent days, weeks, months, some even years, observing NRMs 'in the field', sometimes living in extraordinarily uncomfortable conditions, finding ourselves involved in all manner of strange activities – although most of us will draw the line at participating in certain practices (such as proselytising or joining in sexual orgies). We have interviewed members of NRMs for hours on end. With the exception of the People's Temple and the Manson Family, I have talked with members of almost all the movements mentioned in this book, and many others. I have also listened to ex-members and literally hundreds of relatives and friends of members, opponents and supporters and anyone else who might throw light on the different ways in which a movement operates and is perceived to operate. As researchers, we have also constructed and analysed question-naires; we have waded through literature; and we have studied 'control groups' in order to assess the material we have gathered about the movement by comparing it with data on other 'populations'.[10]

Although most scholars would consider it gross professional negli-gence *not* to spend time with the movements when engaged in such

---

10. For descriptions of some methods used in my own research, see "Brahmins Don't Eat Mushrooms: Participant Observation and the New Religions" *L.S.E. Quarterly*, vol. 1, no. 2, June 1987, pp. 127–152; or "Confessions of a Methodological Schizophrenic", *Institute for the Study of Worship and Religious Architecture Research Bulletin*, University of Birmingham, 1978, pp. 70–89; or "Der professionelle Fremde" in *Das Entstehen einer neuen Religion*, Gunter Kehrer (ed.), Munich: Kösel-Verlag, 1981, pp. 13–40; and Barker (1984) chapters 1 & 5.

research, the very fact that an academic has been in 'the field' can give rise to anxiety and distrust.[11] In an area that is highly controversial and in which strong feelings are roused, perhaps it is not surprising that there will be those who find it hard to understand why a researcher could appear to be fraternising with 'the enemy'. Sometimes the academic is even accused of being an undercover member of the movement – yet few people take the fact that Mrs Thatcher receives hospitality from and appears to be friendly with Mr Gorbachev to mean that she is a communist, or even that she is sympathetic to communism. Even her opponents would tend to agree that without such contact she would be unlikely to get so clear a picture of what is actually happening – nor would she be in so effective a position to attempt to clarify and sort out problems.[12]

Sometimes academics are misunderstood when they talk of objectivity and 'value-freedom'. All that is meant by these terms is that accounts of whatever they are studying should be as accurate as possible and as free as possible of their own personal values. It is, of course, well nigh impossible to be completely objective and value-free when dealing with complicated social issues, but the academic is aware of many of the pitfalls into which the unwary may fall and aims to avoid as many of these as he or she can. The proposition that value-free research is valueless or "useless"[13] seems to me to be just plain silly. While academic researchers might have some skills in acquiring knowledge about a particular subject, they are unlikely to claim any particular expertise in ethical or moral judgements. It is, therefore, difficult to see much value or usefulness in research reports that provide more information about the researcher's personal values than about the phenomenon that has been studied.

To take a practical example, when an academic is called upon to be an 'expert witness' in a court case, it is because the court expects to be given objective information on a subject about which the witness has a specialised knowledge. Whether such a witness personally supports or opposes a particular position should be totally irrelevant to the proceedings. It is, thus, perfectly possible for an expert witness to appear for one side on one occasion and on the other side on another occasion – I have found myself called as a witness for the Unification Church in the *Daily Mail* case, and called by the Attorney General, as a witness against the Unification Church, in the more recent 'Charity Case'.

Yet another misunderstanding arises when it is thought that, because academics are trying to be as objective as possible, they do not care about

---

11. See Barker (1984), p. 34 for an example of a fairly typical 'misunderstanding'.

12. I discuss some of the ethical questions raised in accepting hospitality from an NRM as part of 'participant observation' in "Supping with the Devil: How Long a Spoon Does the Sociologist Need?" *Sociological Analysis*, vol. 44, no. 3, 1984, pp. 197–205.

13. *FAIR News*, October 1987, p. 5.

the problems of those who are personally affected by the situation that is being studied. This too is nonsense; academics are quite likely to have chosen their area of research because they believe that accurate information on that topic could be of practical use. In such instances, the academic believes that there is more value in trying to find out the truth of the situation than in acting from a position of ignorance. There is no reason why academic research cannot be relevant to the practical problems that people face – in fact, there is every reason why it can be.[14]

Social science cannot do everything. Like any other descriptive science, it is limited: it cannot decide between theological or ideological claims; it cannot pronounce moral judgements, telling people what is right or wrong; nor can it tell them what to do. It certainly cannot perform miracles. How then can it be useful for a book like this? Although social science is in itself neutral, its conclusions can become a basis for action. It can try to help people towards an accurate understanding of the situation with which they have to deal, and alert them to some of the possible consequences of their own and others' actions. An awareness of the complexity of a situation might help people to avoid precipitous actions that would later have been regretted. More positively, awareness of a range of possible causes and outcomes might assist in finding a way to improve an apparently intractable situation.

In this book I purposely go beyond mere academic interest. Precisely out of a concern about practical consequences, I go out of my way to spell out some of the implications of the conclusions of academic research. The suggestions should be taken to be of the form 'if you want. . . . then. . . . '; -they are attempts to respond to some of the 'wants' and questions that have been put to me both by relatives and friends who have become worried and confused when someone whom they love has become involved with an NRM, and by people with pastoral or counselling responsibilities who want to know what they might be able to do when someone comes to them for help.

Whether the suggestions that I put forward are accepted is, of course, entirely up to each individual reader to decide in the light of his or her interests and concerns. Having worked in this area for nearly two decades, I am all too aware that there are members of the new religions and several of their opponents who, having reached clear conclusions as to who are the 'goodies' and who are the 'baddies', will scorn the central thesis that the issues examined in the book are complicated and that often there is no simple solution. They will reject many of the conclusions that are drawn from the research, and dismiss many of the suggestions that are put forward. But this book is not really written for them.

---

14. I have discussed these points in further detail in an interview "Moonie Myths" with Pat McNeil in *New Statesman & Society*, 7 July 1989, p. 29.

Acknowledgements and thanks

Although I take sole responsibility for the contents of the book, it would have been impossible to have written it without the expertise, the experiences and the help of many others. First, I must thank those who accepted my invitation to a lunch-time meeting, held at the London School of Economics in October 1986, to discuss the potential need for and "the feasibility of setting up some sort of organisation that would supply objective information about alternative religions" in the hope that we could help those who might be in desperate need of such information. Many of these people now serve on INFORM's Board of Governors. They and those who have joined us since, including INFORM's office staff, have been unfailing in their support, and continually generous in the time, energy and expertise that they have contributed to INFORM – and, not least, in their suggestions for improvements to earlier drafts of this book.

I also owe an enormous debt of gratitude to the friends and relatives of members of new religious movements who have shared with me their experiences, and who have alerted me to what it was that they wanted to know. And I would like to thank those members and ex-members of the NRMs who have (usually) continued politely to answer impertinent questions, even when it was quite obvious to them that not all their answers were being accepted. My thanks are due too to both the Social Science Research Council (now the ESRC), which funded my early research into the Unification Church, and to the Nuffield Foundation, which funded my later research into new religious movements in general. Without their support the research upon which this book draws would not have been possible.

Finally, I would like to thank the many friends who have read and commented upon earlier drafts: colleagues have checked the manuscript for its scholarship; non-academic friends have checked it for vocabulary that could have been irritatingly influenced by the jargon of my academic discipline. I want to thank Judith for the coffee; and, above all, I want to thank one of BBC Radio 3's announcers.

Eileen Barker
London School of Economics and Political Science
1989

INTRODUCTION

Aims of the book

This book has two main aims. The first aim is to provide some general background information about the new religious movements (NRMs). The second aim is to offer some preliminary suggestions to people who are concerned about what should be done when a relative, friend, student, parishioner (or anyone else about whom they have direct or indirect information) has become involved in one of the movements.

One of the important points that the book attempts to make is that NRMs cannot all be 'lumped together'; they differ from one another in numerous respects. Another important point is that, although causes for concern in individual cases may turn out to be far less worrying than might at first have been feared, it is advisable to be alert to real and potential dangers that can occur in some of the movements. Arising from these two points is a third: anyone who is concerned about a particular case should try to get as much accurate information as possible about both the *particular* NRM and the *particular* person.

Readership

The book has been prepared as background reading for parents, relatives and friends of members of an NRM, and for people who wish to offer pastoral care, counselling or advice to relatives and friends and others who either are or could become more directly involved. Thus, it is hoped that it will be of help to chaplains, ministers, professional counsellors, teachers and representatives of the media. It may also be helpful to those who have joined a movement, or are considering doing so, because it draws attention to some of the consequences, such as the degree of commitment that may be involved, and to the kinds of anxieties that may beset 'outsiders' – especially their parents, other relatives and close friends.

But the book has also been written with a wider audience, curious about the new religions, in mind. It is hoped that students and members of the general public who are interested in the movements, and in the practical and ethical issues that are raised by their existence, may be stimulated into further debate concerning the matters raised in the book.

While there are a few instances in which specific details obviously refer to Britain, the general information is drawn not only from the United Kingdom, but also from the rest of Western Europe, North

America, Australia and New Zealand, and nearly all the suggestions would apply equally well to readers in any of these places.

Contents

Part One of the text concentrates mainly on information, Part Two on practical suggestions. The reader is, however, encouraged to read the main text from beginning to end because the issues are complex; the chapter and section headings give only a rough guide to their contents, many of the later sections assume knowledge of what has gone before, and many of the earlier sections contain suggestions that are not repeated in Part Two.

There are several issues that are *not* covered in the book. For example, no attempt is made to evaluate theologically the religious beliefs of the NRMs; nor is any attempt made to explain the rise of the current wave of NRMs, or to discuss many of the wider issues associated with the existence of the movements in contemporary society.[15]

Although several movements are mentioned for illustrative purposes, the book does not attempt a systematic account of any particular movement. Nor is any attempt made to explore in depth any of the specific controversies that surround particular movements. To do such controversies justice would involve going into complicated details that would detract from the book's main aim of providing a practical background introduction. Indeed, the decision whether or not to mention specific movements and to include *Appendix IV* was taken only after considerable deliberation. On the one hand, to give a small amount of information can be misleading, and either the movements or the 'anti-cultists' (or, most likely, both) may consider that they have grounds for concluding that the information is partial in both its senses; that is, the justifiable accusation of 'incompleteness' might be seen as justification for the accusation of 'bias' in one direction or the other.

On the other hand, to 'play safe' by not mentioning any movement by name (as the American Family Foundation, no doubt very sensibly, does in its book on *Cults*)[16] would be to risk allowing the reader who is unfamiliar with the general area either to assume that everything that is known about one movement applies equally to others, or to feel that the whole discussion is unhelpfully abstract.

Since this book is not intended primarily either for adherents to the NRMs or for the anti-cultists, but for people unfamiliar with the 'cult scene' who are seeking as wide and practical an introduction as possible, I decided that the draw-backs inherent in providing limited information about specific movements were less than those inherent in providing

---

15. For an overview of some of these issues, see Eileen Barker "Religious Movements: Cult and Anticult since Jonestown", *Annual Review of Sociology* vol. 12, 1986, pp. 329–46; Beckford (1985); Robbins (1988); Wallis (1983).

16. Ross & Langone (1988).

none. The reader is, nevertheless, asked to be aware of the very real difficulties involved in giving only a few details about only a few groups or movements.

At various points throughout the book, a number of different possibilities are listed. This can be frustrating for the reader who wants to know which is the 'right' description, the 'right' explanation or the 'right' advice. But often the truth is that there *is* no one clear answer. The various possibilities are not mere academic surmises; they are all actual, real-life options, some of which will apply in one instance, and others in another. The purpose is to try to increase the reader's awareness that there *are* all these different possibilities and that further inquiry needs to be conducted before it is possible to reach a conclusion about the appropriate response in any particular situation. Similarly, the frequent use of 'some' and 'may' is not meant to fudge a precise issue, but to alert the reader to a range of possibilities and to suggest a programme for further investigation.

Appendix I gives some information about INFORM (the Information Network Focus On Religious Movements), an organisation that may be able to help readers with more detailed information about particular movements. *Appendix II* discusses the definition of NRMs, the number of movements and the number of members in the UK. It deals with questions that are not, perhaps, of immediate interest to the relative or friend of someone who has just become involved in an NRM, but it does cover a number of issues that are of fundamental importance for anyone who wants to have an overview of the NRMs, and people who are concerned with understanding the phenomenon and some of the debates surrounding it at a more general level are urged to consider its contents. *Appendix III* consists of some excerpts from statements made by individuals who have been 'unsuccessfully' subjected to forcible deprogramming. *Appendix IV* provides a rudimentary introduction to some of the movements about which INFORM has received enquiries. Also at the end of the book there is an *Annotated Bibliography*. The footnotes have been inserted as references for further reading. They can be ignored, without loss of substance, by the general reader. Where a name and date only are given, the full reference is to be found in the *Annotated Bibliography*; 'op cit' is used only when the full reference has already been given within the same section.

Terminology

There are several words or phrases used in the book that have given rise to intense debate, but the use of which should not be taken to imply that a particular view is being endorsed. For example, a distinction is sometimes drawn between those who convert to and those who are recruited into an NRM. Although the distinction is useful in scholarly discussion, the differences between a convert and a recruit are either unknowable or irrelevant so far as the content of this book is concerned. Distinctions can also be drawn between 'the devotee', 'the disciple', 'the adept', 'the client' and the 'patron'.[17] Although the nature of such differences is indicated at several points, the terms 'convert' or 'member' are normally employed, simply in order not to complicate or confuse matters unnecessarily.

Then, just as there can be difficulties in deciding what to call someone who joins an NRM, there can be difficulties in deciding what to call the person who leaves. Terms such as 'apostate', 'defector' and 'leaver' are used in a number of special senses in the literature,[18] but, again, there seems little point in going into such details in this book, and, in order to try to avoid confusion, the term 'ex-member' will normally be used, but, in the section *Leaving a new religious movement*, some possible difficulties arising out of the concept are mentioned.

Another important point to be borne in mind when reading this book is that the terms 'child' and 'children' are almost always used when an *adult* son or daughter has joined an NRM. It should be obvious which are the exceptional occasions when reference is being made to minors.

The application of the term 'new religious movement' does not in itself imply either confirmation or denial of the appropriateness of any particular group's or movement's self-definition – whether the claim is that it is a religion or that it is not a religion, or that it is not new. Many of the movements referred to in this book object to being 'lumped together' with other movements that are referred to.[19] To some extent, the groups and movements mentioned in the book are featured because they are the ones about which people want information. For purely practical purposes, the term should be taken as referring to those groups, movements or organisations that have been called 'alternative religions', 'nonconventional religions', 'cults' or 'contemporary sects'.

It is because the term 'new religious movement' is seen by some people as so controversial, that the problems and qualifications that underlie its use are discussed in some detail in *Appendix II*. There is, however, one point that ought to be made right from the outset: the use of the term 'new religious movement' does not imply that a movement is good or bad, that it is true or false, or genuine or fraudulent. Many scholars working in the field prefer the term 'new religious movement' to 'cult' because, although 'cult' (like 'sect') is sometimes used in a purely technical sense, it has acquired negative connotations in everyday

---

17. See Beckford (1985).
18. Bromley (1988).
19. See, for example, Subhananda dasa *A Request to the Media: Please Don't Lump Us In*, Los Angeles: International Society for Krishna Consciousness, 1978.

parlance.[20] While it is certainly recognised that a number of the NRMs have given rise to legitimate concern, it is neither necessary nor helpful to start from the implicit premise that the movements are always 'a bad thing'.

'Destructive cults' and 'benign cults'

There are commentators who imply that it is comparatively easy to distinguish 'destructive cults' from 'benign cults'; but the world can seldom be divided as easily into such opposing categories as some of the movements and some of their opponents would like to have us believe. Many of the practices that are said to characterise a 'destructive cult' have, at some time, been exhibited by religions that are usually considered perfectly respectable. This is not to suggest that two wrongs make a right – they do not; nor is it to suggest that destructive behaviour may not be recognised – it can be, and there is every reason why such behaviour should be exposed and criticised, and why strenuous attempts should be made to remedy such practices *wherever* they occur. It is merely to suggest that condemning or condoning a group of movements *as a whole* is likely to obscure the complexity of the problems that can arise and, for that very reason, give rise to further problems.

As *individuals*, members of NRMs are not so very different from other people. It occasionally happens that when someone discovers that members of a religious or spiritual community are not the *more*-perfect-than-the-rest-of-us beings that they might claim to be, it is assumed that they must be much *less*-perfect-than-the-rest-of-us. In fact, the majority of members of NRMs, whether or not they or their opponents are prepared to admit it, are unlikely to be much nearer or further from perfection than most members of society – although one may, among their number, find a very slightly above-average peppering of both rogues and saints.

Any general assessment of an organisation's practices depends on *weighing* a number of ethical, social and political considerations. The results, even if done with recourse to as much factual information as possible, are almost certain to differ between individual assessors. There will always be a small percentage of assessors who are uncompromisingly either for or against any NRM, whatever it is like – the 'true believer' being capable of changing from one extreme to the other in a remarkably

20. For discussions about the technical uses of the term 'cult', see Ernest Troeltsch *The Social Teachings of the Christian Churches*, New York: Macmillan, 1931; Geoffrey Nelson "The Spiritualist Movement and the Need for a Redefinition of Cult" *Journal for the Scientific Study of Religion*, vol. 8, No. 1, 1969, pp. 85–93; Colin Campbell "The Cult, the Cultic Milieu and Secularization" in Michael Hill (ed.) *A Sociological Yearbook of Religion in Britain*, No. 5, 1972, London: SCM Press, pp. 119–136; and Stark and Bainbridge (1985).
For examples of use of the term new religious movement in the sociological literature, see, for example, Barker (ed.) (1982); Beckford (1985); Richardson (ed.) (1988); Robbins (1988); Shupe and Bromley (1980); Wallis (1983); Wilson (1982).

short time.[21] Generally speaking, however, it is probable that while most people would consider a few NRMs benevolent and a few almost entirely malevolent (not many would wish to defend the Manson Family), the majority of NRMs would be judged to harbour a motley assortment of both positive and negative attributes.

Although it has already been said that no attempt is made in this book to attempt a theological evaluation of the movements, it should, perhaps, be mentioned that there are people with a deeply religious conviction of their own whose primary concerns are reflected in the concepts of godly and satanic, rather than benign and destructive. The Lausanne Committee for World Evangelization wrote in its Report *Reaching Mystics and Cultists*:

> There are thousands of [new religious] groups of which there is no doubt that they are of satanic origin. But, praise be to God, there are also thousands of new church movements in which, in spite of syncretism, the Spirit of God is at work. Where one ends and the other begins will require discernment that only God can give.[22]

---

21. See Eric Hoffer *The True Believer*, New York, San Francisco & London: Harper and Row, 1951.
22. Lausanne Committee for World Evangelization (1980), p.4.

PART ONE

What are New Religious Movements like?

❧ CHAPTER ONE ❧

Some Characteristics of New Religious Movements

———▶••◀———

T HE TERM new religious movement (NRM) is used to cover a disparate collection of organisations, most of which have emerged in their present form since the 1950s, and most of which offer some kind of answer to questions of a fundamental religious, spiritual or philosophical nature. It is sometimes thought that there are vast armies of people whose lives have been significantly affected by these movements. In fact, the number of those whose lives are affected by an NRM more than they would be by membership of a longer-established religion is relatively small. *Appendix II* discusses both definitions and numbers in further detail.

Variety and generalisation

While it is frequently argued that the role of religion in the more public areas of Western society has diminished,[23] the variety of religious beliefs and practices to be found in Britain has increased dramatically during the second half of the twentieth century. While earlier generations of new religions could usually be recognised as 'deviations' or heresies within the Judaeo-Christian tradition, the religions now to be found come from a wide range of traditions, many of which were quite alien to most of the West until fairly recently.

This is partly because of the immigration of people who have brought their own religions with them to this country, and partly because

---

23. For discussions on 'the secularisation debate', see Peter L. Berger *The Social Reality of Religion*, London: Faber, 1967; Karel Dobbelaere *Secularization: A Multi-dimensional Concept*, *Current Sociology*, vol. 29, no. 2, Summer 1981; Richard K. Fenn *Toward a Theory of Secularization*, Society for the Scientific Study of Religion Monograph Series, no. 1, 1978; Phillip E. Hammond (ed.) *The Sacred in a Secular Age*, Berkeley, Los Angeles & London: University of California Press, 1985; David Martin *A General Theory of Secularization*, Oxford: Blackwell, 1978; Bryan Wilson *Religion in Secular Society: A Sociological Comment*, Harmondsworth, Penguin, 1969.

of the growth and missionary activities of a number of new religious movements. A few of the NRMs, such as the Aetherius Society, the Emin Foundation, Exegesis, The Findhorn Foundation, the Jesus Fellowship Church, the Process, the School of Economic Science and TOPY, have been indigenous to the United Kingdom or, as in the case of the Raëlian Movement and Roux's L'Eglise chrétienne universelle in France, the Ananda Ashram in Denmark, or the Lou Movement in the Netherlands, to continental Europe.[24] But most of the NRMs originated in either North America (frequently California) or the East (frequently India).

It cannot be stressed enough that almost any generalisation about NRMs is bound to be untrue if it is applied to all the movements. Leaving aside the question of whether the beliefs of NRMs may be 'blasphemous' in the view of those committed to certain religious positions, there are those who suggest that all 'cults' are equally guilty of practices such as brainwashing or mind control, financial greed and fraudulent activities, exploitative and corrupt leadership, deceptive practices and sexual perversions – and, possibly, drug-trafficking, gun-running, political intrigue, child abuse and the encouragement of suicide and murder. Some of the movements have certainly been guilty of some of these malpractices. But the extent to which members of the new religious movements are more likely than the rest of us to indulge in criminal or immoral practices has, on occasion, been grossly exaggerated. And the extent to which at least some of the members of some of the movements strive to lead more moral and spiritual lives than is usual in contemporary society tends to pass almost unrecognised.

None the less, despite the dangers of making sweeping statements, there are some characteristics that typify enough of the NRMs to allow certain qualified generalisations to be made. Indeed, several characteristics can follow directly from the extent to which the movements are 'new' and from the extent to which they are religious (using the broad definition given in *Appendix II*). Some of the features that are likely to come to mind when people refer to new religious movements were summarised by Bryan Wilson in the early 1980s in the following way:

> exotic provenance; new cultural life-style; a level of engagement markedly different from that of traditional Church Christianity; charismatic leadership; a following predominantly young and drawn in disproportionate measure from the better-educated and middle class sections

---

24. For notes on some of these British movements and the Raëlian Movement, see *Appendix IV*; for information about the Process, see Bainbridge (1978); for the School of Economic Science see Hounam and Hogg (1984). For Roux's movement, see Anthony B. van Fossen "Prophetic Failure and Moral Hierarchy: The Origins of a Contemporary Messianic Movement" in *Under the Shade of a Coolibah Tree: Australian Studies in Consciousness*, Richard A. Hutch and Peter G. Fenner (eds), Laxham, New York & London: University Press of America, 1984, pp. 239-278; and van Fossen's "How Do Movements Survive Failures of Prophecy?" *Research in Social Movements*, vol. 10, 1988, pp. 193-212. The Lou Movement is referred to in Reender Kranenborg "Churches' Response to Innovative Religious Movements of the Past" in Brockway and Rajashekar (eds) (1987), pp. 119-132.

of society; social conspicuity; international operation; and emergence within the last decade and a half.[25]

First-generation believers

To the extent that an organisation is new, its membership is likely to consist of converts, rather than those who have been brought up in the faith. Throughout history, movements that consist predominantly of first generation members have tended to be far more enthusiastic than mainstream religious traditions, which are likely to have become more staid or 'institutionalised' over time. The new religion typically offers a direct and unambiguous promise of salvation to the community of true believers – or to the individual who follows the true path or practice.[26] The 'Truths' of a new movement are held more fervently, and are often more simple and absolute than the more sophisticated and complicated beliefs of religions that have responded to the shifting and multifarious concerns of successive generations. In the eyes of an idealistic young convert, a new religion may appear passionate and caring, while a traditional religion can appear apathetic or hypocritical.

In short, a new religion is more likely to offer immediacy and certainty than the mainstream religions, which may appear remote and continually indulging in prevarication and equivocation – especially to an impatient youth seeking a clear solution to the complex problems of today's world, or their own personal problems.

Of course, the distinctions are not so clear-cut in reality. One can find enthusiasm and immediacy in some mainstream congregations, and some of the NRMs can seem excessively formal, ritualistic or even boring to the outsider. But an awareness of ways in which movements with first-generation believers can, in very general terms, differ from older religions may alert people to recognise and, to some extent at least, to understand a few of the potential consequences of membership of an NRM. Compared to the mainstream religions, a new religious movement may, for example, be far more demanding of its members' time and commitment; it may be more vigorously convinced that it alone holds the truth and, consequently, it may be less ready to adapt to circumstances (or, from its point of view, to compromise). It may be less experienced in dealing with the problems and challenges of the world – and it may have less to lose by not compromising, because it has less of an investment in the 'establishment'.

Almost all movements with first generation believers have an age distribution that differs from that of the wider society. In new movements which people typically join in their twenties, there will be few babies

---

25. Bryan R. Wilson (ed.) *The Social Impact of New Religious Movements*, New York: Rose of Sharon Press, 1981, p. v.
26. See Wilson (1970) and (1982).

and young children and not many middle-aged or elderly members. It does not take much imagination to realise that this demographic situation can, in itself, account for some of the movements' characteristics. A related characteristic is that many of those in leadership positions will be young and inexperienced – a situation that has been seen as a contributing cause for some of the more extreme actions carried out in certain NRMs.[27]

It is, however, important to recognise that the *average* age of first-generation members increases with the passage of time – although, because there is often a high turn-over rate (with new converts usually being younger than those who leave), it does not increase by as much as a year every twelve months. Furthermore, except in a few instances, where, for example, celibacy is observed, it is not long before a second generation is born into the movement. In both Europe and North America, there is a growing number of children, and there are by now also several young adults, who have been born into a contemporary NRM.

Although, in some instances, the treatment of children in the movements has given rise to new causes for concern (see later sections), the ageing of the first-generation membership and the presence of the second-generation children have been responsible for a number of significant changes. Stuart Wright, in his study of voluntary defectors, argues that:

> The almost exclusive reliance upon young adults in world-transforming movements has its advantages and disadvantages. These movements have unquestionably benefited from the zeal of youth who ... have the expendable time and freedom to make total commitments. However, the distinct disadvantage that these movements face is that they must strive to maintain commitment among persons who are in transition to adult roles and identities. ... Youthful members may change their minds about what they want out of life after a year or two of involvement. ... Thus, simply due to the age group they have targeted for recruitment, the movements face the continual problem of defection.[28]

In other words, parents in their thirties are likely to have a very different outlook on life from that of idealists with few responsibilities in their twenties. A related change that has commonly occurred with the passage of time is that members often find it easier to relate to their parents as the grandparents of their children than they found it to relate to them as parents. Grandparents are often more relaxed with their grandchildren, and many have come to play an important role in their lives.

Furthermore, with the passage of time, with the death of founders, and with the demographic composition of an NRM becoming more like that of the wider community, many of the movements that survive are

---

27. Melton (1986), p. 260.
28. Wright (1987), pp. 65–66.

likely to become 'institutionalised' and more like the established religions against which some of them once railed.[29]

Charismatic leaders

New religions are rarely initiated by a committee. Although sects may be formed by a group of dissatisfied persons breaking away from a larger body, several of the movements have, or have had, a founder or leader who is believed to have some special powers or knowledge, and whom his (or, occasionally, her) followers are expected to believe and obey without question.

Sociologists use the concept of charisma in a sense that differs both from that used in everyday language, when a pop-star may be called charismatic, and from the theological sense in which a person is seen to possess a special kind of grace. The sociologist's use of the term implies merely that the leader's followers *believe* that he or she possesses a very special (possibly divine) quality and that the followers are, as a consequence, willing to grant him or her a special kind of authority over them.[30]

Almost by definition, charismatic leaders are unpredictable, for they are bound by neither tradition nor rules; they are not answerable to other human beings. Thus, in so far as the leaders of NRMs are endowed by their followers with a charismatic authority, the followers accept the legitimacy of their leader's right to pronounce on every aspect of their lives. This might include where they should live, what sort of work they should do, what should be done with their belongings, and, perhaps, with whom they should have sexual and other kinds of relationships.[31]

Not all new religious movements have charismatic leaders. Not all charismatic leaders use their authority in ways that outsiders would deplore. But some do. Some followers 'learn' to recognise the charismatic qualities of their leader only after they have joined a movement. Some followers never accept the charismatic authority claimed by their leader. Many will disobey those commands of their leader (or his lieutenants) which they consider to be wrong, foolish or excessive. Some will come to the sudden realisation that they have ceased to accept that their leader is special in the way that they had come to think of him. Norman Skonovd quotes from a not untypical interview with an ex-member:

29. See David G. Bromley and Phillip E. Hammond (eds) *The Future of New Religious Movements*, Macon: Mercer University Press, 1987. For a discussion of some of the changes that can result directly from the changing demographic composition of an NRM, see Eileen Barker "A Short History, But Many Changes: A New Religious Movement" in *Gilgul. Essays on Transformation, Revolution and Permanence in the History of Religions*, Saul Shaked, David Shulman and Gedaliahu Stroumsa (eds), Leiden: Brill, 1987, pp. 35–44.

30. For the classic statement about charismatic authority, see Max Weber *The Theory of Social and Economic Organization*, New York: Free Press, 1964 (Copyright Oxford University Press, 1947) pp. 358–363.

31. Roy Wallis (ed.) *Millennialism and Charisma*, Belfast: The Queen's University, 1982.

And so then I reflected on things like that and I said "Wow, how could a real messiah treat an old lady like that?" ... It just kind of got to the point where after a while I felt I no longer belonged to the Unification Church and I no longer wanted to have anything to do with it. So, I left.[32]

With the passage of time, charismatic authority is likely to become 'routinized'.[33] The movement and its members become less subject to the unpredictable authority of a single leader. This may be as a result of the death of the original leader, or it may be, especially if the movement has grown in size, that the day-to-day administration of the movement takes on a more institutionalised or bureaucratic form. It is not impossible that the new authority structure is itself unpredictable, possibly in a Kafka-esque manner, and it may exert just as powerful a control over the movement and its members as the original leader. If, however, the other changes that frequently accompany the new religious movement with the passage of time occur, it is likely that the authority will become, in at least some ways, more negotiable.

Socio-economic status and age of membership

While some earlier waves of new religions, and many of those emerging in Third World countries,[34] have appealed to the poor or the oppressed, most of those who join the better-known of the present NRMs in the West come from the more privileged sections of society. By and large, Westerners who become involved in movements such as the Brahma Kumaris, Elan Vital, ISKCON, the Rajneeshees, Sahaja Yoga, the Church of Scientology, Transcendental Meditation or the Unification Church come disproportionately from the middle or upper-middle classes. They will have received a better than average education and they will have had good prospects for their future careers.

There are exceptions. It is mainly disadvantaged black youth from the inner cities who join the Rastafarian movement.[35] TOPY (Thee [sic] Temple ov [sic] Psychic Youth) seems to appeal to young people who will not necessarily have been part of 'the system' that they reject. And, despite the fact that many of the NRMs frequently find themselves bracketed with the ill-fated People's Temple, both it and its members differed in a number of significant ways from the membership, beliefs

---

32. Norman Skonovd "Leaving the 'Cultic' Milieu" in Bromley and Richardson (eds) (1983), p. 98.

33. Weber *op cit* pp. 363–386.

34. Kenelm O. Burridge *New Heaven New Earth*, Oxford: Blackwell, 1969; Vittorio Lanternari *The Religions of the Oppressed: A Study of Modern Messianic Cults*, translated by Lis Sergio, London: MacGibbon and Kee, 1963; Bryan R. Wilson *Magic and the Millennium*, London: Heinemann, 1973.

35. See Cashmore (1983).

and practices of most other NRMs.[36] It is, incidentally, interesting to note that the People's Temple was not branded as a 'cult' or classified as a new religious movement until after the tragic death of its members in Guyana in 1978.

Appendix II discusses different levels of membership, ranging from the vast majority who have little more than a fleeting acquaintance with an NRM to those who dedicate their whole lives to the movement. Not surprisingly, those who join movements that expect the kind of total commitment which involves living in a community and working full time for the organisation are likely to be young adults with few responsibilities; the average age of those becoming 'core members' of the Unification Church, for instance, is twenty-three. Movements that charge fees for their services tend to attract those in a slightly older age-range (many being in their thirties or even older) – if only because such people are more likely to be earning enough to pay.

In a survey of those visiting Atsitsa for "A Holistic Health and Fitness Holiday" or the Skyros Centre for "A Personal Development Holiday" (both on the Greek island Skyros), it was found that the typical participant was "single, professional, over 30 and a *Guardian* reader". Women outnumbered men by two to one.[37]

Some movements have also attracted the elderly, particularly those who live alone and may not see friends or relatives very often. Such movements will usually offer the company of young people and might arrange for someone to help with shopping or odd jobs around the home. It has, however, been pointed out that some members of some NRMs may play upon the loneliness of old people merely in order to get them to hand over their house or their money, or to persuade them to leave a bequest to the movement in their wills. Once they have achieved their purpose, the members may abandon all interest in the old people, leaving them alone and destitute.[38] (Some of the personal predispositions of people becoming involved in NRMs are discussed elsewhere – in, for example, the chapter *What do the NRMs offer potential converts?*)

---

36. James T. Richardson has highlighted differences between the People's Temple and other new religions on eight points: (1) social location and time of inception; (2) characteristics of members and potential members; (3) organizational structure and operation; (4) social control techniques and outside contact; (5) resocialization techniques; (6) theology or ideology; (7) general orientation; (8) ritual behaviours. See "People's Temple and Jonestown: A Corrective Comparison and Critique" *Journal for the Scientific Study of Religion* 19/3, 1980, pp. 239–255.

37. Brochure produced by The Skyros Institute, European Centre for Holistic Studies, London, 1989.

38. See, for example, Marcia R. Rudin "Women, Elderly and Children in Religious Cults", paper presented at the Citizens Freedom Foundation Annual Conference, Arlington, Virginia, 1982.

❧ CHAPTER TWO ❧

Conversion or Mind Control?

———◆••◆———

The brainwashing thesis

ONE OF THE MOST POPULAR explanations that is given for people joining an NRM is that they have been brainwashed or have undergone some kind of 'mind control'. There are various reasons for the popularity of such an explanation, not the least of which is that it tends to absolve everyone (apart from the NRM in question) from any kind of responsibility.

The brainwashing explanation can also provide the rationale for 'deprogramming' – the illegal kidnapping and holding of members of an NRM in 'an involuntary setting' until either they manage to escape and return to their movement, or they convince their captors, in truth or out of desperation, that they have renounced their faith and are 'deprogrammed'. Deprogramming is discussed in more detail in a later chapter.

It is probably true to say that some of the movements would *like* to be able to practise some sort of mind control over both potential and actual members. Certainly, many of the NRMs put the potential convert under considerable pressure to join. The pressure may take the positive form of 'love bombing', when the individual is showered with attention and instant affection, or it may take the more negative form of playing upon the individual's feelings of guilt. It may use both ploys.

Some of the movements are less than honest about who they are, or the amount of dedication and/or money that they are hoping to solicit from their members. Recruitment that employs deception should, however, be distinguished from 'brainwashing' or 'mind control'. If people are the victims of mind control, they are rendered *incapable* of themselves making the decision as to whether or not to join a movement – the decision is made for them. If, on the other hand, it is just deception that is being practised, converts will be perfectly capable of *making* a decision – although they might make a different decision were they basing their choice on more accurate information. It can be argued, and it is indeed frequently the case, that when people who have joined a movement realise that the movement's beliefs or practices are not what they had initially thought them to be, they leave the movement. It can also be argued that once some people have actually joined a movement on the basis of false information, they are more likely to stay because they have become subjected to further influences; they may, for example, have formed strong emotional attachments to members of the movement during the 'extra time' that was gained through the deception.[39] Deception is discussed further in a later section.

There is by now a substantial body of research on the subject of joining and leaving NRMs.[40] This has repeatedly shown that most people are perfectly capable of rejecting the movements' overtures if they so wish. For example, out of a thousand people who had become sufficiently interested in the Unification Church to attend a residential 'Moonie' workshop in the London area in 1979 (when the movement in Britain was at its height and accusations of brainwashing were rife), about 90% resisted the members' proselytising efforts and declined to have any further involvement with the movement. About 8% joined as full-time members for more than a week; less than 4% were still full-time members two years later – and, with the passage of time, the number of continuing members who joined in 1979 has continued to fall.[41] If the calculation were to start from those who, for one reason or another, had visited one of the movement's centres in 1979, at least 999 out of every 1,000 of those people had, by the mid-1980s, succeeded in resisting the persuasive techniques of the Unification Church.

In some years in some movements, there may be more joiners than leavers; in other years, the number of those who leave exceeds the number who join. Subud, for example, has had around a hundred people joining and around a hundred leaving each year, so that its total membership has remained between 1,200 and 1,400 for some time. But whether the general trend is upwards, downwards or steady for any particular movement, it is now incontrovertibly established that members are continually leaving *all* the well-known movements, of their own free

39. A legal battle fought in California and eventually settled out of court, to some extent, hinged on such arguments: *Molko and Leal v. Holy Spirit Association for the Unification of World Christianity et al.* See Barker (1984), chapters 5 and 7, for a more detailed discussion about the relationship between mind control and deception.

40. For further information and discussion on these matters, see Barker (1984); Beckford (1985); Brockway & Rajashekar (eds) (1987); Bromley & Shupe (1981); Bromley (ed.) (1988); Enroth (1977); Levine (1984); John Lofland and Norman Skonovd "Patterns of Conversion" in Barker (1983), pp. 1–24; Melton & Moore (1982); Lewis Rambo "Current Research on Religious Conversion", *Religious Studies Review*, vol. 8, 1982, pp. 146–59; Robbins & Anthony (eds) (1981) (section VI); Rochford (1985); Streiker (1978); David A. Snow and Richard Machalek "The Sociology of Conversion" *Annual Review of Sociology*, vol. 10, 1984, pp. 167–90; Wallis (1983); Williams (1987); and Wright (1987).

41. Barker (1984) p. 146. Similar statistics were revealed by Marc Galanter in "Psychological Induction into the Large Group: Findings from a Modern Religious Sect" *American Journal of Psychiatry*, vol. 137, no. 12, 1980 p. 1575. See also Rochford (1985).

will, even after several years of involvement.[42] (See *Appendix II* for a more detailed discussion of membership figures.) A small number of movements practise techniques that may adversely affect the reasoning powers of those involved (this is discussed in a later section); but, even in such movements, people can and do leave of their own accord. There are those, such as deprogrammers with a financial interest in propagating the brainwashing thesis, who continue to ignore or dismiss such statistics, but they do so without providing any contrary evidence beyond the testimonies of a small number of ex-members, several of whom will have been *taught*, while undergoing forcible deprogramming, that they were brainwashed.[43]

The 'brainwashing thesis' is discussed further in Part Two; the point to be made here is that, whatever individuals might claim as a result of their personal experience, the statistics make it abundantly clear that it simply is not true that 'anyone' is susceptible to the 'lure of the cults'. What *is* true is that there are people whom others might have thought to be immune to NRMs, who do, in fact, become involved in one or other of the movements.

It is, of course, of little comfort to a distraught parent whose son or daughter makes up part of the percentage which joins and remains in a movement to learn that many others have resisted it. But the figures do suggest that it might be sensible to find out what it is that distinguishes those who do not join or who leave from those who have converted and who stay in a movement. In other words, it is not only the movement, but also the personality (the hopes, fears, expectations, and past experiences) of the convert that needs to be taken into account when trying to understand why he or she has joined a movement. Relying merely on the brainwashing thesis to explain a person's continuing membership is more likely to confuse than to clarify the situation.

Conversion processes and techniques of persuasion

Furthermore, serious research suggests that many of the *processes* involved in becoming a member of an NRM differ little, if at all, from the sorts of processes that occur in the family, the school, the army, or, indeed, some traditional religions. There are those who have argued that adult conversion involves less control by others than that which is involved when a child is born into a family with a strongly held religious tradition. The Fellowship of Evangelical Baptist Churches in Canada, in response to a request from the Ontario Government to state their reactions to the

---

42. Bromley (ed.) 1987; Levine (1984); Robbins and Anthony (eds) (1981); Wright (1987).

43. See Margaret Singer's testimony in the *Daily Mail* trial, quoted in Barker (1984) p. 129; Lewis (n.d.); and Trudy Solomon "Integrating the 'Moonie' Experience: A Survey of Ex-Members of the Unification Church" in Robbins and Anthony (eds) (1981), pp. 275–294.

NRMs and the possibility of introducing new legislation to control their activities, came out strongly against the suggestion for a number of reasons, including the argument that:

> Non-physical persuasion is already a widely experienced thing in our society. We ourselves practise it, in our evangelism and in our teaching, commonly with all evangelical churches. Politicians practise it ... Authorities in government practise it ... And parents practise it in the ordinary processes of raising their children.[44]

But, of course, even if the *process* of conversion is rarely of a particularly strange or sinister nature, this does not mean that the *consequences* of conversion to an NRM may not be a cause for concern. It is, indeed, possible that the vocal insistence that 'all cults' use mind-control techniques to obtain their members has, in some instances, deflected attention from some far more pertinent problems.

It is, moreover, possible to argue that *some* of the movements, particularly some of those that Paul Heelas calls the 'self-religions'[45] which claim to transform radically a person's 'way of being', *have* developed some techniques and processes that are unusual in their 'professionalised' packages. People have not, in the past, paid hundreds of pounds in order to be closeted for hours with a number of other 'guests' and have all manner of abuse hurled at them with the express intention of making them realise their true, inner potential. Indeed, the people who pay out these and larger sums of money would be unlikely to do so unless they thought that they were investing in a new technique that *would* 'convert' them in an important sense.

Subliminal suggestion

Another new aspect of modern technology that has given rise to some anxiety is that of subliminal suggestion.[46] One organisation that has an outlet in Britain has taken advantage of the concept of 'subliminal programming' through the marketing of 'Video Hypnosis' in which a number of suggestions, listed on the back of the carton, appear momentarily on the screen and embedded into background music during the course of a talk. The talks cover a variety of subjects such as 'Stop Smoking Forever', 'Channel for the Light', 'Chakra Balance' and 'Develop Psychic Ability Now'. Again, it appears that there are those who are eager to pay around £25 for 30 minutes of tape in the belief that they will have their subconscious mind programmed in such a way that their attitudes and life will be radically altered: "Thanks to incredible new technology and contemporary awareness of how the mind works, change

44. Hill (1980) p. 428.

45. Paul Heelas "Californian Self-Religions and Socialising the Subjective" in Barker (ed.) (1982), pp. 69–85.

46. See Norman F. Dixon *Subliminal Perception: The Nature of a Controversy*. London: McGraw Hill, 1971; Timothy Moore (ed.) "Subliminal Influences in Marketing" *Psychology and Marketing*, 5/4, Winter 1988.

no longer has to be difficult".[47] Another organisation offers the SCWL (Subconscious to Conscious Way of Learning) Human Potential Series, which consists of subliminal audio cassettes "designed to maximise overall effectiveness in achieving your goals", with the boast that:

> This [subliminal] learning technique and the application thereof is an effective and proven solution to the problem we all face . . . how to change our mind in order to change our life.[48]

It is not yet known either how widely used or how effective this method is. Clearly the extent to which such a technique may be effectively used without people's knowledge is a matter for concern, and concern about its deployment in advertising has been the subject of considerable discussion in the United States. As yet, however, there is no substantiated evidence that any of the better-known NRMs have relied upon this method to gain converts – and the statistics would suggest that even if they had been using undetected subliminal suggestion, the technique has not been particularly effective. It has, none the less, been reported that an ex-member of at least one movement claims that the tapes it plays for teaching purposes have occasionally been dubbed with subliminal messages.[49]

The interpretation of unusual experiences

Mention should also be made of the physical experiences that people have had once they have become associated with a movement. These can take a variety of forms. In extreme cases, the individuals concerned may become unconscious or unaware of what is going on around them; they may enter an 'altered state of consciousness'; the experiences may result in what others would consider to be hallucinations. People may report an unusually heightened awareness of colour or sound or some other sense; they may have a tingling sensation or feel a cool breeze; some may suffer from an inexplicable headache, others may find themselves inexplicably cured of a headache or healed of some other ailment.[50] Some

---

47. Leaflet advertising New World Cassettes.
48. Dr Diana J. Hodgson M.D. "A Sound Idea for Personal Growth" *Whole Life* n.d., p. 30, reproduced on the back of a leaflet advertising the Human Potential Series, handed out at the Festival for Mind-Body-Spirit, London, 1989.
49. *Daily News*, 4 February 1982.
50. There is a vast amount of literature about the different kinds of experiences, some of it descriptive, some scholarly, some speculative. It is impossible here to list, even briefly, the books that have been influential or important in this vast area; but those who wish to pursue the matter further could start from a number of different perspectives by looking at, for example, Timothy Beardsworth *A Sense of Presence*, Oxford: Religious Experience Research Unit, 1977; Holger Kalweit *Dreamtime and Inner Space: The World of the Shaman*, Boston & London: Shambhala, 1988; Ioan M. Lewis *Ecstatic Religion: An Anthropological Study of Spirit Possession and Shamanism*, Harmondsworth: Penguin, 1971; Lifton (1961); Abraham H. Maslow *Religions, Values and Peak Experiences*, Harmondsworth: Penguin, 1976; William Sargant *Battle for the Mind: A Physiology of Conversion and Brain-Washing*, London: Pan, 1959; Charles T. Tart (ed.) *Altered States of Consciousness*, New York: John Wiley, 1975;

of these experiences and states can be induced through drugs, some by special techniques and practices. None of the practices will have the same results for all the individuals who take part in them.

Transformative techniques are discussed further in a later section. A point that should be made here, however, is that explanations are not always readily available in contemporary Western society for the mystical, spiritual or 'strange' experiences or altered states of consciousness that people have reported throughout history. This is by no means the norm in other societies. In a project entitled *Cross-Cutural Studies of Dissociational States*, under the direction of the anthropologist Erika Bourguignon, it was found that, of a sample of 488 societies, at least 90% had 'institutionalised' one or more forms of altered states of consciousness – in other words, "altered states of consciousness are widely integrated into the religious institutions of the [vast majority of] societies".[51]

Bourguignon is drawing a clear distinction between the altered states of consciousness themselves and the beliefs that people have about such states. For example, 'trance' is an objective state of consciousness; 'possession' is a belief about a trance state. The belief may be correct or incorrect, but there is no scientific way of assessing its accuracy.[52] The relevance of this distinction is that there are some NRMs that have either arranged for potential converts to undergo experiences that were new and strange to the individual concerned, or who have found out about an individual's hitherto unexplained experience, and have then taken the opportunity to *interpret* the experience in such a way that it would seem to confirm or prove the truth of the movement's doctrine.

There is, however, no guarantee that such interpretations will be accepted, and plenty of people, while admitting that they have had an unusual experience, have been perfectly capable of resisting a movement's insistence that the logical conclusion to be drawn from the experience is that the individual should become further involved in the movement.

Commitment and conversion

By no means all conversions are sudden. Some take place slowly over months or even years so that the convert finds it difficult to point to a specific time when he or she first started seeing the world in a different way. There are people who seem to have started 'preparing' themselves for some of the beliefs or practices that characterise the movement which they will eventually join before they have ever met it or even heard of its existence. Many of those who have joined ISKCON, for example, had become vegetarians some time before they had learned about Krishna.

Although it is often assumed that those who join the NRMs undergo a process that results in their becoming both committed and converted

---

51. See Erika Bourguignon "Cross-Cultural Perspectives on the Religious Uses of Altered States of Consciousness" in Zaretsky & Leone (1974), pp. 230–1.
52. Ibid, p. 228.

to the movement in a very short space of time, this is not necessarily the case. Many people admit to having become committed to the way of life of a movement before becoming converted to its beliefs. For others, it is the commitment to the way of life that follows the conversion to the beliefs. In trying to understand why a particular individual has joined a movement, it may be helpful to bear this distinction in mind.

❧ CHAPTER THREE ❧

What do New Religious Movements offer Potential Converts?

———————◆•◆———————

THE REASONS WHY people join and (which may be different) why they stay affiliated to one or other of the NRMs differ according both to what a particular individual might be looking for or might respond to, and to what a particular movement might seem to be offering. A person's conversion may involve a number of 'pushes' and 'pulls' – a jumble of motives, which may not always be recognised or fully understood by the individual concerned. Furthermore, with the passage of time, converts are likely to develop a story that accounts for their conversion by relying on a highly selective memory of the factors that were involved.[53]

Whatever doubts relatives and friends may have about the NRM, if they want to understand what is going on and to keep reasonable communication between themselves and a convert, it is important for them to acknowledge that those who join and stay in a movement are likely to believe that they are gaining some positive benefit from their involvement – whether this is because they feel that they have developed a deep relationship with God, or because they enjoy the fellowship, the apparent security or the challenge that the movement provides.

Converts may claim that they have been freed from drug dependency, that they have been given self-respect when they had felt worthless, or direction when they had felt aimless. Others may claim that they had gained freedom to develop after years of having been constrained by those around them or by society in general. Furthermore, many of those who leave after a substantial period in an NRM will continue to insist that they gained much from their time in the movement, even if they

---

53. Beckford (1985).

eventually reached a point when they no longer felt it was for them. (See section on *Leaving a new religious movement*.)

Success in careers

Those who attend some of the courses given by the 'self-religions' may claim that they have become far more effective in their work. Precise numbers are unknown, but it would appear that, taking both North America and Europe into account, there are by now hundreds of large corporations, including a number of multinational companies, which have arranged for their top managers and other personnel to take courses run by such movements in the belief that the 'graduates' become more enthusiastic, energetic, responsible, innovative and hard-working employees.[54] In the United States, "Children, prisoners, air force and police personnel alike have been trained [in *est*] with the specific approval of government institutions."[55]

Improved health and longevity

Numerous members of NRMs have testified that their health has improved after they became involved with one of the movements. Transcendental Meditation's literature claims that TM is practised and recommended by over 600 British medical doctors who believe that it contributes to the prevention and alleviation of stress-related illnesses. Among the numerous claims that have been made about the Ayurvedic treatment that TM is providing in the West is one that AIDS victims have shown remarkable improvement. It is, moreover, reported that a Dutch insurance company offers Meditators a 30 per cent reduction in their life assurance premiums.[56]

Perhaps even greater reductions ought to be offered to members of the Flame Foundation, which offers immortality to its members.[57] Pursuing the same goal, Sondra Ray, the founder of Loving Relations Training (LRT) and Leonard Orr, the 'father' of Rebirthing, are busy with research in Life Extension and, with Babaji, the 'Yogi Christ of India', exploring the philosophy of Physical Immortality.[58]

---

54. See, for example, "Trying to Bend Managers' Minds" by Jeremy Main in *Fortune*, 23 November 1987, No. 27; *The Wall Street Journal*, 24 July 1987:19; the editorial and cover story in the 26 September 1987 issue of *Training*; and various brochures put out by the organisations themselves. See also Paul Heelas "Self Religions: Empowering Capitalism", paper delivered at the Annual Meeting of the British Sociological Association Sociology of Religion Study Group, St. Mary's College, Strawberry Hill, Twickenham, March 1989.

55. Peter Finkelstein, Brant Wenegrat and Irvin Yalom "Large Group Awareness Training" *Annual Review of Psychology*, 1982, p. 517.

56. Mentioned at an Introductory Meeting. See also *The Independent*, 10 June 1988; *Sunday Mirror*, 3 January 1988.

57. See *Appendix IV*.

58. See Leonard Orr and Sondra Ray "Physical Immortality", chapter 6 of *Rebirthing in the New Age*, Berkeley CA: Celestial Arts, revised edition, 1983, pp. 150-170.

Community

Many of the movements, including those whose members or clients do not live with other members, offer instant friendship and understanding within a community of like-minded believers. As time passes, the friendliness of the initial proselytisers may well dissipate, but often it is loyalty to those relationships that have subsequently developed which will keep people in the group. This may be so even when the convert has severe reservations about the movement or its leadership. As with more traditional communities, the metaphor of The Family is frequently employed, members calling each other brother or sister and the leaders Mother or Father.

Kingdom building

Roy Wallis draws a distinction between three types of NRM: world-accommodating, world-affirming and world-rejecting movements. The world-accommodating movements, among which he includes Neo-Pentecostalism, the Charismatic Renewal movement, and some non-Christian groups such as Subud, the Aetherius Society and Western versions of Nichiren Shoshu Buddhism, are fairly content with (or indifferent to) the world as it is. The world-affirming movements, which include members of the Human Potential movement, claim to help the individual to cope with the world and its current values. The world-rejecting movement "is much more *recognizably* religious than the world-affirming type":

> The world-rejecting movement expects that the millennium will shortly commence or that the movement will sweep the world, and, when all have become members or when they are in a majority, or when they have become guides and counsellors to kings and presidents, then a new world-order will begin, a simpler, more loving, more humane and more spiritual order in which the old evils and mistakes will be eradicated, and utopia will have begun.[59]

One of the best-known examples of what Wallis calls world-rejecting movements is the Unification Church. Many of those who have become members of this movement have been somewhat idealistic young people, wanting to make the world a better place, but not knowing too clearly how to go about it. While they will have been ready, even eager, to submit to an authority that will give direction and meaning to their life, they tend to be 'doers' rather than the drifters or dreamers who may be attracted to some other movements. Unificationists are likely to be anxious to accept the challenge of a hard-working life of sacrifice in the belief that they are thus contributing towards the establishment of the Kingdom of Heaven on earth. The work in which the members will be engaged takes many forms, but it is likely to include a considerable

---

59. Wallis (1983), p. 9.

period of fundraising and of trying to introduce new members to the movement.

If one turns to other NRMs, it is clear that there is an enormous variety in the accounts of what is wrong with contemporary society and the explanations for these wrongs, and in the ideas about what the future society should look like and the ways in which we ought to proceed if the new society is to be established.[60] It is not one of the aims of this book to describe the ways in which NRMs claim that they can change the world into a better place. It can, however, be noted that many of the movements do have such an ambition and do offer their members a chance to participate in their utopian, millennial, revolutionary or reformist endeavours.

Self development

Wallis' world-affirming category overlaps to a considerable degree with Paul Heelas' category of 'self-religions' – "movements (including Kerista, The Farm, Primal Therapy, Rebirthing, *est*, and Co-Counselling) which exemplify the conjunction of the exploration of the self and the search for significance".[61] The religious nature of many of these movements is not immediately apparent – indeed, people who take part in a weekend workshop with the Forum, who join a group that teaches a technique such as Transcendental Meditation, or who, having taken the personality test offered to passers-by on London's Tottenham Court Road or some other busy shopping centre, agree to sign up for a course in Dianetics, are likely, at least in the first instance, to be wanting to improve themselves, rather than to relate to God or to change the world. When Heelas asked 300 people why they were about to pay £200 + VAT to go on an Exegesis seminar, their motives were invariably concerned with self-improvement, improving personal relationships or greater success in achieving goals. No one mentioned spiritual or religious goals.[62]

Often people start on a course of self-improvement or self-development with no intention of pursuing the matter further, but they may find that further courses (and further money) are needed to complete their training or enlightenment. People who start by paying out modest sums of £20 or £30 may eventually find that they have been 'successful' enough to graduate to a level at which they are eligible to embark on courses costing several thousands of pounds. Inevitably, there nearly always seems to be one more level to which the really serious and committed should aspire. They may find themselves drawn into debt in

---

60. See Eileen Barker *Kingdoms of Heaven on Earth: New Religious Movements and Political Orders*, Centre for the Study of Religion and Society, University of Kent at Canterbury, Pamphlet Library, No. 15, 1987.
61. Paul Heelas "Californian Self-Religions and Socialising the Subjective" in Barker (ed.) (1982), p. 69.
62. Paul Heelas "Exegesis: Methods and Aims" in Clarke (ed.) (1987), pp. 17–41.

order to pay for the courses. They may be offered the opportunity to work for the movement so that they can continue their courses without payment, or at a subsidised rate.

By this time, the seeker may have become convinced that the movement aspires to worthier ideals than the mere personal advancement of its individual members. Heelas reports that Exegesis graduates "have to try to live as gods"; that they have to find god within themselves; and that self-transformation is bound up with world transformation.[63] To take another example, a spokesman for the Church of Scientology responded to the suggestion that becoming a staff member is a way in which Scientologists can pay for expensive courses with the statement that:

> [the fact that] a person who becomes a member of the Church [of Scientology]'s staff will be eligible for reduced or no-charge counselling rates is given, as a matter of policy, minimum stress; what is important is whether the individual wants to achieve the aims of Scientology – "a civilisation without insanity, without criminals and without war, where the able can prosper and honest beings can have rights, and where Man is free to rise to greater heights".

There are, indeed, several examples of movements that offer courses in self-development or actualisation *and* spiritual or religious teachings *and* the chance to change the world into a much, much better place. Just as those who practise Dianetics may also study L. Ron Hubbard's religio-philosophy within the Church of Scientology, so can Rajneeshee 'neo-sannyasins' explore both Bhagwan's philosophy and a wide assortment of yogic and meditative practices; just as Unificationists can believe that they are developing their spiritual nature at the same time as they are contributing to the restoration of the Kingdom of Heaven on earth, so can members of Nichiren Shoshu Buddhism and Transcendental Meditators believe that the personal successes that they achieve through, respectively, their chanting or their meditation will ultimately benefit the rest of society.[64]

Religious experiences

Movements that embrace the more obviously religious systems of beliefs will sometimes attract those who might, in other circumstances, have joined a convent or a monastery in their desire to devote themselves to God or to explore religious questions and pass their lives with others who take such questions seriously. Believers in the New Age will emphasise the spiritual rather than the religious, but they too will often have been seeking for a 'home' in which they can share their experiences and seek, with other seekers, the fruits of the Age of Aquarius.[65]

---

63. Ibid.
64. See Eileen Barker *Kingdoms of Heaven on Earth*.
65. See Rosen (1975); and Roszak (1976).

It is not always easy in modern society for people who have had such experiences, or who wish to examine religious questions, to find a group of people who will 'give them permission' to be religious. It is not only those who are to end up in an NRM who have complained that they have felt isolated among peers whom they believed to be more interested in other matters, and who would have looked upon them as 'religious nutters' had they tried to discuss their religious quest. There are NRMs that offer such people an environment in which it is 'safe' to have such discussions – indeed, where it is the norm for such discussions to take place. (See also the later section on *The opportunity to discuss religious questions*.)

Many members of NRMs explain that their conversion was due to a religious experience which convinced them of the truth to be found in the movement. Although others may question the interpretation that is put on them by a particular movement, such experiences cannot be dismissed lightly – too many people have had them and been profoundly affected by them.[66] The actual form that the experience may take can vary between a general feeling of oneness with the universe to awareness of a presence or a vivid vision.[67] The person may be alone, but those who join an NRM frequently have an experience while they are actually with members of the movement that they are to join. A convert to the Unification Church reported:

> When I actually heard 'conclusion' for the first time I had a rebirth experience completely intoxicated in love and joy – I even inspired my parents about God – in fact the whole week after the rebirth all I was talking about was God – my parents thought I'd gone crazy. But actually I was just so full of spirit, happy, singing, full of love. Amazing experience – I still feel it to this moment.[68]

An ex-member, describing the experience of 'receiving the Knowledge' tells how, when the mahatma (instructor) had entered the room,

> I felt this strange force inside my head. I felt as if I was blasted by some kind of energy coming from somewhere in the direction of the mahatma. I was just loaded with love. It was just pure love, really strong. And it kept getting stronger, more intense. I was feeling like a rickety-framed house about to collapse in a wind storm. *I won't be able to take it*, I thought. Tears were streaming down my cheeks. The emotion was just flowing. I hadn't cried since I was in the first grade. . .

---

66. For documentation of the extent to which members of mainstream denominations, and, indeed, those with no formal religious affiliation, have such experiences, see David Hay *Exploring Inner Space*, Harmondsworth: Penguin, 1982; Alister Hardy *The Spiritual Nature of Man*, Oxford: Clarendon, 1979; and publications of the Alister Hardy Research Centre at Manchester College, Oxford. See also Andrew M. Greeley *Unsecular Man*, New York: Schocken, 1972. And it is still worth reading the classic work on the subject: William James *The Varieties of Religious Experience*, London: Longmans, 1903.

67. Ibid, especially Timothy Beardsworth *A Sense of Presence*, Oxford: Religious Experience Research Unit, Manchester College, 1977;

68. Barker (1984), p. 169.

I worked a couple of days. I was just higher than a kite: I was God talking to God, standing on God, breathing God. My supervisor was angry; he wanted me to resign. Obviously anybody who went chasing off after some guru could not be considered reliable.[69]

69. Enroth (1977), pp. 137 and 139.

❦ CHAPTER FOUR ❧

The New Convert

HOSE WHO JOIN NRMs are by no means always, or even usually, the pathetic, weak, or susceptible characters that it is sometimes assumed they must be. Furthermore, the vast majority of members are unlikely to *become* pathetic, weak or susceptible characters. Members of NRMs are human beings who happen to be in a movement that is considered, both by them and by outsiders, to be 'different'. It can be argued that people who believe unusual beliefs and who engage in unusual practices must be unusual people. But if 'unusual' is being defined as unlike the majority of people in contemporary Western society, then it has to be admitted that most human beings living today, and almost all of those who have lived in the past, could be classified as 'unusual'. Both history and anthropology clearly illustrate that what one group of people considers to be 'natural' or 'proper' behaviour, another group is quite capable of thinking bizarre, insane, 'unnatural', 'improper' or dangerous.[70] Just because a movement is 'different', it does not mean that its members are of a different species. Changes in beliefs and behaviour need not be worrying *just* because they are changes. They could be changes for the worse; they could be changes for the better; most likely, they will be a mixture of both.

So far as the converts are concerned, there may have been a particular moment when suddenly they 'saw the light'. Their life is likely to become defined and interpreted according to the 'before' and 'after' periods, both of which are likely to be seen in the 'new light' – with, quite probably, 'before' being miserable, worthless or evil and 'after' being blissful, valuable or godly. Both the movement and the convert may (consciously or unconsciously) expend quite a lot of effort in reinforcing such an interpretation. Relatives and friends may also feel the need to interpret

---

70. See, for example, Mary Douglas *Purity and Danger: an analysis of concepts of pollution and taboo*, London: Routledge and Kegan Paul, 1966; and R. G. Collingwood *An Autobiography*, Harmondsworth: Pelican, 1939, for discussions about 'cultural relativism' from, respectively, an anthropological and an historical-philosophical perspective.

everything that has happened to the convert in 'before' and 'after' terms – although their evaluation of these two periods may differ quite radically from that of the convert.

The changes that the converts report vary enormously. However, Jeanne Messer's attempt to summarise the changes she noted in Divine Light Mission 'premies' after they had received the Knowledge is helpful because this bears a resemblance to some of the changes reported by others who have gone through an initiation or conversion experience – whether it be the Sahaja Yogi or Yogini who has become 'realized', the Nichiren Shoshu Buddhist who has begun the 'practice' of chanting, the *est* graduate, the Transcendental Meditator or even, in certain respects (if one were, for example, to read 'prayer' for 'meditation'), the 'born again' Christian.

The first obvious change that Messer noted is that meditation is a source of energy:

> Devotees are simply less fatigued, less easily disoriented when they meditate regularly, and they become rapidly dependent on the meditation as a source of rest, energy and personal integration. . .[71]

The second change is an increasing awareness of "that remarkable series of coincidences on which Divine Light Mission runs."

> It is a beginning of an awareness of cause and effect as different from what it once seemed to be. One begins to feel that events in one's life are being arranged for the sole purpose of *getting one's attention*. One devotee reports feeling "directed" to pick up hitchhikers, who turn out to be devotees. Another devotee's car window exploded . . . with no injuries and no apparent cause, and she experienced the event as a demand that she meditate. Most devotees are not consciously looking for signs; they feel *confronted* by signs requesting their cooperation. . . Miracle stories – from pure trivia to the really remarkable – are exchanged by the hundreds and with delight and laughter.[72]

Thirdly, Messer describes how the devotees, convinced that their marriage, their work, their finances and their personal relationships have all obviously improved, develop a growing conviction that:

> One is accompanied, tended, loved, and taught by God, and that the God within is remarkably like the child guru: happy, playful, insistent, unpredictable, loving and perfectly benevolent.[73]

Although a conversion experience can appear quite dramatic, and some of them certainly *are* dramatic, there is, as mentioned earlier, usually both a period of preparation before, and a period of consolidation afterwards. It is during the period following an apparently sudden conversion that

---

71. Jeanne Messer "Guru Maharaj Ji and the Divine Light Mission" in Glock and Bellah (1976), p. 55.
72. Ibid, pp. 56–7.
73. Ibid, p. 56.

the convert is likely to be particularly open to suggestion both from the movement and from relatives, friends and others. Previous beliefs and values will have been questioned, but the new set of beliefs will not yet have been 'lived'. Like new converts to many a faith, new converts to a new religious movement are unlikely to have 'internalised' their new belief system. At this stage, the 'new way of seeing things' consists of ideas and expectations, rather than a comparatively well-integrated system of beliefs and practices.

During the ensuing weeks, new revelations may be incorporated into the convert's previous world-view without resulting in any radical change in his or her life. Alternatively, the new ideas may become incorporated into a new framework that has been supplied by the NRM. Even in this latter case, however, converts will continue to rely on many of their old beliefs and values. This means that, although converts' life-style and adherence to a belief-system may have changed quite radically, new members will usually appear less fanatical, less strange and more recognisably their old selves after two or three months.

There are several reasons why new converts might appear to be more frighteningly changed than they really are. Quite apart from the fact that they may have cut their hair and exchanged shabby jeans for flowing robes or a suit and tie, and quite apart from the fact that they may be giving up a course of study or a promising career, the new converts may not themselves be entirely certain about, or completely understand, the new stand that they are taking. They are, therefore, likely to be on the defensive, particularly if one of the reasons for their joining the movement was that they had felt the need to make a gesture of independence. Indeed, Saul Levine concluded, as the result of fifteen years of work with members of movements and their families, that the need to make a gesture of independence was the primary reason why the young adults whom he had studied joined an NRM.[74]

Because their new beliefs will not yet have become an integrated part of their everyday thinking, new converts are liable to suffer from an inability to be flexible in answering questions. This means that they often resort to the movement's incomprehensible jargon and sound as though they are spouting meaningless rubbish in a parrot-like fashion. They 'know' that it makes sense at some level that they have glimpsed, but they are not yet able to explain it to others. Students often suffer the same disability before they have got 'on top of' a subject. It is also possible that the converts are so excited by the new truth which they believe they have discovered that they are eager to share this with others – especially those whom they most love. As a consequence, they may shower their bewildered parents with zealous admonitions to see the light as they themselves see it.

74. Levine (1984).

Outright rejection or ridicule by the parents in such a situation can lead to withdrawal by the son or daughter and the start of a downward spiral of mutual misunderstanding and recrimination. This process is greatly exacerbated if the parents are also frightened by sensational media reports, or they have been otherwise persuaded that their child is now a brainwashed robot who is incapable of independent thought. The parents might then start to 'see' signs that their children are indeed 'not themselves'. It is, however, unlikely that the converts will have been drastically manipulated by sinister techniques of mind control – and extremely unlikely that they will be suffering from any lasting (or even temporary) physiological damage. It is also very unlikely that they will be suffering from any lasting (or even temporary) psychological harm. In any case, it certainly does not help if converts are repeatedly told that they no longer have a mind of their own.

This is certainly not to suggest that parents may not notice some very real changes in their offspring's behaviour. Parents will, after all, have known their child since his or her birth, and it would be worrying if they were *not* to notice that their son or daughter was behaving differently. The very fact that converts *have* converted and taken on a new way of life will mean that they are more than likely to have changed in some ways. What conversion *calls for* has been described as

> a death and rebirth, the turning away from the darkness to walk in the light, a putting off of the old self to put on the new.[75]

Saint Paul was not the same after his journey on the road to Damascus. 'Born again' Christians who take Jesus into their heart are unlikely to be the sorts of people that they were before conversion – they may have stopped drinking, taking drugs, swearing or sleeping around.

In other words, it is being suggested that relatives and friends of those who join NRMs should not immediately assume that all changes are to be interpreted as signs that something sinister has necessarily happened to the convert. At the same time, those who wish to help should remember that it is the relatives and friends who will be the people who know the convert best, and careful attention should be paid to the kinds of changes that have been observed; some of these may be a genuine cause for concern. To take an extreme example, a deeply distressed father described a personality change in his daughter thus:

> loss of sense of humour; increasing secretiveness; a sort of vagueness; diminished honesty; restlessness; deterioration in handwriting, spelling, grammar (but not spoken grammar); reduced attention to personal appearance or to the home; abandonment of all reading; denigration of any intellectual activity.[76]

---

75. J. Hanigan "Conversion and Christian Ethics", *Theology Today*, vol. 40, no. 1, p. 25.
76. Personal communication.

Other parents have talked of their children suffering from an apparent lack of ability to concentrate, and many have observed that things that once interested the convert can no longer attract his or her attention. These are symptoms that have also been observed in ex-members (see the later section on *Leaving a movement*).

In some cases, apparently worrying behaviour may arise because the son or daughter finds difficulty in relaxing with his or her parents, and it may be advisable to have a less emotionally involved person present on occasion. But it could also be that the NRM and/or the techniques which it employs *are* resulting in significant psychological changes. There is further discussion of this possibility in later sections.

❧ CHAPTER FIVE ❧

Areas of Public Concern

------- ▶ ◆ ◆ ◀ -------

Assessing 'atrocity tales'

THERE ARE SECTIONS of the media, some individuals, and some groups that concentrate on relating 'atrocity tales' with which they aim to demonstrate the essential evil of the cults.[77] Several points ought to be borne in mind when assessing these accounts. First, they may be completely untrue. For example, a young man who claimed that he had been drugged, abducted, and held captive by members of ISKCON has recently been given a three-year suspended sentence in Dublin for making a false statement. The police had carried out an extensive investigation into the movement and the accusations brought against it, and had been able to prove that the whole fantastic story was little more than a figment of the young man's imagination. But the investigation took place only after the young man had made a number of sensational appearances and claims on Radio Telefis Eireann. He was reported to have been encouraged by a local priest who was "concerned at young people being subjected to the degenerate wiles of loony sects".[78] There are further examples of 'exposés', frequently by ex-members, which, upon investigation, have turned out to be fabrications, with the would-be exposer eventually admitting that he or she had made up the story.[79]

Sometimes it appears that the reporter has confused the characteristics of one NRM with those of others – possibly because they are so frequently 'lumped together'. For example, the sweeping generalisation that the leaders of the Unification Church push the members into prostitution and suicide[80] might arise out of a confusion with, perhaps,

---

77. For a discussion on the concept of 'atrocity tales', see Bromley & Shupe (1981); Beckford (1985); Shupe & Bromley (1980); and these authors in Barker (ed.) (1982).

78. See *The Irish Times*, 16 December 1988; *The Irish Independent*, 16 December 1988; and *The Sunday Independent*, 18 December 1988.

79. Melton (1986), p. 243.

80. This was suggested in an article in *La Suisse*, 12 July 1988.

the Children of God and the People's Temple. The idea that 'Moonies' are asked to become prostitutes must seem to be particularly ludicrous to anyone who knows anything about the movement and its beliefs; and although, just after the Jonestown tragedy, rumours circulated alleging that various other movements were preparing their members for mass suicide, there is absolutely no reliable evidence that this was ever the policy, or indeed, the practice of the Unification Church.

More commonly, an action may be described in such a way that it is being clearly labelled as 'bad', while exactly the same action may be labelled as laudable when described in different words. For example, 'conversion', 'recruitment', 're-education', 'secondary socialisation', 'mind control', 'menticide' and 'brainwashing' may all be used to refer to the one process, but each term carries a very different nuance. Similarly, a life-style that is described as one of obedience and sacrificial devotion by one person may be described as one of authoritarian exploitation by another. Depending on the context in which they are used, words such as dedication, discipline, surrender and submission can be imbued with very different values.

And, as suggested earlier, the word 'cult' has come to carry all manner of negative connotations which may not be at all appropriate when applied to certain organisations that are labelled by the term. In a study of media coverage of NRMs, van Driel and Richardson found that:

> Before Jonestown, the various NRMs had been treated as idiosyncratic religious movements existing at the periphery of society. But after the profuse outpouring of information about the incident at Jonestown, the label of 'cult' was firmly attached to a wide variety of movements, and they were all thrown, for a time, into a single, heavily stigmatized category.[81]

In a public opinion survey carried out in Washington D.C. shortly after the mass deaths of members of the People's Temple in Jonestown, over a quarter of the respondents expressed an unfavourable attitude towards a non-existent 'spoof cult'.[82]

More subtly, when reporting some bad news or malpractice concerning an NRM, the story is often presented in such a way as to suggest that the occurrence is more typical of NRMs than it would be of the rest of society. If, for example, a member of an NRM commits suicide, attention is almost certain to be drawn to his or her affiliation to the movement, with the implication that the movement was responsible for the suicide. If, on the other hand, Methodists or Anglicans commit

---

81. Barend van Driel and James T. Richardson "Print Media Coverage of New Religious Movements: A Longitudinal Study" *Journal of Communication*, 36/3 Summer 1988, p. 54. See also James A. Beckford and Melanie A. Cole "British and American Responses to New Religious Movements" in Dyson and Barker (eds) (1988), pp. 209–225.

82. Gillian Lindt and Albert Gollin in an unpublished paper presented at the Annual Meeting of the American Association of Public Opinion Research, June 1979, p. 18.

suicide, it is most unlikely that their religious identity will be mentioned.
For all anyone knows, the suicide rate might be *higher* among Methodists
or Anglicans than among Brahma Kumaris or Scientologists. Not surprisingly, the NRMs themselves are more likely to argue that they *prevent*
people from committing suicide – there are certainly converts who claim
that they would have killed themselves had they not found their new
religion. One well-known NRM makes the point that the only one of
its members who has committed suicide in Britain did so after having
been 'successfully' deprogrammed.

To try to resolve the truth of the matter it would be necessary
(although not sufficient) to make a careful comparison of suicide rates
among people of a similar age and background in the different groups.
Unfortunately this information is not readily available – it is known that
the number of suicides actually recorded in Britain in 1987 was 4,508,
but as it is common practice for compassionate coroners to give an open
verdict if there is any possibility of doubt, the actual number is likely to
be considerably higher.[83]

Similarly, with regard to other issues, nothing but confusion is likely
to arise from noticing *only* those cases that happen to have been brought
to one's attention by the media or a person or group that is interested
only in 'atrocity tales'. In the same vein, it should be remembered that
the breaking up of a family usually occurs without any NRM being
involved, and that the numbers of young people who have no connection
with any cult but are involved in drugs, violence, sexual promiscuity or
who just 'drop out' far exceeds the total numbers of people involved in
such practices in all the NRMs put together.

None of this is to suggest that a tragedy is not a tragedy, or that a
malpractice is not a malpractice – whenever it occurs. It is, however, to
suggest that it might be sensible to look carefully at the facts before
concluding that just because something worrying happens in an NRM it
is necessarily *because* it is in an NRM that it has happened.[84] There may
be other reasons, and it may be that the NRM is being used as a
convenient way of avoiding examining and coming to terms with those
other reasons.

But why, one may still ask, is it that the NRMs *are* associated with
atrocity tales? Is it because middle-class parents with high aspirations for
their children do not like the idea of their child giving up a promising

---

83. John Sweeney "The Marconi Mystery", *The Independent Magazine*, 5 November
1988, pp. 25–7.

84. A more detailed discussion of the methodological procedure necessarily involved
in a responsible examination of such issues, and an example of some unexpected differences
that were revealed through a comparison of (i) members of the Unification Church, (ii)
people who attended Unification workshops but did not join the movement and (iii) a
'control group' of people who had no contact with the movement but were of the same
age and background as the members and non-joiners, can be found in Barker (1984).

career to sell literature on the street, coupled with the fact that middle-class parents tend to be in a position to make a fuss when their child does just that? Is it because to talk about 'my son the Moonie' or 'my daughter the Scientologist' is seen in our society as a shameful admission of failure, while to talk about 'my son the rabbi' or 'my daughter the nun' is more acceptable?

Is it because certain sections of the media and the uninvolved public like a juicy story and exhibit a ghoulish pleasure in exposé-type gossip about the 'exotic', the 'bizarre', the 'sinister' and the 'threatening'? Is it because, almost without exception throughout history, new religious movements (including early Christianity, Methodism, and the Salvation Army) have been treated with fear, mistrust, suspicion and hostility? Is it because the movements' criticisms of the Churches and of the secular, materialistic rat-race are seen to pose a threat to the establishment? – or because the 'alternative' therapies that they offer are seen as a threat to the professions whose conventional wisdom they scorn? Is it because professional deprogrammers can make tens of thousands of pounds by persuading people that they *ought* to be scared stiff?

There could be some truth in all these reasons. But there are also plenty of reasons that arise out of the actions of the movements them-selves, rather than out of the reactions that they have elicited from others.

Criminal activities and other serious charges

Among the obvious causes for concern to which the NRMs have given rise are the crimes, misdemeanours and other unsavoury activities in which some of their number have indulged. There was the terrible tragedy of Jonestown. There were the Manson murders. A poisonous snake was placed in the mailbox of an attorney who had successfully fought a lawsuit against Synanon. Members of the Children of God have been enjoined to become 'Hookers for Jesus' and to engage in 'Flirty Fishing' (the now discarded practice of using sex as a technique to gain money or new members), and several of the internal 'Mo letters' (pamphlets written by the movement's leader, David 'Moses' Berg) can be described as little other than pornographic. Berg has, moreover, been accused by one of his daughters of having had an incestuous relationship with her sister and of attempting to have one with her.[85]

The Manson Family acquired expensive consumer goods by credit-card fraud or with money obtained from drug-pushing. The 'games' that it played included breaking into people's homes, stealing food and other objects, and deliberately moving things around – preferably while the unsuspecting owners were in the house. In 1979, eleven leading Scientologists (including L. Ron Hubbard's wife) were convicted on charges of theft of US government documents. Sun Myung Moon recently served

---

85. Davis (1984), p. 12.

a sentence in a US prison for tax offences. There have been several reports of Krishna devotees in parts of America having engaged in drug-trafficking, child abuse, the stock-piling of armaments and murder. In Oregon, charges against thirty-four Rajneeshees, including Bhagwan himself, are said to have included:

> attempted murder, first-degree assault, second degree assault, first-degree arson, burglary, racketeering, harbouring a fugitive, electronic eavesdropping, immigration conspiracies, lying to US authorities and criminal conspiracy.[86]

There has been a growing number of cases reported in both Western and Eastern Europe and in North America of animals being tortured in ritual sacrifices. In Germany and the United States, teenagers have been convicted of murder after they had become involved in devil worship.[87] It has been reported in the media that the police are investigating the sacrifice of human babies by Satanists in Britain.[88] There are also numerous instances of lesser offences committed by members of some of the movements, such as selling goods without a licence, illegally claiming social security benefits, obtaining visas or overdrafts on false information and obstructing the public highway.

Crimes such as those mentioned have, of course, been committed by many persons other than the members of NRMs. Indeed, several crimes have been committed against NRMs by their opponents. Apart from numerous illegal kidnappings of members of various NRMs with the avowed intent to 'deprogramme the victim', there have been assassinations, arson attacks, shootings, and several bombings of property belonging to ISKCON, the Rajneeshees, The Way and the Unification Church (resulting, in an incident in France, in severe physical injury).[89] On more than one occasion, there have been mob killings of members of the Ananda Marga in India.[90] And in Philadelphia in 1985, police dropped a bomb on a house, burning to death seven members of a confrontational black group, The Move – and four of their children.[91] Sometimes it is a political regime that has violated the basic human rights of members of a group. Just as other religious minorities, such as the Jehovah's Witnesses in Nazi Germany, the Baha'i in Iran or members of the Ahmadiyya

---

86. Milne (1986), p. 313; see also Fitzgerald (1986).

87. *Mobile Press*, 28 October 1988; *Los Angeles Times*, 19 and 20 October 1988. See also *The Arizona Daily Star*, 29 January 1989.

88. *Awareness: New Religious Movements and Cult Activity*, Christian Information Outreach, Spring 1989, pp. 19–20, quoting *Sunday Mirror*, 30 October 1988; BBC Radio 4's *Sunday Programme*, 23 April 1989; *Bella*, 1 April 1989; *Daily Mirror*, 18 May 1989; *The Cook Report: The Devil's Work*, ITV, 17 July 1989. See also *Cook Report: A Crock of Lies*, Leeds: Sorcerers Apprentice, July 1989.

89. For details of some of these incidents, see Melton (1976), pp. 245–8.

90. *The Boston Globe*, 1 May 1982; *The New York Times*, 1 May 1982; and "1974 Report of Mr. W.T. Wells, Q.C." in *The Persecution of Ananda Marga in India*, London: Ananda Marga Publications, n.d., p. 36.

91. *The Times*, 15, 16 and 20 May 1985; *The Observer*, 19 May 1985.

community in Pakistan, have suffered appalling persecution,[92] Krishna devotees in the USSR have died in prison because of their beliefs – although it should be added that, as a result of the recent changes, the Soviet Regime now recognises ISKCON as a religion and the devotees have been released from the prisons, labour camps and mental institutions in which they were previously incarcerated.

Ananda Marga is one of the movements that has denied charges that have been brought against it and its members and vehemently protested against persecution by the Indian regime during the State of Emergency declared by Mrs Indira Gandhi during the 1970s,[93] and there have been instances when they and members of other NRMs who have been accused or even convicted of crimes have, at a later date, had their convictions quashed, or have been pardoned. For example, it has been said that:

> Anand Marg followers were arrested and convicted in UK, Australia, Thailand and the Philippines on charges of violent physical attacks directed against the Government of India officials posted in those countries. . . These acts took place mainly at a time when Mr. P.R. Sarkar was in jail and the Anand Marg followers were demanding his unconditional release.[94]

Charges have, however, been dismissed. Sarkar (Shrii Shrii Anandamurti) was released from prison in 1978 when his conviction for murder was overturned on appeal, and three of his followers who were convicted in Australia of conspiracy to murder were pardoned in 1985, after they had served seven years of a 16-year sentence.[95]

Some of those who have not been involved in the crimes of some of their co-religionists have made strenuous attempts to put their movement in order. For example, the Governing Body Commission of ISKCON has expelled those of its gurus who have been found guilty of malpractices, and has apparently spent much of its time in recent years trying to make sure that none of its leaders will be able to misuse his

---

92. See debate in the House of Commons, 21 December 1984; Peter Smith *The Babi and Baha'i Religions: From messianic Shi'ism to a world religion*, Cambridge University Press, 1987, pp. 178–80; paper delivered by Hugh C. Adamson to the Third International Congress on Religious Liberty, London, July 1989; and *After the Dawn of Democracy in Pakistan*, London: International Ahmadiyya Movement in Islam, n.d.

93. See, for example, *The Destruction of Democracy in India: The Case of Ananda Marga*, Liverpool: The International Committee to Obtain Justice for Shrii Shrii Anandamurti, n.d.

94. Letter signed by B. S. Rathore of the Embassy of India, Washington D. C., 6 November 1979, ref: No.WAS/Pol/551/19/72-vol. IV, a copy of which is lodged in the New Religions Research Collection, Graduate Theological Union library, Berkeley, California. See also David R. Telleen "The Rise and Fall of the Ananda Marg: A Modern Indian Morality Tale", December 1977, unpublished paper, also lodged in the G.T.U. library; Robin Napier "Ananda Marga: New Cult or Terrorist Religion?", *Farrago* 30 June 1978.

95. *The Age* (Sydney), 16 May 1985.

position.[96] And, of course, the majority of the thousand or more NRMs in Western Europe and North America have never had any serious accusations brought against them.

None the less, the fact remains that people who join movements that offer simple answers to the problems of their followers and the world, whose members live in relatively closed communities, and whose leader is afforded charismatic authority would occasionally seem to run the risk of performing actions that they would have considered shameful before their involvement with the movement.

Physical Violence

Physical violence has occurred in NRMs, especially in some of the more cut-off movements, and especially where a leader is accorded complete authority. The previous section mentioned some of the more horrifying instances of beatings, torture and murder that have taken place in NRMs. It is also the case that, as in the rest of society, there are wife-bashers and child abusers to be found in NRMs. Once again, however, it might be helpful to put the general situation in perspective – this time by quoting from the report of a survey of 'cult-related violence' conducted from 1983 to 1984 by the Institute for the Study of American Religion:

> Overwhelmingly, nonconventional religious groups have been free of reported incidents of violence. Most groups in the survey were quite similar to the more familiar and established mainline church bodies; they experienced one or two scattered incidents atypical of their day-to-day life. Those few nonconventional religious groups which have suffered a history of violent interaction with society are very much the exceptions of those groups which have been labeled "cult".[97]

The Report goes on to make an important point that is of relevance not only to the incidence of violence but also to some other potentially worrying aspects of NRMs when it observes that:

> Most of the groups which have shown a long-term tendency for a violent interaction with society have received little or no attention from the anti-cult media. This lack of attention is due, in part, to the primary focus of anti-cult groups upon those cults that concentrate their energy in the recruitment of young adults. The more violent groups have been either predominantly black in membership (anti-cult groups tend to be upper-middle class white) or older in membership.[98]

The Institute, which defined violence as behaviour leading to bodily harm or the significant destruction of property, reached a number of conclusions as a result of its survey. At the most general level, it

---

96. Satsvarupa dasa Goswami *Guru Reform Notebook*, Washington D.C.: Gita-nagari Press, 1986; Steven J. Gelberg "The Fading of Utopia: ISKCON in Transition" in Dyson and Barker (eds) (1988), pp. 157–183.
97. Melton (1986), pp. 241.
98. Ibid, p. 242.

considered that it was unlikely that cult-related violence would ever disappear. This pessimistic prediction was because

> cults participate in the general theme of religious violence: [throughout history, religion has been] responsible for wars, and innumerable acts of violence upon individuals . . . [it has been used to sanction slavery and the exploitation of women and] there is every sign that it will continue to be used to rationalize the impulses of religious leaders.[99]

More specifically, the report concluded that: first,

> *some cults have given and continue to give direct sanction to violent activity.*[100]

Examples of this are to be found among the Black Muslims and the Church of the Lamb of God. Also mentioned is the recent wave of right-wing Christian groups which are avowedly anti-Black and anti-Semitic, and have strong ties with the Ku-Klux-Klan. An example is Richard Girnt Butler's Church of Jesus Christ Christian, which recently tried to establish a stronghold in Britain.[101]

Secondly,

> *more cult-related violence grows out of the indirect sanction of violence from belief systems which intellectually undergird group members' violent tendencies.*[102]

The examples given in the Report include the stereotyping of people so that they are in some way 'dehumanized', whether it is by the Church of Scientology designating people as 'potential trouble sources' or 'suppressives', the Mormons or Unificationists designating others as 'satanic', or the anti-cult movement designating members of NRMs as 'helpless victims', 'zombies' or 'mindless puppets' – who are, thus, in need of 'repersonalisation'.

The Institute also concluded that

> *violence erupts, in most cases, only after a period of heightened conflict between either different factions of a religion or a nonconventional religion and the community.*[103]

The Synanon Church is offered as an example of the process by which a difficult situation can become exacerbated as both sides contribute towards the creation of a climate of increasing distrust, misinformation and hostility that works against a peaceful resolution of problems.

Others have offered a similar analysis of the events leading up to the Jonestown tragedy, and antagonisms between the Church of

---

99. Ibid, p. 257.
100. Ibid, p. 258 (italics in the original).
101. See Leonard Zeskind *The "Christian Identity" Movement: Analysing its Theological Rationalization for Racist and Anti-Semitic Violence*, Published by The Division of Church and Society of the National Council of the Churches of Christ in the USA, 1986; *Time*, 20 October 1986.
102. Melton (1986), p. 258 (italics in the original).
103. Ibid, p. 260 (italics in the original).

Scientology, the sannyasins at Rajneeshpuram, the Mormons and the Unification Church, and their diverse opponents.[104] The point that is constantly made is that it can, at least in some circumstances, be misleading to focus merely on extreme behaviour that arises late in a spiralling process of increasing hostility and deviance without taking account of the dynamics of the interaction that led up to the eventual outcome.[105]

There are people who perform certain actions *because* these are considered evil by society. Among the most sensational and disturbing stories to hit the headlines in Europe and North America in the late 1980s are those concerned with allegations of ritual sacrifice or torture being carried out by Satanists. Especially horrible are cases, such as those referred to in the previous section, in which the victims or even perpetrators are children.

It should not be thought that all, or even the majority of Satanists are intent on harm. Many of the allegations made about Satanists turn out on investigation to be false or unsubstantiated.[106] There are several movements against which there have been no serious charges made, despite the fact that their members swear allegiance to 'His Infernal Majesty'. The Church of Satan specifically admonishes its members to abide by all the laws of the land and not to harm anyone in the pursuit of their satanic goals – in the words of the movement's founder, Anton LaVey:

> We Satanists pride ourselves on being ladies and gentlemen – sinful, perhaps – but nonetheless, ladies and gentlemen.[107]

LaVey, a former police employee, is said to have a chaplain's badge for the San Francisco Police Department and many friends on the force, a few of whom are members of his Church. It is also said that he "still works as a consultant on cases that involve the occult."[108] There has, indeed, been a study of the Church of the Trapezoid, a branch of the Church of Satan, which concluded that Satanism could be positively beneficial for both the individual and society.[109] According to Edward J. Moody:

> [As a consequence of his participating in 'ideological rituals'] the witch or magician need be less anxious or fearful, he is more able socially,

---

104. Hall (1987); Naipaul (1981); and Thomas Robbins "Religious Mass Suicide before Jonestown: the Russian Old Believers" *Sociological Analysis*, vol. 47, no. 1, 1986, pp. 1–20; Wallis (1976), pp. 214–221; Milne (1986); Annette P. Hampshire and James Beckford "Religious sects and the Concept of Deviance: the Moonies and the Mormons" *British Journal of Sociology*, vol. 34, no. 2, 1983, pp. 173-83.

105. See Robbins (1988), p. 189.

106. Melton (1976), p. 251; Richardson et al (eds) (1991).

107. Anton LaVey in an 'encyclical letter' to members, July 1978, quoted in Randall Alfred "The Church of Satan" in Glock and Bellah (eds) (1976), p. 187.

108. Ibid; Melton (1976), p. 77.

109. Edward J. Moody "Magical Therapy: An Anthropological Investigation of Contemporary Satanism" in Zaretsky and Leone (eds) (1974), pp. 355–382.

and he is actually more successful in many spheres of activity due to his enhanced ability to interact with others. . . He has been taught to curb his maladaptive behavior and exhibit "proper" behavior in response to certain cues. If he attributes this new-found power and success to magic rather than to the insights of sociology, or psychology, it is because such an interpretation is more in accordance with his world view and the categories of understanding which he uses to give structure and meaning to his world.[110]

Be that as it may, in genuinely worrying cases there have been several instances of young people who have experimented with satanic practices after they, as individuals or with a small group of friends, have become involved with drugs or heavy metal music or read books about Satanism and satanic rituals.[111] It has been reported that

> of the more than one million crimes reported in the U.S. over the past five years, only about 60 were listed by police as involving Satanism.[112]

Most people who dabble in satanic or black magic rituals quickly get bored and pass on to less unsavoury pursuits, but there seems to be little doubt that certain aspects of Satanism appeal to some psychopaths with sadistic tendencies, and, obviously enough, 60 crimes involving Satanism is 60 crimes too many.

Released at the age of 33 in 1967, after a series of earlier sentences for theft, pimping and numerous other offences, Charles Miles Manson (also known as Jesus Christ and as Satan) became part of the San Francisco Haight-Ashbury scene. Anti-establishment, anti-semitic and anti-black, Manson appears to have despised the 'hippies' and soon formed his own "para-military mystical sect".[113] The ideological lawlessness that ruled the commune where his young followers lived in Death Valley, California, was matched only by the authoritarian control that Manson had over his 'Family'.[114]

In August 1969, Sharon Tate, the film star wife of film director Roman Polanski was ritually murdered, with four other people in her Beverly Hills home. Sharon Tate was eight months pregnant; all the bodies were brutally mutilated. The next day the murder of a millionaire supermarket owner and his wife took place, reportedly because Manson

---

110. Ibid, p. 380.

111. *Los Angeles Times*, 19 and 20 October 1988; *The Tampa Tribune*, 1 November 1988; Melton (1986), p. 250. See also Richardson et al (eds) (1991).

112. Professor Earl Bailey "This Believing World" *The News Herald*, Panama City, Fla., 19 November 1988.

113. Donald A. Nielsen "Charles Manson's Family of Love: A Case of Anomism, Puerilism and Transmoral Consciousness in Civilizational Perspective" *Sociological Analysis*, vol. 45, no. 4, Winter 1984, p. 325.

114. Vincent Bugliosi (with Curt Gentry) *Helter Skelter: The Manson Murders*, Harmondsworth: Penguin, 1977 [Bugliosi was the assistant district attorney investigating and prosecuting in the Manson murders]; Susan Atkins (with Bob Slosser) *Child of Satan, Child of God*, London: Hodder and Stoughton, 1978 [Atkins, one of the Manson 'Slaves', involved in some of the murders, became a 'born again' Christian while in prison].

wanted to make sure that his 'Slaves' would not lose their nerve as a result of the Tate killings.[115] Evidently they did not: after the murders, the five Slaves took a shower to wash off the blood, then sat down to a meal from their victims' refrigerator.

The Manson murders, even more than the Jonestown tragedy, provide a terrifying example of the way in which people can be persuaded to act when they fall under the influence of a powerful charismatic leader. The murders were, by all normal canons, utterly senseless and abhorrent – and yet it appears that it made sense to Manson's followers to perform such acts. (Manson claims never to have 'instructed' Family members to kill anyone.)[116] Such monstrous atrocities occur only rarely, but they do occur. It is as absurd to think that anyone who joins an NRM will find themselves in a position similar to that of Manson's followers as it is to believe that anyone who crosses a road is bound to be run over. At the same time, it is as foolish to forget that such abominations have taken place as it is to forget that people can get killed while crossing a road.

Whatever the motivation, religious belief provides no excuse for the use of violence against the person. In any case where there is good reason to believe that physical violence is practised, the police or some other appropriate authority should be informed.

Deception

It is quite likely that most members of NRMs are neither more nor less truthful than the rest of the population. Some members try to be scrupulously honest about every detail; but, as has already been mentioned, not all the movements are entirely honest about who they are, the precise nature of their beliefs or the details of the practices in which they engage. Converts may be drawn into a movement unaware of the practical 'translation' of some of its tenets. The proselytisers might, for example, put great emphasis on love or on the importance of serving God, without mentioning *how* they express their love or *how* they believe God is best served. It could be that 'love' is expressed in purely sexual terms or 'service' to God entails meting out violence to those who, allegedly, do not serve God.

A few of the movements, or, at least, some of their members, have produced quasi-religious justifications, such as 'heavenly deception' or 'transcendental trickery', for some less-than-honest practices.[117] Some members have excused the practice of not revealing their true identity by saying that, because the media have given them such a bad press, they want to give the potential convert an opportunity to find out

---

115. David Hanna *Cults in America*, New York: Belmont Tower Books, 1979, p. 87.
116. Nielsen, op cit, p. 326.
117. See, for example, Barker (1984), p. 176; Rochford (1985), pp. 195–200; Wright (1987), p. 59.

what the movement is *really* like, without the encumbrance of negative preconceptions.

So far as letting potential converts know what the members' exact goals are, evangelists have, throughout history, justified presenting themselves in a way that will establish a personal relationship or elementary principles before proceeding to a more detailed or sophisticated account of what it is that they want to tell the potential convert.[118] Some members of some movements have gone further than concealing the truth – they have denied the truth, blatantly lying to potential converts and other 'outsiders'. Furthermore, some members of some movements lie to other members of the same movement. It is not unusual for members of certain NRMs not to know what their leaders get up to - how the money is spent, exactly who issues the orders, or what the long-term goals of the leaders are.

Sometimes members have been instructed to say that they are collecting money, food or other goods for the aged, for young people on drugs, or for poor people in under-developed countries.[119] Sometimes these statements are down-right lies; at other times, they are twisting the truth; at yet other times, the members may convince themselves that they are telling the truth, but their understanding of, say, 'Christian missionary work' will not be the same as the understanding of the people from whom they are requesting money.

Several movements have a number of different names or affiliated organisations, and it is not always clear that the off-shoot is connected with the better-known organisation. In this way, a movement might attract people who share its political but not its religious beliefs, or persuade others to sign a petition concerning some particular issue, when they would not dream of signing it were they to know the nature of the parent organisation. People might agree to hire a hall to some 'nice young Christians', not realising that they are members of, say, the Children of God – one way of trying to find out is to ask for an address and telephone number, as this is almost certain not to be given if they *are* the Children of God, and other groups might quickly withdraw their request if too many enquiries are made about who they are and how they propose to use the premises. Parents might send their children to a school that they would keep them away from were they to know the sorts of beliefs that the staff held, and might teach the pupils.[120] People may enrol for a course in Business Management, Philosophy, Economics or some other discipline in order to educate themselves, not realising

---

118. See I Corinthians 3:1–3 and 9:19–23; and Hebrews 5:12.
119. See Thomas Robbins "Profit for Prophets: Legitimate and Illegitimate Economic Practices in New Religious Movements" in Richardson (ed.) (1988), pp. 69–116.
120. Hounam and Hogg (1984), p. 210.

that they are to be exposed to a rather different sort of philosophy or economics than they might be taught at the local Technical College.[121]

---

121. See discussion in Paul Heelas "Exegesis: Methods and Aims" in Clarke (ed.) (1987), pp. 17–41.

❧ CHAPTER SIX ❧

Effects on the Individual

Suicide

I T IS UNKNOWN how many members of NRMs have turned violence upon themselves by committing suicide. As was suggested earlier in the section on *Assessing 'atrocity tales'*, it cannot be assumed that just because people have committed suicide while they are in an NRM, they necessarily did so *because* they were in the movement. It should also be remembered that there are many who claim that they were suicidal before they met the movement that gave their lives a new meaning and direction.

None the less, the meaning of death may be radically transformed by a person's faith,[122] and it is clear that some suicides have been the direct result of involvement in an NRM. Mass suicide is not unknown in the history of religion: in 1190 the Jews of York, like the Jews at Masada before them, committed mass suicide;[123] in the final decades of the seventeenth century, thousands of 'Old Believers' burned themselves to death in Russia.[124] Since the appalling tragedy in Guyana in 1978, countless reports in the media and anti-cult literature have implied that mass suicide is a potential characteristic of numerous other NRMs, usually with no further evidence beyond the fact that the People's Temple and the movements in question have (now) been labelled 'cults'.[125] That the Jonestown affair was horrendous, there is no doubt whatsoever; exactly what led to the tragedy is less clear, but it should be remembered that,

---

122. William Sims Bainbridge in a review discussion, *Sociological Analysis*, vol. 50, no. 2, 1989, p. 192.

123. Philip S. Alexander (ed.) *Textual Sources for the Study of Judaism*, Manchester University Press, 1984, pp. 49–50.

124. Thomas Robbins "Religious Mass Suicide before Jonestown: The Russian Old Believers" *Sociological Analysis*, vol. 47, no. 1, Spring 1986, pp. 1–20.

125. Anson D. Shupe and David G. Bromley "Shaping the Public Response to Jonestown: People's Temple and the Anticult Movement" in Ken Levi (ed.) *Violence and Religious Commitment: Implications of Jim Jones's People's Temple Movement*, University Park & London: Pennsylvania State University Press, 1982, pp. 105-32. See also section *'Assessing atrocity tales'*.

apart from the fact that the membership and the geographical conditions associated with Jonestown differed in a number of crucially important ways from those of almost all other NRMs,[126] there has been growing concern about the numbers of people there who did *not* commit suicide. The tape-recordings of the poisonings and reports by some survivors make it clear that many of those who died were murdered. The chief medical examiner and senior bacteriologist for the Guyanese government is reported as saying that no more than 200 of the victims died voluntarily – many of the victims had died of poison being injected into a part of their upper arms where it would have been virtually impossible for them to have injected themselves.[127] Some commentators suggest that Jones himself was murdered.[128] There seems, however, to be little doubt that there had been macabre 'suicide rehearsals' even before the People's Temple moved from California to Guyana.[129]

Manson is said to have tested his followers' degree of spiritual development by placing a knife to their throats and asking if he might kill them. When a 'true adept' answered "Sure, Charlie, you can kill me", Manson would hand the follower the knife and say "Now you can kill me too."[130] In South Korea on 29 August 1987, the bound and gagged bodies of 33 followers of Park Soon Ja ('Benevolent Mother') were found neatly stacked in a factory attic – drug bottles were found near the bodies and there was no sign that the victims had resisted either strangulation or poisoning. Authorities believed that they had taken part in a murder–suicide pact.[131]

A number of young members of Ananda Marga who immolated themselves provide an example of another type of suicide. They were protesting against the imprisonment in India of their leader. Two of those who were to set fire to themselves in Germany in 1978 delivered a statement which expressed the following sentiments:

> Shrii Shrii Anandamurti has been imprisoned on false charges since 6 years and after a poisoning attempt is fasting in protest since 5 years. . .

126. James T. Richardson "People's Temple and Jonestown: A Corrective Comparison and Critique" *Journal for the Scientific Study of Religion*, 19/3. 1980, pp. 239–255 (see note 36 at beginning of section *Socio-economic status and age of membership* for summary of Richardson's distinctions.

127. See, for example, David Hanna *Cults in America*, New York: Belmont Tower Books, 1979, p. 205.

128. Ibid; Alan McCoy *The Guyana Murders*, San Francisco: Highland House, 1988. See also Naipaul (1980).

129. Jeannie Mills "Jonestown Masada" in Ken Levi (ed.) *Violence and Religious Commitment: Implications of Jim Jones's People's Temple Movement*, University Park & London: Pennsylvania State University Press, 1982, p. 168. See also David Chidester *Salvation and Suicide: An Interpretation of Jim Jones, the People's Temple, and Jonestown*, Bloomington: Indiana University Press, 1988.

130. Donald A. Nielsen "Charles Manson's Family of Love: A Case Study of Anomism, Puerilism and Transmoral Consciousness in Civilizational Perspective" *Sociological Analysis*, vol. 45, no. 4, Winter 1984, p. 329.

131. *Boston Globe*, 30 August 1987.

> Although the socio-spiritual movement ANANDA MARGA is persecuted and defamed all over the world now by the immoralists its workers are sacrificing their lives in selfless service. . .
>
> Our self-immolation is done after personal and independent decision. It is out of love for all human beings, for the poor, the exploited, the suffering.[132]

Further tragedies have occurred when members of an NRM have apparently accepted that they are protected from death and have, therefore, placed themselves in what would, to outsiders, appear to be a suicidal situation. Hundreds of members of the Holy Spirit Movement in Uganda walked to their death after their leader, Alice Lakwena, had told them that oil from the shea tree would protect them from Government bullets.[133] It does, however, seem extremely unlikely that many of those who died went into battle voluntarily – reportedly, Alice Lakwena's press gang proselytised with words such as "Join us or we will cut you with a panga (machete)"[134]

In Memphis, Tennessee, seven black male followers of Lindberg Sanders, who believed police were the anti-Christ and who had predicted that the world would end the following Monday, took a policeman hostage and announced that "The Devil is dead". Police then raided the house, killing the members, who evidently believed that they themselves could not die.[135] It might be said that such cases do not constitute suicide. It might also be said, however, that the members of the groups had invited death because of their actions, and that these actions were the consequence of their beliefs, the influence of a leader, or the dynamics of a situation in which antagonisms between the group and non-members had got progressively beyond the control of either side.

Mental health

Sometimes the very fact that someone has converted to an NRM is taken as a sign that he or she must be suffering from some sort of mental delusion – particularly when the person makes claims about a religious experience or talks about happenings of a non-natural kind.[136] This is nothing new. People who believe things that others find incredible have frequently been labelled as crazy. Sometimes they *have* been mentally ill

---

132. Didi Uma' Brcii and Dada Lokesha Brc. "Statement in Regard of the Self Immolation of a Nun and a Monk of Ananda Marga in Berlin, February 1978" *Mahima*, Berlin Sectorial Newsletter for Ananda Marga Pracaraka Samgha, March/April 1978, p. 16.

133. *The Observer*, 8 November 1987; *International Herald Tribune*, 29 December 1987; *Los Angeles Times*, 2 January 1988.

134. *The Observer*, 8 November 1987.

135. *The Times*, 14 January 1983.

136. An example would be John Clark's "Cults" in *Journal of the American Medical Association*, 242/3, 1979, pp. 279–281. For a critique of this position see Tom Robbins and Dick Anthony "Deprogramming, brainwashing and the Medicalization of Deviant Religious Groups" *Social Problems*, vol. 29, 1982, pp. 283–297. See also Herbert Richardson (ed.) *New Religions and Mental Health: Understanding the Issues*, New York & Toronto: Edwin Mellen Press, 1980.

– when judged by criteria other than their religious beliefs; but it is a dangerous path that a society is treading once it starts defining people as mentally ill *merely* on the grounds of their religious or ideological beliefs, and it is a path that the nations of the West have vociferously denounced.

Another popular conception is that the practices associated with an NRM are likely *to lead* to mental illness. There is, however, very little evidence that members of most NRMs suffer from any more severe mental disorders than do others of their age. For instance, two researchers from the University of California, Los Angeles, Medical Center tested 50 individuals who were either in or had left an NRM, and reported that:

> Varying degrees of insight into their methods of coping and/or handling of problems were demonstrated by the subjects, but all were within the normal range.[137]
>
> No data emerged, either from intellectual, personality, or mental status testing to suggest that any of these subjects are unable or even limited in their ability to make legal judgements. Rather, the groups all emerged as intellectually capable on testing.[138]

Where instances of mental breakdown after a person's involvement in a movement have been investigated, it has not infrequently been revealed that something was amiss *before* the person's involvement and that the movement may have had very little to do with the problem. Sometimes, indeed, an unquestioning, womb-like atmosphere in which clear-cut directives are given can enable a person to cope when he or she had felt unable to do so 'outside'. In fact, there is some evidence that suggests that some people can, in a number of ways, fare better as a result of their stay in some movements.[139]

There are also studies that point to some of the methodological shortcomings of other studies which claim that particular groups have beneficial results. For example, Finkelstein *et al.* conclude a critical assessment of the literature on *est* by saying:

> [The] literature resembles the early literature on encounter groups and other vehicles of the human potential movement; it consists of only a few objective outcome studies which exist side-by-side with highly positive testimonials and anecdotal reports of psychological harm.

137. J. Thomas Ungerleider and David K. Wellisch "The Programming (Brainwashing)/Deprogramming Religious Controversy" in Bromley and Richardson (eds) (1983), p. 207.

138. Ibid, p. 211.

139. See, for example, Marc Galanter, R. & J. Rabkin and A. Deutsch "The 'Moonies': A Psychological Study of Conversion and Membership in a Contemporary Religious Sect", *American Journal of Psychiatry* 136:2, February 1979; Wolfgang Kuner "New Religious Movements and Mental Health" in Barker (ed.) (1983); Tom Robbins and Dick Anthony "New Religious Movements and the Social System: Integration, disintegration and transformation" *The Annual Review of the Social Sciences of Religion*, vol. 21, 1978, pp. 1–27; Michael W. Ross "Mental Health in Hare Krishna Devotees: A Longitudinal Study" *The American Journal of Social Psychiatry*, 5/4. Fall 1985, pp. 65–67.

Reports of testimonials have been compiled by *est* advocates and suffer from inadequate methodology. More objective and rigorous research reports fail to demonstrate that the positive testimony and evidence of psychological change among *est* graduates result from specific attributes of *est* training. Instead, non-specific effects of expectancy and response sets may account for positive outcomes. Reports of psychological harm as the result of *est* training remain anecdotal, *but borderline or psychotic patients would be well advised not to participate.*[140]

The Dutch Government Study of New Religious Movements concluded that

In general, new religious movements are no real threat to mental public health.[141]

and that

No proof has come up . . . that new religious movements would have a serious pathogenic impact on their members. Admittedly former members not seldom [claim] to experience psychic problems, but these are (a) usually not of a serious nature, (b) not of a specific nature and (c) usually on the one hand traceable to problems which existed prior to entry into the movement, on the other hand they are no more than adjustment difficulties. . . . Therefore, in our view, there is no call for protective measures.[142]

Similarly, while the Hill Report to the Ontario Government stated that the experience of some movements might *contribute to* or *be a factor in* some illnesses, it stressed that the evidence could not identify the movements' practices as *the cause of* either mental or physical illness.[143] The Report concluded that "no new government measures were warranted involving the groups' impact on their members' health".[144]

None the less, there are undoubtedly situations in which members have become 'burnt out' or seriously affected in one way or another while in an NRM. For example, as history has shown, strongly held hell-fire-and-damnation beliefs in evil forces or satanic possession can result in states of uncontrollable terror or overwhelming feelings of guilt. In extreme cases, these can contribute to people losing control and possibly harming themselves or others; alternatively, such beliefs can lead to severe withdrawal, with the person losing all confidence and self-respect. And, as discussed in other sections, pressure from fellow believers (and, occasionally, from outsiders) can place converts in situations of severe anxiety, especially when they find themselves torn between old and new values, opposing assumptions and conflicting loyalties.

---

140. Peter Finkelstein, Brant Wenegrat and Irvin Yalom "Large Group Awareness Training" *Annual Review of Psychology*, 1982, p. 538. [Emphasis added.]
141. Witteveen (1984), p. 314.
142. Ibid, p. 317.
143. Hill (1980), p. 550.
144. Ibid, p. 554.

If relatives or friends have serious doubts about the mental health of a member of an NRM (or, indeed, of any other relative or friend), they should not hesitate to seek medical guidance. There may still remain the problem of gaining access to the person concerned or of persuading him or her to accept professional help. This is discussed in a later section.

Drugs

There are a few NRMs that encourage the use of illegal drugs.[145] Rastafarians frequently smoke ganga (a form of marihuana grown in Jamaica) as a sacrament – a ritual that may be referred to as 'taking the chalice'.[146] A small minority of Neo-Pagan groups advocate the use of 'sacred substances' as a 'powerful tool' – so long as they are used only in sacred contexts.[147] In 1972, two members of Love Israel's Church of Armageddon (also known as the Love Family) died after sniffing the chemical toluene, a practice that was at that time occasionally incorporated into the movement's ritual.[148] Substantial quantities of drugs that have been used to influence and control behaviour were discovered at Jonestown, Guyana, fuelling a suspicion that the movement was being used for behavioural modification experiments.[149]

Some movements do not interfere with a member's use of drugs, although they do not themselves advocate such practices. Many movements (ISKCON and the Brahma Kumaris are but two examples) explicitly forbid the use of drugs. Several movements boast that they have been instrumental in curing members of a drug dependency. Unificationists have been involved in trying to fight drug racketeering.[150] Narconon, an organisation devoted to combating drug abuse, is one of the many organisations associated with the Church of Scientology.

Anyone discovering or suspecting the use of illegal or dangerous drugs by a member of an NRM should react in the same way that they would react were the person concerned not a member of an NRM.

It is sometimes suggested that NRMs are *like* drugs in that they are habit-forming, that they create dependency and that they can cause severe damage to a person's mind and body. There are *some* ways in which *some* of the NRMs can produce effects on *some* of their followers which do bear *some* resemblance to those brought about through the use of *some* drugs. Some of the movements will, indeed, boast that they can help people to 'get high on love'. It is also true that when some people leave

145. See Thomas Lyttle "Drug Based Religions and Contemporary Drug Taking" *The Journal of Drug Issues*, vol. 18, no. 2, 1988, pp. 271–284.

146. K. M. Williams *The Rastafarians*, London: Ward Lock Educational, 1981, p. 18.

147. Margot Adler *Drawing Down the Moon: Witches, Druids, Goddess-Worshippers, and Other Pagans in America Today*, Boston: Beacon Press, second edition, 1986, p. 452.

148. Melton (1989), entry no. 860, p. 605.

149. Alan W. McCoy *The Guyana Murders*, San Francisco: Highland House, 1988, pp. 51–60.

150. See, for example, *Today's World*, July 1989, p. 35.

a movement, they undergo experiences that seem, in some ways, to be like withdrawal symptoms.

It should, however, be remembered that there is an important difference between beliefs and actions that are brought about by chemical effects on a person's brain and those that are brought about by social or psychological effects on a person's mind. In trying to understand what is going on and to decide what action (if any) is necessary, the drug metaphor can mislead more than it can help.

Of course, the distinction between mind and body is not as clear-cut as the previous paragraph might seem to suggest. On the one hand, it has been shown that it is not sufficient for marijuana users to learn simply the physical techniques of taking the drug. *Interpretation*, learned through interaction with other users, plays a crucially important role in the process of becoming a marijuana user. Novices have to learn to enjoy the effects if they are to continue in its use. They have to learn to redefine the sensations resulting from the drug as pleasurable (even if they originally found these unpleasant, confusing or frightening) if they are to become accepted within the drug-taking sub-culture as a 'true user'.[151]

And, on the other hand, physiological changes can be brought about without the use of chemicals.

Transformative techniques

There are several techniques or practices, such as fasting, special breathing and certain forms of yoga and meditation, that can result in 'altered states of consciousness'. Just as there are people who claim that, through the use of psychedelic drugs such as LSD, they have been able to glimpse an altogether 'other' reality (that is somehow 'more real' than the mundane, everyday world), so there are those who claim that, through certain non-drug-related practices, they can get in touch with a transcendent reality or knowledge.

Many of these practices are derived from ancient Eastern traditions, some come from Africa, the Caribbean and Latin America, but there are also numerous mystical traditions within Judaism, Christianity and Islam, and some disciplines, such as fasting, have long been observed in all major faiths – the New Testament, for example, tells of Jesus fasting for forty days in the wilderness.[152] Other practices, especially some that have been developed in the Human Potential movement, rely heavily on psychoanalytic and psychotherapeutic theories; further rituals and techniques are derived from pagan and occult practices that have been developed in the West.

Very little is as yet understood about the functioning of any of these practices and there are numerous conflicting accounts of the extent to

---

151. See Howard S. Becker *Outsiders: Studies in the Sociology of Deviance*, New York: Free Press, enlarged edition, 1973, pp. 53–58.
152. Matthew 4:2; Luke 4:2.

which, as well as the ways in which, they operate. What is known, so far as the new religions are concerned, suggests that most of the practices engaged in by young seekers do very little harm, and may produce feelings of extraordinary well-being or of being 'blissed out'.

There is, however, always the possibility that practices which are harmless for most people will exacerbate pre-existing problems for a few. It is also the case that if some of the procedures are performed without proper supervision, or start to take over too large a part of the person's life, the practitioner may develop a dependency on the technique or the movement, or may, in extreme cases, find difficulty in 'coming back to reality'. As a result, there are people who have experienced a frightening incapacity to cope with ordinary life, and who may require professional medical help. Some of those who have taken part in 'mind-development groups' have suffered psychological deterioration as a consequence of 'confrontation techniques'. But others have undergone the same experiences without any noticeable ill effects.[153]

Heelas, having conducted a standard psychological test (MMPI) before and after 50 respondents had taken part in an Exegesis seminar, found no evidence of any statistically significant increase of psychotic malfunctioning after the Seminar. His study led him to remark that while none of his respondents appeared to have sought medical or therapeutic help during or immediately after the Seminar, each year about 5% of the students in the Religious Studies department at his university do seek such help around the time of their final examinations.[154]

In an earlier section (*Conversion or mind control?*), a distinction was drawn between an altered state of consciousness and the interpretation that is put on that state. It has also been suggested that, even in a drug-taking community, a social interpretation of sensations can play an important role in a person's subjective experience of a chemically induced state, and that interpretation by others can play a very important role in a person's belief in, say, possession by evil spirits. The fact that people's subjective *understanding* of a state could affect their behaviour as much as (if not more than) the objective state can have significant implications.

The point to be made is that if a change in that person's situation is to be brought about, then, to revert to the earlier distinction, it is likely that such a change will be effected through the *mind's understanding* (which is influenced by the actions, including the speech, of others) rather than merely through the *physical state of the brain* (in so far as it is influenced by chemical or physical means). Be that as it may in any particular instance, all that can be said here is that those who wish to help others whom they believe to have been influenced by transformative techniques should be aware of the complexity, and make sure that they do not

153. Hill (1980), p. 551.
154. Personal communication.

exacerbate a little understood, but potentially harmful situation by jumping to overly simple conclusions. So far as it is available, expert advice should be sought.

But let it be repeated, only a very small minority of people suffer any permanent harm through transformative techniques. More commonly, and less dramatically, people embrace techniques that *divert*, rather than radically alter, their consciousness. They may then become oblivious to or uncaring about matters that would previously have been of a taken-for-granted importance (such as personal hygiene, outward appearance, earning a living, accepting responsibility for promises made or obligations undertaken). Such negligence can be both worrying and infuriating for others, but friends and relatives should not assume that they are symptoms of the far rarer physiological or psychological changes that result in a serious breakdown of a person's ability to function.

Physical health
Given their youth, it is not surprising that most members of NRMs tend to be strong and healthy. Although food may not always be what a dietitian would prescribe, it is seldom worse than the sort of food that young people might have while they are students or living by themselves. Some of the movements, particularly those from a Hindu tradition, are vegetarian or vegan. Members of many of the NRMs are less likely than their peers to smoke, take drugs or over-indulge in alcohol. Although in some groups living conditions can be fairly primitive, adequate shelter is almost always available.

As mentioned earlier, there are movements that expect their members to fast, occasionally for several days at a time. If continued for too long, without adequate supervision, this can be dangerous. In America, a member of the Kripalu Center for Yoga and Health starved to death after taking Yogi Amrit Desai's teaching of occasional fasts to an extreme, although he had evidently been warned not to fast by one of the ashram's doctors.[155] A movement may demand long hours of work or devotion from its members, some of whom may become exhausted after prolonged periods with little sleep. This can be especially worrying if members drive under such conditions. Movements that encourage 'free sex' may have problems with sexually transmitted diseases, although most of them now encourage the extensive use of prophylactic measures, especially since the advent of AIDS. Bhagwan Rajneesh was, indeed, warning of the dangers of AIDS and insisting on precautions being taken long before the general public was aware of the serious threat of the disease.

Like those of a similar age in the 'outside' world, both elderly and young members of NRMs can become sick, or be involved in an accident. There may, however, be an additional difficulty when, as is sometimes

---

155. Melton (1986), p. 256.

the case, movements are irresponsible about their members' health – especially when, as employers, they do not take out the usual health insurance or make it difficult for their members to take time off work for health reasons. This is slightly less worrying in Britain, where there is a generally reliable and free Health Service, than it is in a country such as the United States, where medical and dental costs can be prohibitive for those without insurance. Parents may wish to arrange for insurance for their offspring in such circumstances.

Parents may also be anxious when their offspring travels to a country in which the facilities for emergency treatment are minimal and/or of a low standard. Here they should do all they can to persuade their son or daughter to take as many precautions as possible, and to accept responsibility for his or her health. See the later section, *When a member is in a country other than the UK*.

A further difficulty can arise with movements in which ill-health is interpreted as a sign of sin, spiritual weakness or possession by evil forces. In such cases, the movement may insist that it alone is privy to the correct remedy, and that the use of Western medicine would be counter-productive or a sign of lack of faith. Mahikari, one of the groups that came to the West from Japan, has urged its members to be highly critical of modern medicine and refuse any surgery.[156] More often in the West, however, problems have arisen because of strict adherence to certain Biblical admonitions by a number of conservative Christian groups of a sectarian nature. The 'No-Name Fellowship' was disbanded after a 10-year old boy who was dying of untreated diabetes was reportedly spanked "to try to make him confess sin they believed was causing the illness".[157] Hobart Freeman, a Pentecostal minister who founded the Faith Assembly in the 1970s, denounced medicine as a derivative of pagan religion and rejected the use of any medical services, and, as a result, several of his followers died when they could have been saved by minimal medical attention.[158] The withholding of medical attention on religious grounds continues to give rise to controversy over older groups such as the Church of Christ, Scientist and, where blood transfusions are concerned, the Jehovah's Witnesses.

If a member falls seriously ill or is dissuaded by a movement from taking a vitally important medicine (such as insulin), this can be a cause for very real concern. Relatives or friends who become aware of such situations should not hesitate in seeking advice from a medical and, if necessary, a legal expert.

---

156. Laennec Hurbon "New religious movements in the Caribbean" in James A. Beckford (ed.) *New Religious Movements and Rapid Social Change*, Beverly Hills: Sage, 1986, p. 158.
157. *Seattle Times*, 19 October 1988. See also *The Spokesman Review Regional*, 25 October 1988; *Chicago Tribune*, 21 June 1988.
158. Melton (1986), pp. 255–6.

Further education and careers

Not infrequently, a consequence of conversion or commitment to an NRM has been either that students have given up their studies altogether or that they have started to spend so much time engrossed in the movement or its practices that their academic performance has gone badly down-hill.

So far as dropping out is concerned, it should be remembered that students drop out for a number of reasons and that joining a NRM might be used as an escape route for someone who was not wanting to continue his or her studies anyway. Some perfectly happy students do, however, leave their course of further education because of involvement with an NRM. This may be because they themselves want to devote their time and attention to their new beliefs, or it may be because the movement exerts pressure on them to leave. Usually the outcome is the result of some sort of collaboration between the movement and the convert, but there are converts who will continue their studies in the face of quite severe pressure to drop out, and there are converts who will insist on dropping out even when the movement encourages them to complete their studies.

Quite often, converts will return to their studies at a later date. Wright found that those who have not completed a college education may later experience reservations over the fact, and when some 'trigger', such as a row with a superior, occurs the member may decide that he or she wants to leave the movement and return to university.[159] Others may take up their studies, or start them for the first time, while they are still in their movement – and they can perform very well. Practising members of the Unification Church, for example, have obtained First Class Honours at Cambridge and Ph.D.s at American universities such as Harvard, Yale and Chicago; others have passed exacting Bar examinations.

Parents who do not want to abandon hope that their offspring will ever complete his or her education, might be advised to check with the College or University to see whether a place could be kept for their son or daughter – or, even better, they might try to ensure that the convert arranges that the door is left open for opportunities that it might otherwise be difficult to renew at a later date. It might also be worth trying to find out if the convert's membership of the movement reflects or has led to an interest in a different kind of career or course of study – see the later section on *Getting information about the convert*.

When relatives, friends or teachers suspect that involvement with an NRM is resulting in under-achievement by a student, it may be advisable to discuss the matter with the student, with his or her tutor, or possibly with the Chaplain or a professional student counsellor. In some instances,

---

159. Wright (1987), pp. 63–65.

it may also be productive to speak to someone whom the student respects within the NRM itself. It should, however, be remembered that students under-achieve for numerous reasons and it is notoriously difficult to persuade them to concentrate on their studies if they are drawn by a distraction that has a more immediate interest for them.

As mentioned earlier, there are numerous people who will testify that they have become far more effective in their careers as the result of attending a course with one or other of the 'self-religions', and there are firms that have become so convinced that such courses can improve a person's capabilities that they will pay considerable fees for employees to go on them. On the other hand, there have been cases where people have been dismissed from a post because it has been discovered that they are associated with an NRM.[160] There is also a significant number of cases in which converts to some of the NRMs have given up successful careers, or started performing so badly that they have eventually lost their job. Again, this may be because they were never really happy in their work; it may be that their new set of beliefs leads them radically to alter their priorities; or it may be that they are under pressure from the NRM to do something different. Discussion with confused converts might help them to clarify in their own minds what is happening.

Finances

There are leaders of NRMs who not only take a vow of poverty, but also adhere to such a vow. A brochure prepared by the Brahma Kumaris World Spiritual University tells how the movement's founder, Dada Lekh Raj, gave up a prosperous jewellery business and handed over all his wealth to a trust of eight women so that it could be used for the "spiritual service of uplifting humanity". There are movements that eke out an existence without putting any pressure on their followers to contribute more than the minimum expenses necessary to scrape by. Some NRMs may have gone out of existence because of lack of funds. There can, however, be no doubt that many of the movements which offer spiritual, religious or personal development to the modern seeker know how to make an inordinately large profit. Even in cases where the leaders do not officially receive a large income, it is not uncommon for them to live in the lap of luxury, enjoying a splendid array of the material benefits of modern society, while their followers *cease* to live in the manner to which many of them had previously been accustomed, leading instead a decidedly frugal life.

There are several ways in which the movements obtain their money. Some take full advantage of the *labour* of their followers, unhampered by union rates or restrictive practices. Others may rely more on the practice

---

160. See Eileen Barker "Tolerant Discrimination: Church, State and the New Religions" in Paul Badham (ed.) *Religion, State and Society in Modern Britain*, New York, Toronto & Lampeter: Edwin Mellen Press, 1989, pp. 197–8.

of *tithing* or the solicitation of *donations*. Yet others will accumulate most of their wealth by charging *fees* for courses or services.[161] All of these methods have, of course, been used by mainstream religions throughout history, and there is certainly no lack of evidence that many of the mainstream religions have enjoyed immense wealth, not infrequently at the expense of their flock. None the less, some of the NRMs have shown a remarkable ability to acquire a remarkable amount of wealth in a remarkably short time.

Some of the movements are quite unscrupulous in their pursuit of wealth. They may persuade their followers to sign over all their assets, to mortgage or make a gift of property, to realise and hand over their capital investments, or to go heavily into debt in order to prove their commitment to the cause, or to pay for the course which, they are told, will solve all their problems – including the problems that they may find themselves in as a result of their having become involved in the movement.

Ideological justifications for the accumulation of wealth by religious leaders who offer not only spiritual, but also material rewards to their followers were by no means unknown before the rise of the current wave of NRMs. Such explicit ideologies seem, however, to have reached new heights in the contemporary West, where they are most evident in the pleas and promises made by some of the American 'Televangelists'. 'Prosperity theology' provides an unusually explicit example of the way in which a number of biblical texts are used to promise financial riches to those who are prepared to demonstrate their faith in God by giving just a little bit more than they think they could possibly afford to 'God's messengers on earth' – a favourite text being: "Beloved, I wish above all things that thou mayest prosper and be in health, even as thy soul prospereth".[162]

Individuals have, of course, the right to dispose of their money as they see fit – so long as it really is their money. But not all of those who become involved with a movement realise just how much money, or earning power, they may be expected to give. Potential donors would be well advised to consider carefully, before they part with money to an NRM, what they or others may have to give up as a result of their donations – and whether they can be confident that their money will be used in the way that they would want. See also the later section, *Money*.

Confessions
An unpleasant situation that can lead to a group's having a hold over an individual may arise when it has collected intimate details about their

---

161. See Richardson (ed.) (1988).

162. Third Epistle of John, v. 2. See Denis Hollinger "Enjoying God Forever: An historical/sociological profile of the Health and Wealth Gospel Movement in America", paper presented to the Annual Meeting of the British Sociological Association Sociology of Religion Study Group, St Mary's College, Strawberry Hill, Twickenham, March 1989.

members' lives before they joined the movement – or has subsequently involved them in practices of which they are likely to feel ashamed if others were to learn about them. There are movements that ask members to write down a list of their previous sins on the understanding that the exercise is merely a means of putting the past behind them, so that, purified, they may move to a new phase of their lives. The members may be told that their confessions will be ritually destroyed or, at least, that they will be treated as utterly confidential; but it has not infrequently happened that the confessions have been used at a later date for either implicit or explicit blackmail.

Individuals would be well advised to consider very carefully just how far they can trust members of a movement not to misuse information that they are asked to reveal either in writing or in a counselling session. They should also consider seriously the extent to which they are prepared to indulge in, for example, sexual or illegal practices that they would not want other people to find out about. And, of course, they should remember that they themselves are responsible for any practices in which they take part – whoever it was who made the suggestion or issued the command.

❧ CHAPTER SEVEN ❧

Personal Relations and the Family within the Movements

Sexual practices

SEXUAL PRACTICES vary from the celibacy observed by the Brahma Kumaris to the promiscuity that has been encouraged by Bhagwan Rajneesh and the 'Revolutionary Sex' of The Children of God, in which the calculated use of sexual intercourse (justified on the grounds that it is for Jesus) has been practised in order to attract money and new converts to the movement.[163] Some of the nastiest reports concerning NRMs relate to the involvement of children in ritual sexual practices that have been carried out by some devil worshippers.[164] Any kind of sexual abuse of children is, of course, a serious criminal offence and should be immediately reported to the police or some other competent authority.

Between these extremes, ISKCON devotees are permitted to have sex only within marriage for the procreation of children. Thus, couples who do not want children do not consummate their marriage, although they may live together. Members of the Unification Church are forbidden sex with anyone except those with whom they have been 'blessed' in marriage by the Reverend Moon. Even then, they are not permitted to consummate their marriage until at least 40 days after the ceremony, and

---

163. See, for example, *The Basic Mo Letters* by Moses David, no. 258. For a sociologist's account of the policy of "F'fing" (Flirty Fishing), see Roy Wallis "Yesterday's Children: Cultural and Structural Change in a New Religious Movement" in Bryan (1981), pp. 97–134. See also James T. Richardson and Rex Davis who give graphic details of the instructions and theological justifications that 'Mo' offers his flirty fishers (and their husbands) in "Experimental Fundamentalism: Revisions of Orthodoxy in the Jesus Movement", *Journal of the American Academy of Religion* LI/3, 1983, pp. 397-427; For an illustrated French-language exposé by an ex-member, see Jane Hervé and Marie-Christine C. *Confession d'une enfant de Dieu*, Paris: Rochevignes, 1985.

164. See Robert J. Gillespie, Jr. "Investigating Satanic Cults" in *Justice for Children*, Washington D.C., 1985, p. 6.

there are a few couples who have not been allowed to do so for seven or more years.

In a study of 144 Pagans in the United States it was reported that:

> Many Witches perform the Great Rite – ritual sexual intercourse between the high priest and high priestess inside the circle as part of the religious ceremony. . . In some covens, because the roles . . . rotate, each member of the coven will eventually have ritual sex with every other member. The rite can be done 'in reality' or 'symbolically'. . . 47 percent [of the respondents] felt that some sort of ritual sex was justified. They used words like ritualistic, symbolic, magical, sacramental, holy and spiritual to describe religious-oriented sex. Only 17% felt that sex had no place in Paganism and only 4 percent felt that sex should be limited to husband and wife.[165]

The study has, however, been criticised: one well-known expert on Witches doubts whether more than a tiny percentage of Neo-Pagan Witches *actually* practise the Great Rites or any form of sex magic – even if many of the Witches wish they did and would like people to believe that they do so regularly.[166]

Charles Brown of the Flame Foundation has announced that:

> We of the Immortal Species relate differently on a sexual level than death oriented man. We are not homosexual, heterosexual, bisexual or asexual. We are androgynous flesh.[167]

Other movements, such as the Church of Scientology or Nichiren Shoshu Buddhism, are unexceptional in their sexual practices, the members behaving no differently in this respect from the rest of society. Obviously enough, outsiders' concerns about sexual practices in the NRMs will depend on their own views about what is 'normal' and desirable. One worried father complained that there must be something seriously wrong with his son because, on joining an NRM, he had stopped 'sleeping around'.

It can be argued that people's sexual habits are their own business, not anyone else's. But some of the movements have given rise to worries about sexually transmitted diseases and unwanted pregnancies. Abortions or sterilisations carried out at the suggestion of leaders have been bitterly regretted at a later date. Many ex-members have felt either guilt from a sense of over-indulgence, or resentment or feelings of acute anxiety as a result of having had to repress sexual emotions during their time in an NRM. Furthermore, there are instances in which either guilt or resentment has been experienced concerning a partner in a sexual liaison.

165. R. George Kirkpatrick, Rich Rainey and Kathryn Rubi "Pagan Renaissance and Wiccan Witchcraft in Industrial Society: A Study of Parasociology and the Sociology of Enchantment" *Iron Mountain: A Journal of Magical Religion*, 1984, p. 37.

166. Isaac Bonewits "Quibbles with Kirkpatrick", ibid, p. 42.

167. *The Eternal Flame*, January 1979, p. 4.

Marriage

It is common in many of the Eastern traditions that have come to the West for parents to arrange their children's marriage. Some of the NRMs have adopted the practice of selecting marriage partners for their members. The Unification Church's arranged marriages, and mass weddings, have been widely publicised. It should, however, be pointed out that not only can members refuse to be married to the partner whom Moon suggests, but that many of them have actually done so, either at the time of the 'matching', or at a later date. Most commonly the rejection has occurred before the marriage has taken place, or at least before it has been consummated.

There are other movements, such as ISKCON, in which a person in a position of leadership may make suggestions (that may or may not be accepted) as to whether a member should get married and who the partner might be. The leader of Sahaja Yoga, Shri Mataji, states explicitly that her disciples may not choose their own marriage partners:

> ... people start choosing their life-partners in Sahaja Yoga. That is not allowed. *That is not allowed.* You are not to spoil your Ashrams, your centres – using them for a marriage searching society.... For all practical purposes you are brothers and sisters. And that's why I always encourage marriage between people who belong to another country or another centre...
>
> As we are now having a big marriage programme, I would say that most of the marriages which were done like that, are 'very' successful... *It's very wrong to do such a thing as to arrange your marriage with a Sahaja Yogi by yourself.* It will be dangerous. I don't want to say anything; but it wouldn't turn out to be good because it is anti-God activity. Absolutely anti-God.[168]

In a movement such as Rastafarianism, however, the question of inter-racial marriages may be seen as undesirable on religious grounds, especially when there are children. As one worried Rasta summed up his position by writing:

> We as Rastafarians are against anything that doesn't promote the wholeness of Africans at home and us abroad.[169]

Some NRMs do not make any pronouncements or suggestions about the marriage arrangements of their members, but, not surprisingly, as people often choose a partner with interests or beliefs similar to their own, members are quite likely to find themselves a husband or wife in their NRM. There are several cases of divorce or separation that result from one partner converting and the other not, or of one partner leaving a movement while the other remains a member. This is discussed in the later section, '*Mixed marriages*'.

168. Shri Mataji "Rakshā-Bandhan and Maryādās for Sahaja Yogis", *Nirmala Yoga*, vol. 4, no. 23, September-October 1984, p. 27.
169. Letter to the Editor, *Rastafari International News*, July-August 1989, p. 3.

Some movements are strongly opposed to the very idea of marriage. For different reasons, and with different consequences, the Children of God, the Raëlians and the Manson Family have all derided the institution of marriage. In some movements, such as the Children of God, the Rajneeshees and Synanon, the exchange of partners has been encouraged.[170]

Attitudes towards women

The New Age movement and a number of pagan groups tend, in their different ways, to stress the importance, and sometimes the primacy, of the Feminine. There are movements, such as Sahaja Yoga, where the founder and leader is a woman. Sometimes men take over leadership roles on the death of the female founder; this has happened in several of the Japanese NRMs. Sometimes women take over from a male leader: all the present leaders of the Brahma Kumaris are women, their (now deceased) founder, Dada Lekh Raj, reportedly having stressed the importance of the spiritual role of women and expressed the utmost confidence in their administrative ability.[171] The Church Universal and Triumphant has been led by a woman, Elizabeth Clare Prophet, since her husband died in 1973; and there are other movements, such as Programmes Ltd., in which women play a powerful or highly respected role.

Many of the movements (especially those from an Eastern tradition) appear, however, to see women as inferior beings whose main role in life is to serve men – even when (or especially when) the officially stated policy is that women are 'equal but different'. This can mean that men in leadership roles, including husbands, have to be obeyed without question – which has occasionally provided a rationalisation for a number of physical and psychological abuses.

Children

Children born into the NRMs are usually brought up with at least as much love and care as are children in the rest of society. The number of cases for concern is small, but such cases do exist. Of the nine hundred plus who died in the Jonestown tragedy, about 260 were children. Sometimes children have, as in other circumstances, been ill-nourished or inadequately clothed or sheltered. Occasionally they have been denied medical attention. Sexual abuse has already been mentioned, as has the accusation of the incestuous behaviour of the leader of the Children of God, David Berg, who, in his 'Mo letters', has used the Bible to justify incestuous relations and to encourage children to engage in sexual

---

170. See Davis (1984); Milne (1986); and Richard Ofshe "The Social Development of the Synanon Cult: The Managerial Strategy of Organizational Transformation" *Sociological Analysis*, 41/2, 1980, p. 123.

171. Vieda Skultans "The Brahma Kumaris and the Role of Women", mimeographed paper presented to the London School of Economics Graduate Sociology of Religion Seminar, n.d.

exploration.[172] Sexual abuse, although obviously a matter of real concern, should not, however, be seen as a problem confined to new religious movements; there has also been a disturbing number of cases of child molestation by clergy of mainstream Churches.[173]

As mentioned elsewhere, there have been some horrific stories concerning children's involvement in satanic rituals – these include tales of children being placed in coffins and tortured, and of young girls being made pregnant in order to give birth to babies who are then ritually sacrificed.[174] Although many, possibly most, of the stories of ritual abuse of children have turned out to be unfounded or based on a hoax,[175] if a child gives any indication that he or she may have been involved in such activities, the claims should be thoroughly investigated with, if necessary, the help of the police or some other competent authority. Even if the details of the case turn out not to be true, the fact that indications have been given would seem to suggest that the child is in need of help for some reason or another.

As a result of its survey of cult-related violence (see earlier section on *Violence*), the Institute for the Study of American Religion concluded that violent tendencies can be nurtured by a group's belief in strict discipline and an advocacy of corporal punishment as a proper means of controlling behaviour. Public concern had grown after a mother was convicted of involuntary manslaughter of her child; the mother was a member of a small Black Jewish group, the House of Judah, whose leader advocated strong discipline and corporal punishment for disobedient children. Following this case, the Institute looked into the other reports of child abuse that were assembled as evidence of violence towards children in cults. It found that

> the child abuse charges did not come from the major nonconventional religions (i.e., those most identified as cults in the public mind) but from [a number of] conservative evangelical Christian Church groups.[176]

These groups tended to sanction their practices by reference to Biblical passages such as the twelfth chapter of Paul's Epistle to the Hebrews:

> 6. For whom the Lord loveth he chasteneth, and scourgeth every son whom he receiveth.
> 7. If ye endure chastening, God dealeth with you as with sons; for what son is he whom the father chasteneth not?

---

172. See Davis (1984); Mo Letter no. 258.

173. See Rorie Sherman "Legal Spotlight on Priests who are Pedophiles" *The National Law Journal*, 4 April 1988. See also *The Atlantic Journal*, 30 April 1988.

174. Maureen Davies in "Satanic Ritual Abuse", a paper distributed by the Reachout Trust, Twickenham, n.d., lists some repulsive rituals in which children have allegedly been involved.

175. Melton (1989), p. 145; J Gordon Melton "The Evidence of Satan in Contemporary America: A Survey", paper presented to the Pacific Division of the American Philosophical Association, Los Angeles, 1986. See also Richardson et al (eds) (1991).

176. Melton (1986), pp. 255 and 258.

8. But if ye be without chastisement, whereof all are partakers, then
are ye bastards and not sons...
11. Now no chastening for the present seemeth to be joyous, but
grievous: nevertheless, afterward it yieldeth the peacable fruit of
righteousness unto them which are exercised thereby.

Sometimes members of an NRM can believe so fervently that it is God's
will that they are to save the world or restore the Kingdom of Heaven
on earth that, although the ideal is to have happy families with a loving
relationship between parents and children, they will exhort others to
sacrifice the immediate happiness of their children for the sake of fulfilling
God's will and, in the longer term, creating a better world for their
children.[177]

Worries are frequently expressed over whether a separated parent,
grandparents or other non-members can have sufficient access to young
children, and over what kind of upbringing the children are receiving.
Usually the concern is whether the children are being indoctrinated into
the beliefs and practices of the movement to the extent that options are
no longer open to them in the way that they were to their mother or
father who converted into the movement. In fact, there are several cases
of children who, having been born into an NRM, have now grown up
and decided to leave it. Indeed, while there are numerous cases of parents
who are worried about their children's conversion to an NRM, there are
also cases of children who, having been brought up strictly in their
parents' religion, are worried about the fanatical or 'closed' nature of
their parents' beliefs.

Clearly if children born into a movement are going to an 'outside'
school, non-members are likely to feel less cause for concern about
'undue influence' than if they are attending one of the number of schools
that the NRMs provide for the children of their members. Ananda Marga,
the Children of God, the Church Universal and Triumphant, ISKCON,
the Rajneeshees, Sahaja Yoga, the School of Economic Science, Transcendental Meditation and the Unification Church are among the movements
that run schools, some of these being attended also by children of non-
members. In Britain, schools are subject to visits from Her Majesty's
Inspectors and have to be registered with the Deparment of Education
and Science if there are five or more pupils over five years of age, and
registered with the local Social Services Department if the school is for
children under five years of age. Any one who suspects that a school is
not up to standard can serve a 'notice of complaint'.[178]

---

177. Jin Hun Moon "True Family's Natural Inheritance" *Today's World*, July 1989,
p. 11. See also Eileen Barker "Doing Love: Tensions in the Ideal Family" in *The Family
and the Unification Church*, Gene G. James (ed.), New York: Rose of Sharon Press, 1983.

178. Further information can be obtained from INFORM or from ISIS (Independent
Schools Information Service), 56 Buckingham Gate, London SW1E 6AG; Telephone: (071)
630 8793/4.

More difficult is the question of whether children should be isolated from other children and from the influences of modern industrial society. This is not a new problem. It is merely one that adds to the debate about the extent to which parents have a right to bring up their children according to their own beliefs. Given the availability of necessary facilities and certain safeguards, many of which have already been alluded to, parents in Britain do have that right under the present law.

❧ CHAPTER EIGHT ☙

Separateness

Exclusive language

ANY GROUPS develop a special language of their own. The outsider trying to comprehend a memo full of acronyms emanating from the Civil Service or the BBC can feel completely lost; the new student attempting to read a sociological dissertation may undergo a similar feeling of bewilderment. Sometimes the use of special concepts and terminology in an NRM can contribute, consciously or unconsciously, to cutting members off from non-members and providing the means whereby the members are reinforced in their distinctiveness and, perhaps, separateness from non-members. The Rastafarians provide an example of a language ('soul language', 'ghetto language' or 'hallucinogenic language') that is unintelligible to most outsiders. Leonard Barrett suggests that Rasta speech symbolises an identification with other sufferers.[179] The non-Rastafarian who has tried to understand Rastas talking among themselves is, however, likely to feel isolation rather than identification. When written, the language is slightly easier to understand, but the uninitiated may still have to make several wild guesses:

> Is like seh I n I have a good news fi di I dem, seen. . .
>
> I n I have a mini-bus so ah posse ah wi can go allround de place now, dat is good. Dred n Dred can hire I n I minibus if dem want to mek ah trip go some weh; dat cool; price will be reasonable, ah just wan love. . .
>
> Ina the 1980's InI ah step fast. You see this place that we get and de sheckels InI ah go use it wisely for ah we guarantee fi step eena Africa! Jah Know Dat!
>
> I man ah look fi si all positive minded dreda dred fi come work the resources for ah Zion wi ah go.[180]

---

179. Leonard Barrett *The Rastafarians: Sounds of Cultural Dissonance*, Boston: Beacon Press, 1977, p. 144; see also K. M. Williams *The Rastafarians*, London: Ward Lock Educational, 1981, pp. 22–3.

180. *Voice of Rasta*, Monthly Publication of Ethiopian World Federation Inc. no. 38, September–October 1982, p. 1.

To take another example, some of the jargon and acronyms used by the Church of Scientology can leave the outsider quite nonplussed. By opening L. Ron Hubbard's *Dianetics* at random, one may come across the following paragraph:

> The aberree goes into his own valence of the time of the sympathy engram in his bid for sympathy and his denial of his own dangerousness. The valence of himself, of course, is complicated by the age-tab and somatic of the engram in which he was immature and not well.[181]

Apart from being a means of either facilitating or blocking channels of communication, language is used to define – and to redefine – reality. It may deny normal meanings in order to stimulate new thoughts in those who meditate upon what is said. One form of this may be found in the Köan – a problem in enigmatic language that cannot be rationally solved, but is used in meditation by the Rinzai sect of Japanese Zen Buddhism: What is the sound of one hand clapping? is an example.

Manson provides another example of using perfectly ordinary words to deny normal sense and thus introduce a normless, confusing and unpredictable situation:

> you are my dad, I'm your mom, you are my wife, I'm your sister, you are my woman, I am your tree . . . you are my grass and I am your feet, you are my finger and I am your nose, you are my nothing, I am your something and together we are alikin.[182]
>
> All words are without meaning.[183]

Incompatibility of beliefs

Potential converts or their parents sometimes want to know whether or not an NRM's beliefs are compatible with their own; or ministers may want to find out whether a group that wants to hire the church hall is going to be teaching something that is in direct opposition to the teachings of their Church.

Logically, it is possible to point out that certain aspects of a particular belief system would seem to be incompatible with, or even directly contradict, aspects of another belief system. It has to be recognised, however, that many belief systems contain *internal* contradictions – some religions celebrate paradox as part of Divine Mystery. Just which beliefs are compatible with other beliefs or actions must be left to the individual believer or organisation to decide.

---

181. L. Ron Hubbard *Dianetics: The Modern Science of Mental Health*, Copenhagen: New Era Publications, 1950, p. 356.

182. Letter from prison by Charles Manson, quoted in Sy Wizinski *Charles Manson: Love Letters to a Secret Disciple, A Psychoanalytical Search*, Terre Haute: Moonmad Press, 1977, p. 109, cited in Donald A. Nielsen "Charles Manson's Family of Love: A Case of Anomism, Puerilism and Transmoral Consciousness in Civilizational Perspective" *Sociological Analysis*, vol. 45, no. 4, Winter 1984, p. 328.

183. Ibid.

Some NRMs expect their members to adhere unswervingly and exclusively to the movement's belief system, or to associate exclusively with fellow believers. Others, such as most New Age or Human Potential groups, are more likely to insist that people can belong to any or to no religion and still be a member, follower or 'student' of their group. In an introductory leaflet describing Subud, it is stated that:

> Nobody is expected to believe anything, only to recognise and to trust what he experiences. People of different religions find their faith deepened, and practise the latihan in complete harmony with each other and with those who have no religion.[184]

Sometimes, as in the case of Freemasonry, there is strong disagreement within the mainstream religions as to whether a declared compatibility does in fact exist.[185] Not all Christians would accept that the techniques of Transcendental Meditation can be divorced from their Hindu origins,[186] yet TM can boast a special group of Christian meditators "with a principally Catholic theological understanding of the world, man and the Church", which meets for a long weekend twice a year, and which seeks "to promote among Christians generally a clearer understanding of the value of TM for spiritual growth".[187] A Church of England curate, who is said to have practised TM for 13 years, denied that TM conflicts with Church of England teachings when he reportedly declared:

> The process of Transcendental Meditation is simple and straightforward. It is not particularly related to Christianity; it can be practised by anyone. I find it helps me with my Christian faith.[188]

Converts may believe that their new beliefs are compatible with the beliefs in which they were brought up, but then find that they are expected to take part in a practice that appears blatantly to contradict their previous beliefs. The movement may then try to produce an interpretation or a justification for the activity in terms that could seem compatible with both belief systems. An example is provided by David Van Zandt's study of the Children of God. A convert was experiencing difficulties with the newly introduced 'access strategy' of flirty fishing. He had been brought up in a conservative Christian home and interpreted

---

184. *A Brief introduction to Subud*, leaflet distributed in the UK, n.d.
185. See reports of the Methodist Conference, 1985, the General Synod of the Church of England in 1987 and the General Assembly of the Church of Scotland in 1989 for debates on the compatibility of Freemasonry and Christianity. See also Stephen Knight *The Brotherhood: The Secret World of Freemasons*, London: Granada, 1984 and Clifford Longley "Warning Triangle for Masons" *The Times*, 4 March 1989 for further discussion of this controversial topic.
186. See, for example, John Allan *TM: A Cosmic Confidence Trick*, Leicester: Inter-Varsity Press, 1980; James Bjornstad *The Transcendental Mirage*, Minneapolis: Dimension Books, 1976.
187. Adrian B. Smith (ed.) *TM: An Aid to Christian Growth*, Great Wakering: Mayhew McCrimmon, 1983, p. 143.
188. *Kent Messenger* (North Kent), 2 January 1987.

the new practice, from the vantage point of his previous background, as a form of religious adultery. The following exchange between the 'shepherd' [leader] and the member was constructed from Van Zandt's field notes:

> *Shepherd*: The only law once you're saved is the law of love. Salvation frees you from other laws. It repairs the damage done by Adam. The church is too cautious: a girl in church is afraid of what you'd think if she held out her hand. It's bad to be cautious. For example, the Song of Solomon is pornography: it tells you exactly how to make love.
> *Doubting member*: But it's adultery.
> *Shepherd*: It's done in love. Yes, there is adultery, but it depends on your motive. Adultery means betraying marriage. You must "have the faith" to engage in Flirty Fishing... [My wife] knows what I'm doing... The partners in a marriage have to decide together... Fornication is just lustful sex – you just want to bang her and leave her; it gives you nothing spiritual. God looks on your heart and will judge your works. If you do it just from lust, He will punish you. It's really radical, huh?! You have to be willing as a Christian to give everything. There will be sex in heaven, as we are all the Bride of Christ.[189]

Although few non-members of the Children of God are likely to think that flirty fishing *is* compatible with conservative Christianity, it is clear that the 'doubting member' had found himself in a situation in which it would be more difficult to disagree with the practice of flirty fishing than it would have been if he had not already become a member of the Children of God and publicly declared himself to be in general agreement with the movement's beliefs. Van Zandt does not tell us what the outcome of this particular case was; it may, of course, have been that the doubting member decided to leave the movement. But the shepherd's interpretation of what 'being a Christian' involves was almost certainly given added weight not only by the fact that the shepherd was someone who had, by then, been accepted as a person with a certain authority, but also by the fact that the exchange took place in the presence of other members who appeared to be in agreement with the sentiments that were being expressed.[190]

Opinions differ as to the extent that exclusivity of beliefs is desirable, and both the Children of God and conservative Christian groups tend towards the exclusive end of the spectrum. Like members of many other

---

189. David E. Van Zandt (1991), p.161.

190. For group pressure towards conformity, see the now-classic experiments carried out by Solomon E. Asch, described in most social psychology text books and by Asch himself in, for example, "Studies in the Principles of of Judgements and Attitudes: II. Determination of judgements by group and ego standards" *Journal of Social Psychology*, vol. 12, 1940, pp. 433–465; "Opinions and Social Pressure", *Scientific American*, vol. 193, 1955, pp. 31–5. See also Stanley Milgram "Nationality and Conformity" *Scientific American*, vol. 205, 1961, pp. 45–51. Also see Stanley Milgram "Some Conditions of Obedience and Disobedience to Authority, *Human Relations*, vol. 18, pp. 57–75; and Milgram's *Obedience to Authority*, New York: Harper and Row, 1974 (also described in most social psychology text books).

religions (old and new), they are of the opinion that followers should stick to fundamentals and that exposure to other ideas is a danger to their faith; they may believe that openness or dialogue with other belief systems invites compromise. One of the London Church of Christ's Evangelists has analysed the fall in membership of the 'old' Churches of Christ as being largely the result of:

> **Liberal theology:** biblical criticism, which undermined the authority of the Bible and raised more questions than it answered, swept through the brotherhood.
>
> [And] **The ecumenical movement:** churches increasingly looked to the denominations for their organisation, level of commitment, and even doctrine.

The Evangelist concluded:

> . . . if we stick to the "High Road" and the "Narrow Road," Churches of Christ can once again ascend the "Up Road".[191]

For members of other religions (old and new), the more open a system is to alternative interpretations or perspectives, the more it is to be welcomed. People who advocate the open approach might talk about the 'many ways' of understanding or worshipping God, or truth, or the spiritual nature of human beings; they may believe that while approaches may appear different at a 'lower' level they are complementary and, in some way, lead eventually to a broader or deeper understanding at a 'higher' level. Such people are likely to approve of, and possibly encourage, inter-denominational and inter-faith dialogue.

No attempt can be made here to evaluate the relative merits of theological openness or exclusivity. What is of concern, however, is the extent to which an NRM may expect its members to cease *associating* with non-members – a practice that is sometimes, but not only or necessarily, associated with theological exclusivity.

Detachment, isolation and dependency

The Exclusive Brethren, as their name suggests, provide an obvious example of a longer established movement that gives theological reasons for keeping its membership strictly separated from others. This is seen as a way of "dealing with evil":

> The Lord knows those that are his; and let everyone who names the name of the Lord withdraw from iniquity. [Timothy 2:19][192]

Not infrequently, converts to NRMs are unaware of the extent to which they will be expected to 'keep separate' from people (and activities)

---

191. Douglas Jacoby "Are You an American Church?", *A Light to London*, vol. 5, no. 8, August 1986, p. 3.
192. See Bryan R. Wilson "The Exclusive Brethren: A Case Study in the Evolution of a Sectarian Ideology" in Bryan R. Wilson (ed.) *Patterns of Sectarianism*, London: Heinemann, 1967, p. 310 *passim*.

associated with their past. In one NRM, where new converts are drawn gradually into the movement, relatives and friends may initially remark on how they seem to have taken on a new lease of life, to have become happier, more open and ready to share their thoughts than had previously been the case. After a few months, however, the convert may be invited to visit India or to go to another country for some special occasion. It is after the convert's return from this intensive period that the relatives and friends may notice that they are made less and less welcome; they may be told that they cannot stay in the same house as the convert because their 'vibrations' have a bad effect. There are other movements that refuse to eat with non-members, and withdraw almost totally from any contact with the outside world.

It has already been suggested that the most serious causes of potential danger may arise when a community cuts itself off from the rest of the world geographically as well as socially. One thing that Rajneeshpuram (Bhagwan Rajneesh's former settlement in Oregon), New Vrindaban (the settlement in West Virginia that has now been expelled from ISKCON) and, above all, Jonestown (the People's Temple settlement in Guyana) had in common was a certain degree of geographical isolation. There are, of course, established sects that are now regarded as perfectly respectable and are even highly respected despite the fact that they have cut themselves off both geographically and socially; examples can be found in the Hutterites or certain Amish and other Mennonite groups in parts of North America.

Convents and monasteries of all religious traditions, including enclosed orders, are frequently held in high esteem – sometimes *because of* their strict rules of withdrawal from the world. It tends, however, to be easier for parents to see their child disappear into a long-established order than into a new group or movement – fear of the unknown is less probable; it is usually much easier to imagine the kind of life that people will be leading in an institution that has been around for a number of centuries. Furthermore, religious orders are part of a wider religious tradition and, although they may have considerable autonomy, they are liable to control by an external authority within that tradition in a way that the NRM is not.[193]

Occasionally one may suspect that it is the very fact of exclusiveness that, to some extent, accounts for the attraction of a movement. For example, a young person who has been brought up in a liberal home in which 'anything goes' may long for a single, clear boundary that divides truth from falsehood, right from wrong – and good people from bad

---

193. See Michael Hill *A Sociology of Religion*, London: Heinemann, 1973, p. 84. See also Michael Hill's *The Religious Order: A Study of Virtuoso Religion and its Legitimation in the Nineteenth Century Church of England*, London: Heinemann, 1973; and Michael Walsh *The Secret World of Opus Dei*, London: Grafton, 1989.

people.[194] An unambiguous boundary that separates the group (its beliefs and its members) from the rest of society may provide confused or bewildered young people with the certainty they lacked throughout childhood. Alternatively, if they had previously felt guilty about, say, a sexual liaison, it may provide a certainty that they are now 'on the right side'. It may be that it was the group that had instilled the guilt by re-interpreting a rather undefined feeling that 'everything wasn't quite right'.

It is, however, widely acknowledged that most people's definition of reality – of what is or is not happening to them, to others and to the rest of society – and their judgements of what is right and wrong, or good and evil, can be particularly vulnerable to suggestion, influence and, in some cases, manipulation, when they are cut off from alternative sources of information.[195] 'Reality testing' is not easy when only one interpretation is available, when that interpretation is apparently shared by one's fellow believers and when even to think of questioning is seen as lack of faith in the truth, or betrayal of the cause.[196]

Furthermore, the more isolated (socially and geographically) a group is from the rest of society, the easier it is for paranoia about outsiders to set in. Paranoia may then develop about those within the community itself. Members may be asked to report to the leaders those who question the beliefs or practices; then the leaders may place under covert surveillance anyone who could conceivably be suspected of questioning their authority.[197] The more that a leader insists that his is a divine revelation (or that he IS God), the more unquestionable must his pro-nouncements be, and the more extreme may his demands become. The question 'Why?' was expressly forbidden in Charles Manson's 'Family of Love'.[198]

Some of the more worrying aspects of certain NRMs can be traced, at least in part, to the leader's single-minded pursuit of idealistic goals. In some instances these goals have been used to justify means which contradict the idealism of the goals. In fact, there is a variety of striking contradictions within a number of the movements. In some self-development movements, for example, one can observe a rigid conformity to individualism, or the bureaucratic organisation of spontaneity; and absolute obedience may be demanded as a means of achieving absolute freedom (see the section on *The quest for freedom*).

194. For a discussion about groups and boundaries, see Mary Douglas *Natural Symbols: Explorations in Cosmology*, London: Barrie and Rockliff, 1970.
195. See the references to Asch and Milgram cited earlier in this section.
196. For a discussion of the ways in which a 'plausibility structure' may be constructed and maintained or 'negotiated', see Peter L. Berger and Thomas Luckmann *The Social Construction of Reality: everything that passes for knowledge in society*, London: Allen Lane, 1967; and Peter L. Berger *The Social Reality of Religion*, London: Faber, 1969.
197. Milne (1986).
198. Donald A. Nielsen "Charles Manson's Family of Love: A Case Study of Anomism, Puerilism and Transmoral Consciousness in Civilizational Perspective" *Sociological Analysis*, vol. 45, no. 4, Winter 1984, p. 329.

A religion which believes that it alone holds the One Truth can view non-members not merely as mistaken, but as evil and deserving of treatment appropriate for a lesser species. It is not uncommon for parents to be told by children in such movements that they are satanic, or that they are suffering from some kind of mental disorder. There is, for instance, a group that would appear to specialise in attracting the children of (otherwise undiagnosed) 'schizophrenic' mothers. One of the mothers concerned reported feeling greatly relieved of niggling doubts about herself and her previous relationship with her daughter after having been introduced by INFORM to another mother whose daughter had labelled her in a similarly cruel way after she had joined the same group. The suspicion that it was the group's attitude, rather than her own behaviour, which had precipitated her daughter's accusations was strengthened even further when it was learned that a third mother had also been accused of being schizophrenic. The accusation had been particularly hurtful as each of the children had used it as a reason for discontinuing their relationship with their mothers until they (the mothers) had 'sorted themselves out'. The breaking up of families is discussed further in a later section.

Even when a group is not geographically isolated, individual members of it may become socially and psychologically dependent on it, especially if they have cut off ties with other people so that, eventually, they can feel that they have nowhere else to turn (this is discussed further in Part II where stress is laid on the importance of trying to keep in touch with the convert). It may be that part of the movement's teaching is that ties with one's past prevent one's development. Shri Mataji, for example, warns her disciples that they must be prepared to overcome all their attachments:

> . . . to develop this power [of Ekädasha Rudra] one has to develop a tremendous power of detachment, *power of detachment – detachment from negative*. For example, negativity can come from very near people like brother, mother, sister; could come from relatives. It could come from a country, it could come from your political ideas, economic ideas, anything like that. Any misidentification can destroy your power of Ekädasha Rudra. So *it is not only sufficient to say that "I am surrendered to Sahaja Yoga and I am Sahaja Yogi"*. . .[199]

Totalitarian Authoritarianism

Again, it must be stressed that most people do not suffer as the result of a brief flirtation with, or even from a longer attachment to, one of the NRMs. But there are undoubtedly those who *have* suffered within the confident, unquestioning structure of an NRM at the hands of unprincipled, power-hungry zealots – and, on occasion, at the hands of perfectly

199. Shri Mataji "Ekädasha Rudra Puja", *Nirmala Yoga*, vol. 5, no. 28, July-August 1985, p. 20.

well-intentioned visionaries who, in their fervent pursuit of what they consider to be godly or utopian goals, are unrestrained by the checks and balances to be found in situations that contain less certain mortals and less uncompromising beliefs.[200]

It sometimes happens that a movement has been operating without any serious problems for the members, but then a person who abuses his or her position is put in control of a particular group or centre. The movement's *organisational structure* or its beliefs might facilitate the exploitation of grass-root members, even when such exploitation goes against the intentions and normal practices of the movement. For example, a movement that believes in living a life of sacrifice, obedience and service, and which delegates responsibility to local leaders, can operate without problems when the local leader is concerned with serving his or her obedient subordinates, but it can be a recipe for disaster when the local leader is concerned only with self-serving interests. Needless to say, it is extremely difficult to know with certainty when such a situation is likely to arise in an otherwise non-manipulative movement, especially if the local leader happens to be devious. But such a development should always be considered a possibility, particularly when a group is geographically or socially isolated so that it is difficult not only for outsiders, but also for the members themselves to recognise what might be happening before the situation becomes too serious.

Some of the characteristics of NRMs that were discussed in earlier sections can contribute to situations in which either the leaders or the group as a whole can exert considerable pressure on the individual member to conform. The characteristics of charismatic authority have already been touched upon. What may be underlined here is the extent to which these may become authoritarian because the leader who is accorded charisma by his followers is answerable to no traditions, no rules, no person. When the follower ceases to believe that the leader really has the authority of charisma, things can be seen in a very different light. One ex-member, bitterly describing the man upon whom he said he had "mistakenly transferred my belief in Jesus Christ", wrote:

> The system he has created has nothing to offer the world, it is as corrupt as any other system he condemns, in fact his is worse in that he perpetuates this injustice in the name of God and brings total misery into many people's lives by getting them to believe that God's will and his will are one and the same. They become so confused that they no longer have the ability, in my opinion, to make rational decisions about their lives any more, he makes them all. If they don't do what he says they will go to hell and be rejected by God. If you really believe in this God, this is a very scary experience. After all, what could

---

200. See Edgar W. Mills "Cult Extremism: The Reduction of Normative Dissonance" in Ken Levi (ed.), *Violence and Religious Commitment: Implications of Jim Jones's People's Temple Movement*, Pennsylvania State University Press, 1982.

be worse than being rejected by God himself and to be unforgivable and unredeemable as well, and all of this for eternity. That's a long time.[201]

The quest for freedom

Belief systems with an emphasis on self-realisation would seem, at least at first glance, to espouse libertarian or even anarchic values in that they frequently make a point of rejecting the rules and constraints of society. But here too one can observe that movements which, in theory, embrace unbridled licence may, in practice, manifest a totalitarian authoritarianism, albeit of a somewhat different nature from that found in some of the 'world-rejecting' movements where control is more explicitly formulated.[202]

Freedom is one of the foremost values that many of these movements are (literally) in the business of promoting; and, indeed, many people have experienced feelings of liberation and a new sense of being in control of their own destinies after experimenting in one or other of the groups. As mentioned earlier, thousands will testify that their health has improved; that their social life has become more relaxed, more interesting, more fulfilling or more exciting; that their careers have prospered; that they have become happier, more spiritually aware; and that they have been released from the bonds of their past or the restrictions of society – they have been set free.

But, while getting rid of socially inflicted 'hang-ups' may help people to feel happier and 'more fully their true selves', freedom from guilt and conscience and a constant preoccupation with 'the real me' can also result in what others would describe as downright selfishness. When the self becomes the centre of one's concern, the risk of becoming self-centred must be considerable. Rejection of social mores and/or rational thought can remove all notions of accountability. The liberated self may (as is often claimed) become more sensitive to the needs of others and may develop wonderful, honest relationships with other liberated selves; but it may become an imperious animal, demanding constant attention, displaying little empathy with, or interest in, the feelings of the non-liberated souls around it.

It is also possible that, for some people, rejecting too many of the constraints of social life results not in freedom, but in a newer, even stronger dependency upon the group. The leader who asks his followers to cut themselves adrift from all previous ties, to trust him implicitly, to feel rather than to think, to surrender to his all-encompassing love and knowledge and to commit themselves to his service (or, perhaps, to sign the cheque for the next session) may be untying some knots, but he is

---

201. Personal communication.
202. See Milne (1986); Rosen (1975); and Judith Thompson and Paul Heelas *The Way of the Heart: The Rajneesh Movement*, Wellingborough: Aquarian Press, 1986.

also likely to be forging new bonds and new dependencies. Indeed, if new bonds are *not* forged, the newly liberated individual, rather than feeling exhilarated by his or her release from the constraining accretions of society, can come to feel helpless, hopeless, and very lonely.

Withdrawal or escapism

One of the more frequent worries which friends and relatives report that they have about someone who has become involved with an NRM is that the person has lost touch with what is really going on – that they have withdrawn from the world or that they are escaping from facing up to reality. This withdrawal can take a number of different forms, some more worrying than others. Perhaps the most worrying is when people appear to have become catatonic – they seem to have gone into a stupor and become completely cut off from everything that is going on around them; they have the appearance of being a robot or a zombie; they may be completely 'burnt out' after years of fund-raising for eighteen hours a day, seven days a week. They may have been persuaded that they are worthless or possessed by evil spirits and be terrified of not only the world, but also of themselves. They may have become addicted to a powerful practice or technique that enables them to detach their rational mind from their immediate surroundings, so that it has become increasingly difficult to 'return' to the mundane world and cope with ordinary, everyday reality. Such people may be seriously sick and every effort should be made to ensure they receive the proper medical treatment as quickly as possible.

It should, however, be added that although such severe cases do occur, they are very rare. More frequent is physical exhaustion after long hours of work and lack of adequate sleep which results in members 'cutting off' if they have a chance to do nothing (apart from getting some sleep) when they visit home. It is also possible to observe converts behaving like perfectly normal human beings within the NRM environment, but dropping down a curtain to distance themselves from non-members. 'Zombie-like' behaviour may arise when there is a strain between members and their parents (or spouse). A glassy look appears in the members' eyes when they decide that they do not wish to discuss their movement - or their future. (It is not only converts to NRMs who practise this selective social withdrawal.) Such behaviour can be infuriating, but it is unlikely to be a symptom of mental disturbance.

Another kind of escapism is what might be called the 'Peter Pan' syndrome. Here converts seem to be reverting to the emotional state of a childhood in which they are told what to do by strict but loving parents who make all the major decisions. Such converts may be working hard for the movement, but they have no responsibilities. Parents have reported that their concern in such cases is not that their children are miserable, but that they are blissfully happy, with absolutely no thought for the morrow. Indeed, in some cases, the converts might not believe that there is to be a morrow – or, at least, a year 2000. They may be contentedly waiting for the imminent end of the world and their ecstatic future in the next life.

As suggested in some other sections, the sorts of world view adopted by some NRMs can lead to what non-members might consider to be an escape from moral responsibility. This may take a form that presents a mirror image of the guilt instilled by the 'hell fire and damnation' type of movement. Messer, in her account of Divine Light Mission premies, reports that many of them undergo a change in their relation to right and wrong as they move from an adherence to a strict moral code to a desire to respond to internal cues, without reference to fixed standards:

> With that change, devotees indicate that guilt disappears; that is, there is no pool of guilt that is evoked by wrongdoing.[203]

Messer, herself a devotee, comments:

> One regrets a lack of "responsibility" in its generic sense, but the self-hatred associated with shame is lacking. One begins to feel and act toward one's self and others as one experiences God acting within the self: playful, loving and benevolent.[204]

Finally, social withdrawal may result, curiously enough, from attending some of the courses that promise the furthering of people's "highest aspirations" by helping them to experience "fulfilment in all areas of their lives". One ex-member of Lifespring reported:

> I learned the idea that I was responsible for 'choosing' everything, whether it was bad vision, or cancer, or even my own parents. I came to believe that if I really concentrated on something, it would happen by magic. They tell you, Be open to the possibilities,. I became open to crystals, which I thought were looney before. Then I went to a channeler and I thought, O.K., maybe there really is a spirit speaking through him. Basically, I went from action to inaction. If you can visualize the perfect world, why do anything about the world as it is?[205]

203. Jeanne Messer "Guru Maharaj Ji and the Divine Light Mission in Glock and Bellah (eds) (1976), p. 57.

204. Ibid.

205. Jon Ruth quoted in Fergus M. Bordewich "Colorado's Thriving Cults", *The New York Times Magazine*, 1 May 1988. It should, perhaps, be noted that Ruth had been deprogrammed and could, therefore, have had his erstwhile perspective influenced – see, for example, Trudy Solomon in Robbins and Anthony (eds) (1981), pp. 275–294.

❧ CHAPTER NINE ❧

Effects on the 'Outside Family'

The breaking up of families

SOMETIMES IT IS the parents who insist on breaking off contact with a child who has converted to an NRM. Sometimes an NRM is blamed for the disruption of a family that was already in a sorry state. Some commentators have argued that it is the break-up of the modern family which has led individuals to seek family values in the NRMs – that, in other words, the attraction of youth to the movements is a symptom, not a cause, of disintegrating family life.[206] And there are several instances of families that say that they have been brought closer together because they have shared experiences or beliefs that one member of the family has introduced to other members.[207] Some movements publish literature containing testimonies which say that the writer's family has been brought closer together because of the movement.

The fact remains, however, that many previously happy families have been put under enormous strain as the result of one of their number joining a movement. This is not peculiar to the current wave of movements, for there have always been those who believe that their duty to God must over-ride all other interests. Throughout the ages, religious leaders (including Jesus and Buddha) have expected their disciples to be prepared to sever their relationship with their families.[208] Similar demands

---

206. See Brock K. Kilbourne and James T. Richardson "Cults Versus Families: A Case of Misattribution of Cause?" *Marriage and Family Review*, 4/3–4, 1982, pp. 81–101.

207. For a discussion about 'networking', see Stark and Bainbridge (1985), chapter 14.

208. See Luke 14:26:

If any man come to me, and hate not his father, and mother, and wife, and children, and brethren, and sisters, yea, and his own life also, he cannot be my disciple.

See also Matthew 10:35–6. There are, of course, other passages in the Bible that can be quoted to the opposite effect, not least of which is the Fifth Commandment [Exodus 20:12; Deuteronomy 5:16; Mark 7:10–12; 10:19]. See also *The Teaching of Buddha. I. Duties of the Brotherhood, 1. Homeless Brothers*, p. 384:

A man who wishes to become my disciple must be willing to give up all direct relations with his family, the social life of the world, and all dependence upon wealth.

have also been made by more established figures: the Protestant theo-
logian, Paul Tillich, declared that anyone who would truly know God
"must risk tragic guilt in becoming free from father and mother and
brothers and sisters".[209]

Some converts will have left home several years before their conversion. Having had only spasmodic contact with their parents in the
intervening years, they may not see any reason why things should change
merely because they have joined an NRM. Other converts are so absorbed
with the excitement of their new lives that they just do not bother to
think about their parents, and they can be genuinely surprised to learn
that their parents are suffering from extreme anxiety because they have
failed to visit, to write or to telephone home.

Several of the movements are now trying to make sure that their
more thoughtless members do keep in touch with their parents, and clear
policy statements have been issued stating that any problems which arise
ought to be sorted out with the parents. The fact remains, however, that
even when a local leader may tell members that they are perfectly free
to go home if they wish, he or she may, at the same time, bring
contradictory psychological pressure to bear. It may, for example, be
suggested that those who express a desire to visit their family might also
wish to consider that God (or the movement) needs them, and that they
may want to sort out the list of their priorities a bit more carefully –
the implication being that parents come, at best, second in such a list.

There are also a few NRMs that explicitly discourage, or even forbid,
their members from having any contact with their family or anyone from
their past life – unless they can be thought of as potential converts. There
are cases where parents have not been allowed to know where their son
or daughter is living, and they have had to wait to be contacted. Parents
of members of the Children of God (Family of Love), for example, have
to write to a Post Box number; other parents may not even be told of a
Box number. In such circumstances, the parents may become afraid of
complaining too strongly on those occasions when they are contacted
lest the response is to sever all connection. There are a few, but only a
few, cases where parents, after years of silence, say that they have no
means of knowing whether their child is still alive.

Apart from imposing feelings of guilt at letting down the group or
God, a common reason that is given for severing ties with one's family
is that the parents might be planning a deprogramming attempt. A further
rationale is that the convert is entering a new, spiritual plane which
cannot be reached if he or she is continually looking backwards or feels
constrained by past ties and values. There are religious traditions which
teach their followers that the path to enlightenment or a mystical union
with God involves detachment from worldly matters. As suggested

---

209. Paul Tillich *The New Beginning*, 1955, p. 108.

earlier, some of these traditions, and the NRMs that derive from them, insist that those who seek true enlightenment ought to detach themselves not only from material possessions but also from all previous attachments to family and friends. In such movements it can be interpreted as a proof of one's faith or one's stage of development to be able to turn one's back on one's parents.

It would seem plausible to believe that the fewer the contacts that new members, particularly those in their late teens or early twenties, have with their family and previous way of life, the more likely these new members will be to accept the movement's perspective. There are, however, people who have left a movement because they rebelled against the movement's insistence that they should stop seeing their relatives and friends. For example, one of Skonovd's interviewees reported that, after four years in the Unification Church,

> I was typing this speech out and it went "Your parents and your family . . . are like an anchor and they're tied around your leg. Your parents and all the deprogrammers and all the fallen people are on this side trying to pull you away from me. But run to me, run to me." . . . I was just sitting there typing this stuff, you know, and I said "Oh, God! This is crazy, and this is not right." . . . I just stopped typing and I said to myself: "I've got to get out of here."[210]

Strains between non-NRM members of the family

It is not only the relationship between parents and the child who has joined a movement that may put a family under strain. Other children may be affected by the 'loss' of their brother or sister. They might have a certain amount of sympathy for the member which they feel unable to express in the home, and difficulties may arise if the parents forbid them to have contact with the member because of a fear of 'losing' another offspring to the movement.

At the same time, brothers and sisters can experience resentment or hurt because of what may seem to them to be the disproportionate concern for the convert that their parents display. Parents should try not to forget that their other children may need just as much understanding and help as the child who has joined an NRM.

There are, furthermore, situations in which parents start to blame each other for their child's involvement in a movement. It is not uncommon for the parents of a child to react in different ways, and occasionally these differences can be divisive – if, for example, the father (although it might just as easily be the mother) is bitterly against the child's involvement and no longer wants to have anything to do with him or her, while the mother desperately wants to keep in touch, but

---

210. Norman Skonovd "Leaving the 'Cultic' Religious Milieu" in Bromley and Richardson (eds) (1983), pp. 95–6.

feels under considerable pressure because of divided loyalties. The mother may then feel guilt because she is keeping in touch, or because she is not. The guilt can lead to resentment and to a growing estrangement between the parents.

'Mixed marriages'

Marriages have also been put under strain or even broken down completely when one of the partners has joined an NRM without the other. Sometimes both have joined, but one partner has eventually left, or, while remaining a member, has stayed with far less enthusiasm than the other partner. Some NRMs will suggest that the individuals would make better progress (develop further or become more enlightened) were the partners apart and no longer dependent upon each other. This can, of course, result in the separated individuals becoming more dependent upon the group than they were previously upon their partners.

While there are certainly plenty of cases when a husband and wife can lead a very happy life while one belongs to one religion and the other to another or to none at all, the intensity of commitment that is characteristic of many of the NRMs can result in very great strains for such a marriage. The non-converted partner may feel that, like a lover or a mistress, the movement has come between them.

Husbands or wives who have become involved with a movement may continue to live at home, but they may cease to confide in, or to discuss important matters with, their partner. They may lose all interest in doing things as a couple – their thought is concentrated on the new 'Truth', and most of their leisure time is taken up with the practices of the NRM or with their fellow members who, they believe, 'really understand' in a way that the rejected spouse does not. The non-member may well suffer even more anguish and loneliness than the parents whose child joins an NRM, for often there will be no one at all with whom he or she feels able to discuss the situation.

It may be that the member makes the non-member feel uncertain and, perhaps, foolish for fearing that something is wrong with the marriage. With no-one to talk to, the non-member can come to feel that he or she might be paranoid – especially if the member, secure in a certainty bestowed upon members that they are the ones in 'the right', intimates such is the case. Occasionally, the partner's behaviour changes in a manner that can cause the non-member severe unease and discomfort, although it would hardly be the kind of thing that could be considered grounds for divorce. For example, a wife who had been told by her husband that if he had to choose between his marriage and his guru, it would be the marriage that would have to go, reported:

> A lot of the time during this early period he would not make eye contact with me. It was a strange experience, but I thought I was going crazy as something was amiss and I couldn't quite put my finger

on it. One day I realised what he was doing and asked a psychologist of the significance of eye contact who informed me it was quite important. I asked my husband if Mataji had made any statement about eye contact and he said that she had. If someone was angry with you or vice versa then you should not make eye contact with that person. This small gesture can be quite devastating and destructive.[211]

Sometimes the member will give to the movement money that rightfully belongs jointly to both partners. Such a situation can become particularly unpleasant in that it is likely to be the spouse, not the movement, who would have to be sued if the non-member wants to get the money back. Few marriages can survive such a battle in the courts without its leaving some very deep scars. In cases where it looks as though such a situation may arise, or when, for example, it looks as though the partner who is not a member might be forced to sell the house that he or she has been living in, it would be advisable to consult a lawyer as soon as possible.

As in the wider society, conflict between separated or separating partners becomes especially poignant when children are involved. There have been some painful legal battles between members and non-members over gaining custody of children.

---

211. Personal communication.

❧ CHAPTER TEN ❧

Parents' Reactions

A T ONE END of the spectrum, there are parents who have said that they would rather their child was doing *anything* else – or was dead. At the other end of the spectrum, there are parents who have expressed positive delight at their son's or daughter's involvement with an NRM, some even following their offspring into the movement. Parents who themselves have strongly held religious beliefs may experience first incredulity, then horror and fear when they learn that their child has embraced a new set of beliefs that appear to the parents to be heretical, blasphemous or just plain crazy.

Most parents, at least in the early stages, would much prefer their child to be doing something else – if only because they are sceptical about the beliefs and claims of the movement, and are convinced that their son or daughter could be leading a better – a happier or more useful – life. Several parents have, with the passage of time, changed their attitude towards their child's membership of an NRM. Some, originally having paid little attention to what they had initially taken to be a passing phase, have become more concerned. Others, having been upset at the start of their child's involvement, have become reconciled to having a Krishna devotee or a Divine Light Mission 'premie' in the family. One mother, already beside herself with anxiety over her son who had previously taken up drugs and then attempted to commit suicide, was even more appalled when he joined a 'cult-like' Christian group. She was horrified that a child of hers, who had been "brought up to question authority and to think rationally for himself", could have accepted so enthusiastically what she considered to be little more than superstitious rubbish. Within a few weeks, however, she had reached the conclusion that while having a 'Bible-thumping' child was a problem for her, it was not a problem for her son.

Parents may have talked to their children and to friends about the problems of drugs, of drink, of sex, of money, of getting into university, of finding a new job and all manner of other potential difficulties. But not many parents will have anticipated, let alone seriously discussed, the possibility of their offspring's joining an NRM. Only a small proportion of parents have the faintest idea of what the movements are like, beyond some vague memory of reading or hearing about them as 'bad' and 'dangerous'. Few parents will escape at least some misgivings. Most will find themselves confused and uncertain as to what to do or to whom they might turn. Many will suffer untold anguish.

One of the first, and perhaps one of the most difficult, things that parents need to do is to come to recognise and cope with their own reactions. They may experience a frightening array of emotions, among which there is likely to be a combination of feelings of rejection, anger, frustration, guilt, loneliness, bewilderment and anxiety.

Rejection

Many of those who join the current wave of NRMs come from close-knit families in which the parents had correctly believed that they were an important part of their child's life, and in which the child had been an important part of the parents' life. When the child joins an NRM, the parents may feel that they themselves have been rejected or that the values and beliefs in which they brought up their child have been rejected.

In most cases, the rejection is far more likely to be a show of independence than a permanent, outright rejection of either the parents or their beliefs. It is not uncommon, in fact it is very common, for young people to rebel at some point during their adolescence. Nevertheless, even when this amounts to little more than part of a perfectly healthy growing-up process, it can be a very painful period for the parents, especially if a parent defines him or herself primarily *as* a parent.

Enthusiastic young converts can feel less need to be involved in their parents' lives than the need their parents feel to be involved in their child's life – at least to the extent of knowing what their child is doing. At the same time, and perhaps somewhat perversely, these same adult children can feel quite hurt and may sever the relationship if they believe that their parents are *not* sufficiently concerned about what they are doing.

When children grow up to 'do their own thing' in a way that involves their rejection of the beliefs and values in which they have been carefully nurtured and that are important to their parents, this can be particularly painful for the parents – whether the latter are Orthodox Jews whose son joins the Jews for Jesus, devout Baptists whose daughter turns to Bhagwan Rajneesh or, as the example in the previous section suggested, secular humanists whose child joins one of the new, fundamentalist Christian groups. Some parents will have very real fears for the state of their child's eternal soul; others will be more concerned about their child's capacity for rational thought.

It is possible that, in at least some cases, the difference in beliefs is not as great as it may at first seem. Sometimes it is beliefs that have much in common which can seem more threatening than beliefs that are completely alien. It is also possible, even probable, that the values which the parents have taught their children have *not* been rejected at a fundamental level, but that the children are trying to live these values in their own way. Many of those who join the Unification Church, for example, would seem to have done so not in spite of, but, to at least some extent, *because* of ideals (such as devotion, duty and sacrifice for others) that were instilled in them by their parents during childhood.[212] Sometimes it is the intensity with which the movement is accepted that is taken as a rejection. A member of the Unification Church was not atypical in saying "My parents wanted me to make religion a *part* of my life, but not to make it a *way* of life".[213]

Sometimes the rejection is the other way around. The parents reject the child who has joined an NRM. In the words of one parent, writing a letter, a copy of which was sent to his son for circulation in the movement:

> On the day we realised that X for the first time in his life was committed to a cause rather than pursuing yet another fleeting enthusiasm, I with my wife's understanding, dropped him from my will and, to the extent possible, from my thoughts. . .
>
> [My wife] and I made a major investment of time and energy in giving X the best in physical and intellectual capability which his potential could utilise. We are however wise enough to know that that is not necessarily enough and that sometimes you have to write off the investment as being fundamentally flawed. That we have done.

The rest of the letter contained a number of cruel statements about the son, who, when he eventually decided to leave the movement, did not reveal his whereabouts to his family.

Anger and frustration

Many normally gentle and loving parents have reported feelings of uncontrollable anger when they discover that their son or daughter has adopted a set of alien beliefs and seems to have sacrificed everything they had wanted for his or her future. It is not uncommon for the parents themselves to have sacrificed willingly many comforts or pleasures for what they believed to be the more important goal of giving their child the opportunity to get on in the world – not to join a 'cult'. Sometimes the anger will be directed towards the son or daughter, sometimes it is directed towards the movement – more commonly it is directed towards both. Frustration is especially likely to arise when parents feel that their

---

212. Barker (1984), especially pp. 210–215 and chapter 10.
213. Quoted in *New Religious Movements* a Handbook (Section G13), compiled by Maureen Edwards for the Methodist Association of Youth Clubs, p. 1

child will no longer listen to reasonable arguments, or when they believe that the movement is stopping them from presenting their case.

Such reactions are totally understandable. But they can result in parents' resorting to desperate measures that could worsen their relationship with their child. However angry or frustrated they feel, parents should try to be careful that their emotions do not lead them into a situation in which they themselves start to talk or act in a manner that their child can interpret, or the movement can represent, as unreasonable.

Guilt

It is not uncommon for children to blame their parents for problems that they experience when they are adult. Some of the NRMs encourage their members to do this. It does not, however, follow that there is any necessary connection between blame and guilt, whether it be members of an NRM blaming their parents, or parents blaming an NRM.

Most of us with children have at some time wondered where we went wrong, but there is no evidence to suggest that parents of converts to NRMs are likely to have done anything particularly 'wrong'. With hindsight, some may feel that they have been over-protective or over-demanding, and there will be a few who have special reasons for feeling guilty, but the vast majority will not have been any worse than most parents. In fact, according to a number of criteria, it is possible that they have been better.[214] Despite the fact that there may be a few instances where guilt-ridden parents need help, parental guilt is usually unfounded. It is almost always unconstructive.

Loneliness

Many parents whose child (or husbands and wives whose partner) has joined an NRM feel bewildered, isolated and alone when they find themselves in what is, for most of them, a totally unexpected situation. Given the stigma that is commonly attached to the NRMs, some may feel ashamed to admit what has happened. Those who do confide in others risk having to face friends and relatives who make it obvious that they suspect that the parents or the spouse are to blame, or (and this is sometimes more difficult to bear) that they are to be pitied. Several parents have reported that people have gone out of their way to avoid mentioning a child who has 'been lost to' an NRM, while asking, with studied interest, about the welfare of their other children - "as though X had committed suicide".

In trying to overcome the less helpful reactions of relatives and friends, a lot of misapprehensions might be dealt with quite simply by getting the relatives and friends to *meet* the convert. Clearly, if the convert is overseas or unable or unwilling to come home, this may be difficult,

---

214. Levine (1984); Barker (1984), especially pp. 210–215.

or even impossible. But if 'outsiders' *do* meet the member on a face-to-face basis on more or less neutral territory, they might be amazed to discover how 'normal' he or she is. Even when the parents are worried at the change that has taken place, it is unlikely to be nearly as great as the relatives and friends could be imagining. Some years ago, a technician who was assigned to process a film about one of the movements telephoned the producer to check whether he really had been sent the 'cult one' as the people in it looked so ordinary.[215]

The experience of a close relative or friend joining an NRM has been likened to a bereavement. In both situations, the 'bereaved' may experience fear, disbelief, shock, anger and feelings of having been abandoned; they may share feelings of helplessness in that something which, neither decided nor wanted by them, has happened *to* them, resulting, perhaps, in the need to make a radical adjustment to their way of life or to their self-definition. As with a death, there are various 'stages' of adjustment that people may go through, with the sharpness of the pain of being alone and feeling lonely eventually easing, even if it never entirely disappears.

Some people have said that, especially in the first few months, death might have been easier to bear because at least death is final; one is not left in a state of uncertainty, never knowing whether one is doing the right thing, or what is going to happen to the convert in the future. But the analogy of bereavement should not be taken too far – after all, the convert *is* still alive and quite likely to return; and even if it does sometimes seem that coping with a death might be easier, very, very few people would really prefer that option were they given the choice.

If the strain is not to become intolerable, people with a close friend or relative who has unexpectedly joined an NRM should try to share their experiences with at least one or two other people. They may also find it easier to cope with their relationship with the convert if they can share their experiences and their fears with others. Of course, one wants to make sure that those in whom one confides can be as informed, sympathetic and sensible as possible, and that the confidants' response will be neither unrealistically hysterical nor unrealistically complacent or dismissive.

However lonely parents or other close friends and relatives might feel, they should try to remember that they are not alone. There are other parents, husbands, wives or friends who have been in a similar situation, who really do understand the agonies that parents can go through at such times and who are willing to listen and to share their experiences. And there are others who want to help. INFORM can put enquirers in touch with parents or other relatives and friends of members

---

215. The BBC producer, Noella Smith, was making two films for the Open University about my research into the Unification Church.

of a movement, or with professional counsellors and ministers associated with the mainstream religions who understand something about the movements and the problems that can arise as a consequence of their existence.

Fear and anxiety

Fear, fear of the unknown in particular, has resulted in parents suffering extreme anxiety on learning that their child has joined a movement. One of the main messages which this book hopes to communicate is that the worst should not immediately be assumed. Nevertheless, a certain amount of anxiety is understandable – it is, indeed, sensible.

It is sometimes helpful for anxious parents (and for their relationship with their son or daughter) if they are to sit down with pencil and paper, possibly with the assistance of someone outside the family, and ask themselves *why* they are worried. If the answer goes no further than saying "because my child has joined a cult" then the exercise is unlikely to be helpful. A list of clearly stated worries can be faced far more easily than vague, unexpressed fears; some of the fears may fade away in the light of honest and informed examination; genuine problems can be approached more calmly and effectively.

In cases where there does seem to be a cause for concern, however slight, it may be helpful to continue to keep a written record of what happens, including the gathering of information about the movement and the convert, and the reactions of relatives and friends. This could be useful not only for assessing changes, but also for informing others who might be asked to help at a later date. Obviously, the keeping of such records should not be allowed to become an obsession that merely fans anxiety.

◆ PART TWO ◆

What Can Be Done?

EVERAL SUGGESTIONS have already been made about the courses of action that anxious relatives or friends might consider pursuing. This second part of the book reinforces some of these and offers a number of further suggestions – but they can only be suggestions. Once again, it should be stressed that each case is unique. Actions and responses to a particular situation need to be carefully considered in the light of the particular circumstances. And, it should always be remembered, it is the close relatives and friends, most commonly the parents, who know and care most about the convert; and it is they who will have to accept responsibility for whatever course of action they decide upon.

Outsiders can, however, help by offering friendship, information and, perhaps, counselling. Such help may contribute to reducing unnecessary confusion and helping those who are most concerned to reach decisions and to come to terms with their own feelings.

Laissez-faire

It might be said that nothing should be done; that if adults want to join an NRM then that is up to them: that so long as they do not involve themselves in criminal activities, they should be left to believe what they want to believe, and to lead the kinds of lives that they wish to lead. In a free society, people should be free to sort out their own lives – and, if necessary, to make their own mistakes.

At a more pragmatic level, it might be said that there is little point in doing anything because one would only be risking making the situation worse. Or, rather more positively, it might be argued that a person's conversion to an NRM is an occasion for rejoicing because that person is now experiencing a fuller, happier, more spiritual or, in some other way, more satisfying life than he or she was leading previously.

But while one may unreservedly accept the principle that people should be free to *believe* whatever they wish, and while one may recognise

the right of individuals to *manifest* their religion,[1] one can also recognise
that such manifestations must be circumscribed for the protection of the
rights of others.[2] That is to say, some *practices*, even when these are
carried out in the name of religion, can be a cause for concern on the
part of the rest of society. Once such practices have been investigated as
rigorously as possible, it may be deemed necessary for action to be taken
by an appropriate authority. Moreover, some of the practices of some of
the movements, while not deserving of state intervention or control, may
result in help being needed either for those who have been attracted to
the movement (before, during or after their involvement), or for their
relatives or friends.

A decision to do nothing might emerge as a consequence of research
and careful consideration, but it would be prudent to ensure that the
research and careful consideration came first.

---

1. According to the United Nations' Universal Declaration of Human Rights:
Article 2: Everyone is entitled to all the rights and freedoms set forth in this Declaration,
without distinction of any kind, such as race, colour, sex, language, religion, political or
other opinion, national or social origin, birth or other status.
Article 18: Everyone has the right to freedom of thought, conscience and religion; this
right includes freedom to change his religion or belief, and freedom, either alone or in
community with others and in public or private, to manifest his religion or belief in
teaching, practice, worship and observance.
2. Ibid. Article 29:
1. Everyone has duties to the community in which alone the free and full development of
his personality is possible.
2. In the exercise of his rights and freedoms, everyone shall be subject only to such
limitations as are determined by law solely for the purpose of securing due recognition and
respect for the rights and freedoms of others and of meeting the just requirements of
morality, public order and the general welfare in a democratic society.
3. These rights and freedoms may in no case be exercised contrary to the purposes and
principles of the United Nations.
And, as stated in the European Convention on Human Rights and Fundamental Freedoms:
Freedom to manifest one's religion or beliefs shall be subject only to such limitations as
are prescribed by law and are necessary in a democratic society in the interests of public
safety, for the protection of public order, health or morals, or for the protection of rights
and freedoms of others.

❧ CHAPTER ELEVEN ❧

Forcible Deprogramming

———————◆◆◀————

A
T THE OPPOSITE extreme from the *laissez faire* position, there are those who suggest that, as members of NRMs are almost certainly the victims of brainwashing, or are under such pressure that there is no hope of their ever leaving of their own free will, the only viable option is to arrange to hold them in a secure environment so that they can be 'deprogrammed'. Sometimes professional deprogrammers contact parents directly, playing on their fears in order to persuade them that, if they really care about and want to save their child, the only option open to them is to hire the deprogrammers to 'rescue' the child. More frequently, the suggestion is cautiously dropped into the conversation by someone connected with a 'cult-watching' organisation which the parents have contacted in order to try to get help and information about the movement that their child has joined.

Deprogramming has involved members of a movement being kidnapped by being set upon while walking along a street then being bundled into the back of a van;[3] in other cases, unsuspecting members have gone to their parents' house for a visit, only to find that they are unable to leave and that their erstwhile home has been turned into a prison with locked doors and barred windows.[4] They may find themselves handcuffed or tied up with rope. Sometimes they have been forced at gunpoint to do what their kidnappers have demanded.

Despite the threats frequently made to kidnap-victims that they may be locked up indefinitely if they do not comply with the deprogrammer's demands,[5] the majority of deprogramming attempts are likely to last for less than two weeks (the average length of the deprogrammings instigated

---

3. Several vivid descriptions are to be found in Patrick (1976).
4. Case Number V in *Appendix III* is an example.
5. See, for example, Patrick (1976), pp. 15 and 91.

by respondents to the American Family Foundation survey was 8.5 days),[6] but there have been attempts that have lasted for several months.[7]

In both Britain and North America, the use of this illegal practice has spread beyond the area of NRMs. There are examples of Protestant parents hiring professional deprogrammers to 'rescue' their offspring from Roman Catholicism,[8] of Catholic parents arranging for the kidnap of their daughter from a convent that was reportedly run by a follower of Archbishop Marcel Lefebvre;[9] of Jewish parents kidnapping children who had converted to evangelical Christianity;[10] or a daughter kidnapped after she had married a Muslim;[11] and various other cases when parents have disapproved of their adult children's choice of marriage partner or the political causes that they have espoused.[12]

Sometimes deprogrammers have been gentle in manner; sometimes the methods used have been anything but gentle. The 'Father' of deprogramming, Ted Patrick, has written with pride about some of the more brutal practices that he has employed:

> I believe firmly that the Lord helps those who help themselves – and a few little things like karate, Mace, and hand-cuffs can come in handy from time to time.[13]

Apart from the instances of physical violence that are described in Patrick's book, there is a disconcerting number of sworn testimonies by victims of 'unsuccessful' deprogramming attempts, including those made by British deprogrammers, that tell of physical violence, intimidation by guns and by unwanted sexual advances.[14] Even when the parents are present and physical violence has not been employed, forcible deprogramming is almost invariably an experience that has terrified the 'victim' during at least its early stages. (See later sections and *Appendix III*.)

The Dutch Government Report concluded "Actions, aiming at enforced resignation of members (deprogrammation) we deem unjustified

---

6. Michael D. Langone "Deprogramming: An Analysis of Parental Questionnaires", American Family Foundation, n.d. p. 8. The survey is discussed further in the later section, *"Success Rates"*. Patrick (1976) suggests a shorter time – see p. 15.

7. See Cases I & II in *Appendix III*.

8. M. Darrol Bryant (ed.) *Religious Liberty in Canada: Deprogramming and Media Coverage of New Religions*, Toronto: Canadians for the Protection of Religious Liberty, 1979, pp. 11–18; *The Toronto Star*, 11 March 1975.

9. *New York Times*, 11 August 1988; *New York Post*, 21 July 1988; *Newsday*, 29 June 1988.

10. James Bjornstad "The Deprogramming and Rehabilitation of Modern Cult Members", paper presented at the Eastern Sectional Meeting of the Evangelical Theological Society, Lancaster Bible College, PA, 1 April 1977, p. 17.

11. *Mail on Sunday*, 2 December 1984; *The Guardian*, 30 October 1985.

12. For further examples of the 'scope' of deprogrammings, see, for example, Bryant, op cit; *Deprogramming: Documenting the Issue*, prepared for the American Civil Liberties Union and the Toronto School of Theology Conferences on Deprogramming, 5 February 1977 (New York) and 18–20 March 1977 (Toronto); "Now – Deprogramming for Everyone" *The Washington Star*, 18 December 1976; Associated Press 2 July 1980.

13. Patrick (1976), p. 63.

14. See literature cited elsewhere in the notes in this section.

and not to be tolerated".[15] In 1986, the Dutch Secretary of State for Health defined deprogramming as being "against the fundamental rights and freedoms of men". The Hill Report to the Ontario Government declared that "forced deprogramming is repugnant to the study."[16] In their 1974 *Resolution on Deprogramming*, the National Council of the Churches of Christ in America (a cooperative agency of 32 Protestant and Eastern Orthodox religious bodies with an aggregate membership of over 40 million persons) declared that:

> The Governing Body of the NCCC believes that religious liberty is one of the most precious rights of humankind, which is grossly violated by forcible abduction and protracted efforts to change a person's religious commitments by duress. Kidnapping for ransom is heinous indeed, but kidnapping to compel religious deconversion is equally criminal. . .
>
> The Governing Board is mindful of the intense anguish which can motivate parents at the defection of their offspring from the family faith, but in our view this does not justify forcible abduction. We are aware that religious groups are accused of 'capturing' young people by force, drugs, hypnotism, 'brainwashing' etc. If true, such actions should be prosecuted under the law, but thus far the evidence all runs the other way: it is the would-be rescuers who are admittedly using force.[17]

It might also be noted that there are many ex-members of NRMs, including those who have themselves been forcibly deprogrammed, who have spoken out against the practice, declaring it to be unhelpful or destructive. And, as has already been mentioned, every time a forcible deprogramming is attempted, it can provide the movements with ammunition with which they may persuade their members that parents are not to be trusted and should not be seen without 'adequate safeguards'.

Lest there be any possible misunderstanding, let it be stated unequivocally that the argument in this book is *not* one against people trying to talk other people out of their beliefs when the decision to talk has been agreed by both parties and when either party can walk away or terminate the conversation at will. It is the use of physical restraint (when a person is unable to leave a location) that is regarded as totally unacceptable. It is this practice, involving physical restraint, that is being referred to when the term 'deprogramming' is used in this book.

There may have been between 40 and 75 British members of NRMs deprogrammed since the practice was started – the number could be even higher. The number of cases continues to grow. A score or more British 'experts' are prepared, having convinced anxious parents that their child is being held by irresistible mind control techniques, to recommend the

---

15. Witteveen (1984), p. 314.
16. Hill (1980), p. 585.
17. "Religious Liberty for Young People Too" *Resolution on Deprogramming*, adopted by the Governing Board of the National Council of Churches, February 28, 1974.

services of a professional deprogrammer. Sometimes deprogrammers come over from North America or elsewhere, but there are, at the time of writing, at least five British deprogrammers, four of whom were themselves once members of an NRM.

In the American courts, several deprogrammers have been convicted of offences such as kidnapping, false imprisonment and assault. Two British deprogrammers were recently convicted in Germany of causing bodily harm and *Freiheitsberaubung* (causing deprivation of liberty).[18] For this assignment, the deprogrammers were charging the relatively modest fee of £3,000 (plus expenses), but it is not unknown, or unusual, for parents to have landed themselves in severe debt or to have had to mortgage or sell their house in order to pay the fee and expenses for a disastrous deprogramming. A third British deprogrammer, who has been reported as saying that he has successfully deprogrammed 175 people,[19] (and who could have certainly added a not inconsiderable number of unsuccessful attempts to that figure) has recently been given a six-month suspended sentence after being held in custody in another European country. This was as a result of his involvement in an attempted deprogramming which, according to several newspaper reports, involved handcuffs and tear-gas.[20]

American deprogrammers may ask for up to $80,000, plus expenses. Parents may also have to pay damages and legal costs if their child subsequently brings an action for unlawful imprisonment. In the American Family Foundation inquiry, 16% of all the reported deprogrammings resulted in lawsuits, but Langone suggests that the unrepresentative nature of the study may have resulted in this being rather a high figure.

Rates of voluntary defection

Forcible deprogramming is not only illegal[21] and morally repugnant to most people, it is also based on a highly tenuous assumption, and it is liable to cause far more problems than it solves. As will be apparent from an earlier section (*Conversion or Mind Control?*), scholarly research has seriously undermined the basic premise which is used to justify deprogramming – the assumption that members of NRMs have been programmed in such a way that they are literally unable to leave the movement by themselves. Far more people have left the very NRMs

18. *The Guardian*, 30 December 1987; *Sunday Telegraph*, 17 January 1988.

19. *SonntagsBlick* (Zurich), 25 June 1989. The same deprogrammer was reported in 1986 to have claimed that he had "dealt with up to 150 cases all over Europe in the last six years." *Woman* 1 March 1986.

20. *The Mail*, 25 November 1990, *Western Daily Press* Bristol, 22 March 1989, 27 March 1989; *Gloucestershire Echo* Cheltenham, 22 March 1989; *Birmingham Post*, 23 March 1989; *South Wales Echo* (Cardiff), 23 March 1989; *24 heures* (Lausanne), 21 March 1989; *L'Express* (Neuchatel), 20 March 1989; *Libera Stampa* (Lugano), 21 March 1989; *Il Dovere* (Bellinzona), 21 March 1989; *Giornale del Popolo* (Lugano), 25 March 1989; *Blick* (Zurich), 21 March 1989; *Berner Zeitung* (Berne), 21 March 1989.

21. *Archbold Criminal Pleading, Evidence and Practice* 43rd edn, Vol 2, para 20–243.

from which people are most commonly deprogrammed than have stayed in them, and the overwhelming majority of these people have managed to leave without the need for any physical coercion.

Bird and Reimer found in their survey of 1,607 adults in Montreal that 75.5% of participants in NRMs were no longer participating five years later; the drop-out rate ranged from 55.2% for Transcendental Meditation to 100% for the Church of Scientology.[22] Rochford found that over half the devotees who had been initiated into ISKCON between 1974 and 1976 had defected within a year, and that there was an even higher attrition rate, starting in 1977, after the death of Prabhupada.[23] In my study of the Unification Church, I found that at least 61% of those who joined the movement during a four month period in 1978 had left within two and a half years.[24] Levine, in his study of over 800 members of NRMs, found that over 90% left within two years and

> are able to resume the sorts of lives their parents had hoped for them and to find gratification and significance in the middle-class world they had totally abjured.[25]

The fact that there is a high defection rate from those NRMs from which deprogrammers attempt to 'rescue' their members does not, of course, mean that any particular individual will leave. But this does not mean that these statistics are irrelevant to the concerns of parents who might be considering hiring a deprogrammer. The implication to be drawn from the statistics is simply that the movement is not as efficient at keeping its members as the deprogrammer is likely to argue, and that it is quite possible (especially if the convert has only been in the movement for a short time) that he or she will leave anyway; or, if the member has been in for a longer period, that he or she is there for reasons other than the coercive techniques of the movement. (See the next section.)

Before deciding on forcible deprogramming, parents might like to examine carefully their assumptions and motives – and the assumptions and motives of those who may be trying to persuade them that deprogramming is the only or the wisest response to the situation. They might also like to consider some of the potential consequences.

Deprogrammers' 'success' rates
Given that it is an illegal practice, it is not surprising that it is difficult to gain accurate statistics of the 'success' rate of deprogrammings – 'success' being defined according to the deprogrammers' intention of

---

22. Frederick Bird and William Reimer "Participation Rates in New Religious Movements" in Barker (ed) (1983), pp. 221–2; see also *Journal for the Scientific Study of Religion*, 21/1, March 1982, p. 5.

23. Rochford (1985).

24. Eileen Barker "Defection from the Unification Church: Some Statistics and Distinctions" in Bromley (ed.) (1988), p. 167.

25. Levine (1984), p. 15. See also Bromley (ed.) (1988); and Wright (1987).

removing people permanently from the movement to which they had belonged. Deprogrammers claim to have only a few failures; the NRMs claim that the deprogrammers have only a few successes. The Director of Research of the American Family Foundation (AFF), America's 'Center on Destructive Cultism', in his analysis of 94 (admittedly unrepresentative) responses to a questionnaire at the back of the AFF newspaper, reported that over a third (37%) of 62 forcible deprogramming attempts were said to have failed; one quarter of these 'failures' later left the movement voluntarily, but several respondents (15% of the total of all 94 respondents) returned to their movement after having left it.[26] Of the 32 (again, admittedly unrepresentative) cases of deprogrammings in which British members of NRMs were involved and about which I have some documentary evidence, 11 were 'successful' and 21 resulted in the person returning to his or her movement.

In the mid-1980s, I estimated that:

> About two-thirds of those who are deprogrammed do not return to the Unification Church [in the West], but I would also guess that well over two-thirds of these would have left the movement of their own accord within a year or so. In other words, although deprogramming definitely 'works' in some cases, it is probably unnecessary and/or counterproductive in the majority of cases.[27]

I now consider that this estimate could have been over-cautious in the light of a study by David Bromley that involved the analysis of 397 cases of deprogramming from the Unification Church. Just under two thirds of these cases (64%) were 'successful', but:

> Nearly all (96.3%) deprogrammings involving individuals who had been members of the [Unification Church] for less than two months were successful, while only somewhat more than a third of those involving individuals who were members for more than four years were successful.[28]

The important point that Bromley makes is that

> The apparent ease with which some individuals have been deprogrammed has led to interpretive confusion. NRMs have attributed such results to coercive techniques (and consequent fear and intimidation) employed by deprogrammers. The ACM [anti-cult movement] has argued that such results demonstrate that cult attachments dissolve when individuals have been liberated from the effects of coercive mind control mechanisms. . . . Both positions are based on the presumption, albeit for different reasons, that attachments to NRMs are strong. This assumption is incorrect, however. NRMs like the [Unification Church]

---

26. Michael D. Langone "Deprogramming: An Analysis of Parental Questionnaires", American Family Foundation, n.d., p. 7. The questionnaire was printed in the spring and summer of 1982.

27. Bromley (ed.) (1988), p. 175.

28. Ibid, p. 201.

experienced both high conversion and high defection rates during the 1970s, when coercive deprogrammings were most frequent. Thus at any given time *most members were in the process or either affiliating or disaffiliating.*

Feelings of ambivalence and uncertainty were relatively easy to create in an individual whose link to a group had been unidimensional, who already has had some disillusioning experiences, who has felt uncertain about making the kinds of sacrifices the group has required, who has not been privy to the group's politics and esoteric beliefs and practices, or who has not given thought to the long-term life-style implications of group membership. At the same time the individual in a deprogramming situation has been faced with expressions of love and concern, recollections of the warmth and caring of family life, guilt for having abandoned family members and educational plans, the prospect of being detained indefinitely if group membership is not renounced, and reminders of the bright future ahead outside the group. *Thus the high rate of deprogramming success is consistent with the fragility rather than the tenacity of [Unification Church] members' group attachments.*[29]

This strongly reinforces the suggestion made in the previous section that, on the one hand, it is more than likely that new converts will either leave of their own accord, or they can be encouraged to reassess their affiliation by someone whom they trust and respect, without the potentially counter-productive measures involved in a deprogramming. On the other hand, it is likely that those who have remained in the movement for a longer period will be more familiar with its beliefs and practices and have reached a firmer decision that, at least for the time-being, they wish to pursue a Unification career; and for such people, the likelihood is that an attempted deprogramming will fail.

Consequences of 'failure'
So far as the consequences of forcible deprogramming are concerned, those that are unsuccessful (in the sense that the kidnap-victims return to their movements) almost invariably result in the situation becoming significantly worse than it was before. Even if no physical violence was used, people who have been unable to leave a place where they were being held captive against their expressed desire will almost certainly be badly shaken and they are often imbued with a deep distrust of their parents which can take several years to heal. Furthermore, returning members frequently become far more zealously committed to their movement as a consequence of the experience – and less likely to leave than they might otherwise have been.[30]

In two recent deprogramming attempts in England (by different deprogrammers), women were told that if they persisted in their beliefs

---

29. Ibid, pp. 199–201, emphasis added.
30. See Eileen Barker "With Enemies Like That. . .: Some functions of deprogramming as an aid to sectarian membership" in Bromley and Richardson (eds) (1983), pp. 329–344.

they could be committed to a mental hospital.[31] As has already been made clear, it is not denied that there are cases when those who have been associated with an NRM may need to be put under psychiatric care. What is being objected to here is that those who are involved in deprogramming can, by virtue of their having taken the law into their own hands, be in a position to threaten someone with committal unless that person renounces his or her allegiance to an NRM. Whether or not the people concerned would have actually gone ahead with an attempted committal is beside the point; the threat of such a possibility can result in a very genuine terror, especially for anyone who has heard of some of the cases that have been recorded in the United States where people, whose only apparent sign of mental illness has been their membership of an NRM, *have* been committed to hospital with, on occasion, very disturbing consequences.[32]

In cases where the subjects of an attempted deprogramming have managed to escape and return to their movement, it is not uncommon for them to have subsequently refused, for varying lengths of time, to let their parents know where they were living (as happened in the two cases referred to in the preceding paragraph). Such people have occasionally said that their feelings of hurt and their belief that they had been violated have been made all the worse by the apparent inability of their parents to acknowledge that they (the parents) could have done anything wrong. Parents, by publicly blaming the movements for the situation, and continuing to deny that their children could possibly have minds of their own, have persisted in exacerbating the situation in the eyes of their children.

In other cases, parents have come to the conclusion that what they did was mistaken or wrong, and they have managed to patch up their relationship with their child. There are parents who, because of what they have come to believe was false information and self-interested advice, subsequently feel bitter that they were persuaded by the deprogrammers to pursue such a course of action.

Stories of how 'victims' have been maltreated while 'in the clutches' of some 'sinister, bizarre cult', and how they 'managed to escape' or how their parents 'had to kidnap them' have become almost a common-place in the media. Practically untold, however, are the stories of the people who have undergone harrowing experiences at the hands of deprogrammers, especially when the person has suffered from a mental breakdown

---

31. See Cases IV & V in *Appendix III*.

32. See, for example, "Using Psychiatry to Fight 'Cults': Three Case Histories" by Lee Coleman in Brock K. Kilbourne (ed.) *Scientific Research and New Religions: Divergent Perspectives*, Proceedings of the 64th Annual Meeting of the Pacific Division, AAAS, and the 59th Annual Meeting of the South-Western and Rocky Mountain Division, AAAS, vol. 2, pt. 2, San Francisco CA 94118: Pac. Div. AAAS, 1985, pp. 40–56. See also Herbert Richardson (ed.) *New Religions and Mental Health: Understanding the Issues*, New York & Toronto: Edwin Mellen Press, 1980.

following the deprogramming. The excerpts in *Appendix III* come from a growing number of testimonies by those who have suffered from deprogramming attempts. They are included not so much to give a comprehensive account of any particular attempt as to indicate to those who may be considering taking such action how the 'victim' might interpret what has happened.

Consequences of 'success'

There are those who are delighted with the results of a forcible deprogramming. But, despite the claims that 'successful' deprogramming allows the erstwhile member to return to a normal life, the deprogrammed individual may well face a number of problems that are not shared by those who leave a movement of their own free will. Those who leave by themselves may have concluded that *they* made a mistake and that *they* recognised that fact and, as a result, *they* did something about it: they left. Those who have been deprogrammed, on the other hand, are taught that it was not they who were responsible for joining; they were the victims of mind-control techniques – and these prevented them from leaving. Research has shown that, unlike those who have been deprogrammed (and thereby taught that they had been brainwashed), those who leave voluntarily are extremely *un*likely to believe that they were ever the victims of mind control. They are far more likely to say that things did not turn out the way that they had thought they would, or that the movement helped them over a particular period, but that they now want to move on to something else.[33] (See also the later section on *Leaving a movement*.)

If the mind-control thesis were true, it might provide some excuse for the physical coercion involved in deprogramming. If it is *believed* to be true, it can certainly provide both those who have been deprogrammed and their parents with an explanation of cult involvement that exonerates them from all blame. But it is also the case that, in so far as the brainwashing thesis is believed by those who have been deprogrammed, it leaves them with the belief that twice in their lives they have been incapable of controlling their own destiny – not just in the way that any of us can feel blocked by circumstances, but in a more fundamental way that can severely threaten their sense of personal identity. They may find themselves with exactly the same problems that they were experiencing before joining the movement – except that they have now lost confidence in their ability to decide their own future. In the words of Saul Levine:

> Halted in their radical endeavour before they have been able to utilize
> the group self in their own behalf, former members are thrown back

---

33. For comparisons between those who leave through involuntary and voluntary methods, see Beckford (1985); Bromley (ed.) (1988); Levine (1984); Lewis (n.d.); Wright (1987); James R. Lewis "Reconstructing the 'Cult' Experience: Post Involvement Attitudes as a Function of Mode of Exit and Post-Involvement Socialization" *Sociological Analysis*, 47/2, 1986; and Trudy Solomon in Robbins & Anthony (eds) (1981), pp. 275–294.

upon just the psychological dependency on parents they had attempted to break away from. The more the parents have achieved their purpose – that is, the more children now realize their 'mistake' – the less former members trust their own ability to make wise choices and the more dangerous it seems to them to do anything on their own. In other words, they find it all the more difficult to grow up.[34]

Although some of those who were thought to have been successfully deprogrammed will return to their movement during the so-called 'floating' stage, others do settle down to a normal life on the 'outside'. The length of time that it takes for them to readjust will depend on a number of factors, including the kind of help and understanding that they receive from others. But the abruptness of their departure can create a very considerable gap in their lives. When they come to accept that the faith which they had believed in, the friendships which they had thought they enjoyed and the love which they had assumed was bestowed upon them were all illusory, they are more than likely to feel disillusioned and to experience feelings of helplessness and hopelessness – unless they are given something else as a substitute.

One Briton, about six months after he had been 'successfully' deprogrammed, described his situation in the following way:

> I know the [Unification] Family wasn't actually providing the answers I needed, but now I'm out, I realise just how badly all those questions are still bothering me. I feel so guilty about all the anxiety and trouble I've caused my parents . . . I feel I have to go back to my studies just to make up for some of the hurt I've caused them – but I can't believe that this is what I'm really meant to be doing. I know I can't go back, but there's nowhere to go forward to.[35]

For some who have been deprogrammed, a new faith fills the gap and gives renewed hope. For others, and, indeed, for some of those who have discovered a new faith, it is joining a deprogramming team or becoming actively involved in the 'anti-cult movement' that allows the deprogrammed person to adjust. Through becoming anti-cult, such people may be offered many of the attractions of being a member of an NRM: they know clearly what is right and what is wrong; they are playing a saving role with a purifying purpose; they belong to a small, often misunderstood community of like-minded believers who know 'the truth' and are prepared to make a stand and, if necessary, suffer for the sake of that truth.

34. Levine (1984), p. 177.
35. Personal communication, which was originally quoted in Bromley (ed.) (1988), p. 176.

❧ CHAPTER TWELVE ❧

A Middle Way

———◆◆◀———

PUT BRIEFLY, the two positions considered so far in Part II are: Either that the child is 'lost to the cult' and is incapable of leaving; for parents who really love their children and want to rescue them, deprogramming is the only option. Or, nothing should be done because either to do anything would be to intrude upon another's religious liberty, or the 'victim' is controlled by such effective mind-control techniques that anything short of deprogramminng is useless – and deprogramming is dangerous, expensive, unpredictable, and often exacerbates the situation.

Experience, backed by scholarly research, has left an increasing number of people unconvinced of the moral or the practical sense of either of these positions. The assumption underlying this book is that, while neither deprogramming nor *laissez-faire* are appropriate responses, there *is* a great deal that can and should be done. The following sections suggest that there is a middle way – or, rather, that there are a number of middle ways, the appropriateness of each depending on the precise circumstances of any particular case.

Keeping in touch
One of the most important actions that parents, other family members and friends are advised to take throughout a person's involvement with an NRM is to keep in touch with him or her.

Keeping in touch may be difficult for a number of reasons. Sometimes it is the intemperate handling of an extremely difficult and testing situation that leads to the breakdown in communication between converts and their parents. Relatives and friends are strongly advised not to issue a convert with any kind of ultimatum, whether or not they intend to keep to it. Even when it is patently obvious that the problem lies primarily with the movement or the convert, relatives and friends should do everything in their power to make it clear that they still love, respect, and are interested in the convert and that they want to maintain a close relationship with him or her.

Quite apart from the fact that parents are unlikely to want to 'lose' their child to an NRM, and that they have every right to want to keep in touch, the convert who is *not* otherwise in touch with the 'outside world' may need to be reminded what the outside world is really like – to be reminded that his or her family and the rest of the world are not to be thought of merely in terms defined by the movement but according to his or her *own* experiences. This is particularly important in those movements whose members are socially isolated, because these are often the very movements that see the world in starkly positive and negative terms – everything associated with the movement being defined as good, godly, true and desirable and everything (and everyone) not associated with the movement defined as evil, satanic, false and despicable.

Even if letters are not answered, they can still be written. Even if telephone calls are not returned, they can still be made. Even if invitations to visit are never accepted, the invitations need not be withdrawn and friends and relatives can always try to visit the convert.

Several parents have admitted to being frightened of visiting the movement that their child has joined. There are those who have been explicitly warned against doing so by people and organisations which believe that any contact with any NRM is either dangerous or compromising – or both. Obviously it could be foolhardy to send young brothers or sisters to visit some movements, but there are very few instances in which parents who want to find out what their son or daughter is doing would be ill-advised to visit the movement in question. Parents might not want to go by themselves, at least for their first visit; and clearly if a confrontation develops, the visit is unlikely to be helpful. But normally, if visiting the movement is the only way in which contact can be maintained with a convert, parents should try, if at all possible, to make the effort. Even when it has not been the only way of keeping in touch, parents have found it helpful to visit a centre and learn more about their child's new beliefs and friends, and many converts have expressed disappointment and hurt that their parents have not, it seems to them, been interested enough in them and their new life to make the effort.

It is very rare indeed for any NRM to constrain its members by physical means, but a few of the movements have been known to intercept mail and telephone calls. Mention has already been made of some other measures (justifications and pressures) that some movements impose upon their members in order to dissuade them from keeping in touch with friends and relatives. Add to this the fact that fear of deprogramming may also be given as a reason why some parents who are able to see their offspring find that they cannot talk to their son or daughter in private but are obliged to meet in the presence of at least one other member of the movement, and it is not altogether surprising that this has led to parents becoming convinced that forcible kidnapping was the only way to 'get through' to their child, even when they had previously rejected so drastic an action.

In those rare cases when it seems to be impossible for parents to locate their children, INFORM may be able to put them in touch with someone who has established some sort of neutral contact with the movement. If parents or friends suspect that a person is being put under undue pressure or is suffering from mental or physical ill-health and is not getting the necessary treatment, then such contacts may be able to get help in investigating the matter further. If all else fails and access is persistently denied, it may be advisable to consult a lawyer about the possibility of taking out a writ of Habeas Corpus so that the person has to be brought before a court or judge.

But such total separation is rare. Most parents do keep in touch with their children, and, unless there are exceptional circumstances, friends and relations should not become so enthusiastic about 'keeping in touch' that either they appear too intrusive in their child's life, or they allow the situation to dictate or disrupt their own lives beyond all reason.

Keeping the relationship positive
Assuming that contact is not completely severed, relatives and friends should make every effort to ensure that their continuing relationship with the convert does not worsen, even if it changes, as a result of his or her joining the movement.

It is usually much easier to give advice ('don't join' 'get out') or to tell the convert what is wrong with a movement than it is to listen to what it is that the person finds attractive about it. It is, however, crucially important for the maintenance of their relationship with a convert, and for ensuring that the convert is encouraged to think about what he or she is doing, that **relatives and friends should be prepared to listen to what the convert wants to say**.

Parents may have to show a considerable degree of restraint in the face of converts who enthusiastically declare that they have discovered a truth or life-style which, they imply, their parents are too bigoted, closed-minded or stupid to accept. There is no doubt that new converts (and not only those who have joined NRMs) can appear insufferably self-righteous and scornful of other positions which, a short time previously, they would have treated with respect. It is quite understandable that the parents can become bewildered, and then angry and resentful. It is, however, important that parents should recognise that the convert also might be under considerable strain, and that this may result in their child behaving in a less helpful manner than he or she would ideally want. The parents should try to draw on whatever strength their maturity can offer them, and try *not* to get hysterical, *not* to transfer vindictive feelings about the NRM onto their son or daughter, *not* to say things that they will later regret, and *not* to attack their child's new faith in a manner that will seem totally unreasonable to the convert.

This does not mean that the parents should smile blandly and feign delight at every turn of events. Far from it. Parents have the right to respect for their own views. While they should try to engage the convert in an open discussion without hostility, they should also recognise that if they do lose their self control, it could well be that an honest row will have helped to clear the air. Indeed, it will almost certainly be preferable to a suppressed, but smouldering resentment. After a row, it is, of course, advisable to try to make sure that broken bridges are mended as soon as possible.

Some parents have found that it helps to agree to do something special, even if it is only going for a walk, when the convert comes to visit them, rather than just aimlessly sitting in an uneasy atmosphere with no obvious means of reducing the tension. Tension between the parents and a member of a movement might also be assisted through the presence of an emotionally neutral third party.

As suggested earlier, showing respect for their sons' or daughters' right and ability to reach their own decisions is particularly important in those cases where the parents might have been over-protective and the young adults could have joined their movement as a way of proving to themselves that they could stand on their own two feet – while, at the same time, they still feel (consciously or unconsciously) that they 'need' a family atmosphere in which to make such a stand.[36]

Parents who are most successful in 'getting through' to their children would appear to be those who, on the one hand, manage to avoid a cynical or contemptuous dismissal of their child's new-found beliefs and life-style and, on the other hand, do not go in for an unquestioning endorsement of whatsoever their child espouses. Stuart Wright reports that:

> While the influence of families seemingly never [is] identified by defectors as triggering disillusionment they are frequently mentioned as contributing in other ways.[37]
>   ... It was found that both parental disapproval and a smooth adolescent experience with one's family were related significantly to disaffiliation.[38]
>   ... among converts who reported a closeness to family prior to entry, stayers were four times more likely than leavers to report parental approval.[39]
>   ... Though parental disapproval appears to have a significant impact – at least when adolescent socialization and preconversion bonds are strong – it should not be equated with extreme parental

---

36. See Levine (1984).
37. Wright (1987), p. 60
38. Ibid, p. 61.
39. Ibid.

reactions. . . . These were said to be ineffective and even counterproductive.[40]

In other words, Wright's research suggests that young people are most likely to feel that, without losing face, they can leave an NRM with less difficulty if their parents have made it clear that, while they respect their children's right – and ability – to make their own decisions, they do not agree with the beliefs and/or practices of the movement.

Melton and Moore, writing for an American readership, advise parents to communicate to their children along the following lines:

> You are my daughter (son). Any child of mine has resources for adapting to life. I have confidence in you. I know that whatever our differences now, we will continue to relate and love each other through the years. I recognize your right to your own opinion and your own style of living. I may not agree with you about your current involve-ment, but I know it is meaningful to you. Because you are an intelligent person, you must be getting something out of it or you would leave the group. If you decide that it is not living up to your expectations, you will leave it on your own. If this time should come, I will be willing to help you explore other options. If this time does not come, we can still love each other.[41]

In brief, it is important that parents and friends should not over-react towards someone who is thinking of joining (or has just joined) an NRM, and it is important that they should try to reassure the convert of their continuing love and that they respect his or her right to make decisions. At the same time, there is no reason why it should not be pointed out that the movement in which someone is interested, or which he or she has joined, may expect a lot more money or commitment than is immediately apparent – or whatever the particular worries are in the particular instance. In fact, if there *are* genuine causes for worry, there is every reason why such things *should* be brought to the person's attention as quickly, calmly and accurately as possible. It might, however, be noted that pointing out that a movement will demand a great deal from converts is not necessarily the best way to discourage them. The opportunity to sacrifice – to give rather than to receive – can be a welcome challenge to an idealistic youth. (See the later section on *The opportunity to improve things*.)

If the parents feel that such warnings would be more effective if made by outsiders, and if the convert is willing to discuss the matter with outsiders, INFORM may be able to suggest someone who could help in providing further information about the movement.

Furthermore, representatives of several movements (including, but by no means only, the Aetherius Society, the Brahma Kumaris, the

---

40. Ibid. See also James Beckford "A Typology of Family Responses to New Religious Movements" in Florence Kaslow and Marvin B. Sussman (eds) *Cults and the Family*, Boston: Haworth Press, 1982, p. 50.
41. Melton and Moore (1982), pp. 114–5.

Church of Scientology, ECKANKAR, Elan Vital, ISKCON, the Jesus Fellowship Church, the London Church of Christ, NSUK, Sahaja Yoga, the Summit Lighthouse, Transcendental Meditation and the Unification Church) have expressed to INFORM a desire to try to help resolve misunderstandings or other problems that might arise between their members and their members' parents as a result of the former's involvement in their movement. Some parents may wish to take up such offers, either themselves or through someone who is, for example, in a pastoral role in their own church, or a secular counsellor acting on their behalf.

Getting information about the movement

To repeat, all those concerned should try to get as much accurate information as possible as quickly as possible. This is especially urgent if the convert gives any hint of being likely to leave the country or to enter into some commitment (legal, financial or marital) that may later be regretted.

There are many reasons why getting information about the movement may be crucially important, not the least of which is that, while parents can be alerted to possible problems, they may also find that many of their worst fears can be allayed. Another reason is that, while to understand is not necessarily to approve, the convert will be far less able to throw 'you-can't-possibly-understand' accusations at relatives and friends who have made a genuine attempt to understand. It is almost certain that the understanding will lead to a more fruitful dialogue between the convert and the outsiders, especially when the convert, while desperately struggling to explain, could be sounding utterly incoherent or ridiculous to those with no background knowledge of the movement.

Although attempts should certainly be made to get as much information as possible about the movement from the potential convert and other members, it should be recognised that not all movements can be trusted to divulge all the information that the enquirer may want. As has already been suggested, there are some movements that have no qualms about telling outright lies; more frequently, members will be evasive of the truth. Few groups (be they NRMs or other organisations) are likely to parade the skeletons in their cupboards in public, or, indeed, to provide anything other than what they consider to be their most attractive features to outsiders. It is, therefore, advisable to refer to further sources for information. INFORM may be able to help, either directly or through its network of specialist organisations, individual scholars, counsellors, ex-members or parents.

Many people will want information about the ways in which the philosophy, ideology or theology of an NRM differs from their own beliefs. The tenets of some NRMs can be explained quite simply in a few minutes. Other movements have so complicated or diverse a set of beliefs that it could take years of study before they were understood in any detail. Yet other movements may not have very complicated beliefs, but they are secretive about their more esoteric doctrines so that it is difficult for the outsider to find out what the members believe. INFORM will try to supply as much factual information about the beliefs of NRMs as it can, but it is not prepared to pass judgement on theological matters. If asked, however, it will try to put those who wish to have a movement's beliefs evaluated from the point of view of their own faith in touch with someone who is conversant with the doctrines of both the enquirer and the NRM.

Again, it should be stressed that *all* information, whether it comes from 'insiders' or 'outsiders', should be assessed as carefully as possible. It is advisable to be especially suspicious of sweeping generalisations that are offered in place of detailed facts about the NRM in question. For this reason, some reports in the media and some of the more sensationalist or horrifying information that is disseminated about the NRMs should be treated with caution as potentially biased and possibly untrue. This is not to say that valuable information may not be obtained from biased sources – it undoubtedly can be.

The point is that there is no need to add *unnecessary* anxiety to what is possibly already a worrying situation. Furthermore, action taken on the basis of inaccurate information is unlikely to be effective. It is of little use presenting members of an NRM, especially if they have been involved in the movement for some time, with a barrage of unsubstantiated accusations. All that is likely to do is to confirm the proposition that outsiders misrepresent or cannot recognise the 'real truth'.

Getting information about the convert

Apart from finding out as much as they can about the NRM in question, those who want to help should try to elicit two further pieces of information: what the person might find attractive about the movement, and whether he or she may be trying to escape from some unresolved difficulty.

The point has already been made that the fact that most people are able to resist the so-called 'lure of the cults' suggests that, rather than the movements employing irresistible recruitment techniques, there may be something about either the personalities or the situation of those who *do* join an NRM that makes them more likely than others to find the movement attractive. There is no reason to suppose that the characteristics which dispose a person towards an NRM are necessarily 'bad' or undesirable characteristics; they may well be traits that many members of the wider society would wish to foster, even if they do not wish to see them employed in the service of an NRM.[42]

Some of the attractions that NRMs might offer their members have already been mentioned: a means of developing a closer relationship with God; a way of improving one's spirituality, one's IQ, one's communication, business or management skills or one's personal relationships; or a chance to find friendship, to be given a direction and meaning to life, or to feel that one is making a genuine contribution to the creation of a better world. The recognition that converts almost certainly believe that they have found something of immense importance to their lives can provide the basis for building a crucial bridge across the gaping chasm that might seem to be separating them from their relatives and friends. By expressing an interest in what they are told are the positive aspects of the movement, enquirers will be showing an interest in what a convert believes to be his or her new-found self, not merely his or her previous self.

It is also possible that there may be negative pressures or tensions in converts' lives from which they are trying to escape or with which they feel incapable of coping. They might, for example, be suffering from loneliness after a recent loss through death or the break-up of a close relationship, or from feelings of uncertainty, inadequacy or lack of purpose while there is a burning desire to *do* something. It sometimes happens that those who had been big fish in little ponds while at home or at school discovered that they were little fish in big ponds once they moved on to further education or a job.

There are some converts who might be escaping from what they felt were their parents' unrealistic expectations to 'succeed' in an area in which they themselves felt unsuited or uninterested. While some may have felt the need to escape from what they felt was an over-protective environment, possibly even a 'claustrophobic' smothering of their adult personality by their parents, others may be seeking direction and absolute certainties in reaction to the 'agoraphobic' laissez-faire liberalism and permissive values either of their parents or of society.

Some movements might be helping the convert over a difficult patch; others might be offering an anaesthetic to ease the pain without actually tackling the problem; yet others might be actively worsening the situation. Whatever the particular reason (or, more likely, reasons) for the conversion or commitment, getting as clear a picture as possible from the

---

42. For some studies which indicate that characteristics such as compassion, a sense of fair exchange or the idealistic desire to improve the world are to be found among members of at least some NRMs see, respectively, Ted A. Nordquist *Ananda Cooperative Village: A Study in the Beliefs, Values, and Attitudes of a New Age Religious Community*, Uppsala: Borgstroms Tryckeri, 1978; Brock K. Kilbourne "Equity of Exploitation: The Case of the Unification Church" *Review of Religious Research*, 28/2, December 1986, pp. 143–150; and Barker (1984).

convert's point of view will help those concerned to assess the situation and may provide a basis for further action.

Assessing the situation with the convert
It is very unlikely that anyone (including the person concerned) will elicit every reason why someone wants to be a member of an NRM, or will acquire a comprehensive knowledge of the movement's beliefs and practices. But in so far as those concerned about a relative or friend succeed in learning about the movement and understanding the convert's point of view, they could become better equipped:

(a) to suggest (and, where suitable, to provide) alternatives to whatever positive appeal the movement offers;

(b) to recognise that the convert was facing some kind of problem, and was (and, perhaps, still is) in need of help;

or (c) to accept that the NRM might indeed be able to offer the convert something of genuine value for at least a short time, but possibly throughout a lengthy involvement.

But knowledge and understanding by themselves are not enough – especially if it is not a shared knowledge or understanding. Even if non-members believe that they have reached an understanding of why a person has joined an NRM, and are convinced that they could help the person concerned, it by no means follows that the convert will agree with their conclusions. Just as converts may feel that it is impossible for them to communicate the truth of their movement's message and the essential rightness of its practices to their parents, parents may feel it is impossible to communicate their doubts and their worries to a convert. Enough has already been said to suggest that just insisting that one side has the truth and the other has not is unlikely to produce anything other than an increased polarisation and a reinforced commitment to the position from which each started.

For many converts, it would be seen as a lack of faith to admit that the teachings or the practices of the movement provided anything other than the true answer to all their problems. This means that it is all the more important to try not to reinforce too clear-cut a definition of the situation in terms of good and bad or true and false. It is only when each side is prepared to listen to the other and to examine critically their own position that any progress is likely to be made. If parents want to ensure that their children are thinking and questioning for themselves, they must be careful not to push them into corners where all they can do is defend themselves and their movement – or escape back into it.

Perhaps one of the most important objectives of such an exchange is to ensure that converts have not lost, or are not in danger of losing, their sense of individual responsibility. Merging with the unconscious, submitting to God, surrendering to the guru or just 'swimming with the tide' can result in a person's forgetting or suppressing the fact that he or she *is* an individual person with both rights and responsibilities. Of course, individuals have the right to merge, submit, surrender or float, but they ought, at very least, to be prepared to accept responsibility for abrogating their individual responsibility if that is what they truly wish to do. They ought to be clear in their own minds what they are doing and be able to recognise the possible consequences of *their* decisions.

One of the main assumptions of this book is that, almost always, people *can* make decisions for themselves. Even when the influence of others may seem well nigh overpowering, individuals can and do continue to resist such influence. Rather than telling members of NRMs that they have been brainwashed and that they must, therefore, submit to a 'de-programming', it is almost certain to be more honest and more constructive to encourage converts actively to examine what they are doing. The underlying *challenge* to be conveyed to the convert is, in other words, that while others care and want to help, it is he or she who must accept the ultimate responsibility for his or her own life. No one should be allowed to get away with blaming anyone else – even a divine being – for abandoning his or her sense of personal responsiblity.

Encouraging people to think *for themselves* is not the same as making them think *like oneself*. However, it is possible that by inviting converts to talk about their beliefs and experiences one can encourage them to review the movement in a way that does not involve merely the repetition of the pat phrases or cliché-ridden jargon with which some movements isolate their members from non-members. It is usually possible, although by no means easy, gently to question converts in such a way that they will need to explain to a questioner who has not accepted the whole package of their belief system how one could make sense of the movement's practices, or, say, the demands that leaders make of members.[43]

The enquirer who does not accept the movement's beliefs can encourage the convert to think of the movement's beliefs and practices according to principles which the convert and the questioner can agree that they share – principles such as those of love, goodness, truth, honesty, respect for the individual and personal responsibility. The questioner should not try to force responses or conclusions onto the convert, but give the convert the opportunity to consider, in an environment that is not perceived as threatening, some of the information, assumptions and implications that he or she may not otherwise have had the inclination or opportunity to deliberate.

Lest all this has sounded too academic or intellectual, it should, perhaps, be stressed that it is not only by discussion, but also by showing

---

43. In rather different ways, and from somewhat different perspectives, Melton and Moore (1982), Levine (1984), Hassan (1990) and Ross and Langone (1988) offer some helpful suggestions on how to go about this process.

love, respect and concern in hundreds of little ways that people can help converts to develop their love, respect and feelings of concern about the people and the happenings of the world beyond their movement.

And, in this final analysis, if adult human beings persist in their desire to remain involved in a movement, it should be acknowledged that they *are* adult human beings. So long as their actions do not impinge upon the rights of others, their right to lead their own lives in the manner of their choosing has to be respected. It is not impossible that they are correct in believing that membership of the NRM is right for them – even when others are convinced that they are making a mistake.

When the convert is in a country other than the UK

On a purely practical level, people going abroad should be advised to make sure that they have received the necessary protection against disease. Information and immunisation can usually be obtained from one's General Practitioner or from various other centres such as the Hospital for Tropical Diseases,[44] or British Airways, which has two London-based immunisation centres.[45]

If parents feel that they have cause for worry when their child joins an NRM while overseas, the convert should be encouraged to return home for a visit, but if this seems unlikely to happen, one or more members of the family might try to visit the convert - if they can afford it. Again, if the parents can afford it, they may have more success in persuading their child to visit them if they offer to provide a *return* ticket, which might help to assuage fears that may have been instilled into the member that he or she will be unable to return to the movement if the invitation to visit home is accepted.

Whether or not the parents are worried about the immediate well-being of an offspring who has joined in (or moved to) another country, it might be helpful if the convert could be told that a prepaid airline ticket (that cannot be cashed for money) is available at a convenient airport.

Converts should also be told that, if necessary, they can enter the United Kingdom *without* their passport, so long as they can satisfy the British immigration service of their entitlement to enter the UK – which should not be a problem for a British citizen. It is advisable to find out further details relating to particular countries and to make sure that converts know how they can get home if they want. INFORM may be able to help, either directly or through its network, with specialised information.

---

44. By appointment, 4 St Pancras Way, London NW1 0PE. Tel: (071) 387 4411.
45. 156 Regent St, London W1R 7HG, Tel: (071) 439 9584 (Monday–Friday 8.30am–4pm) and Victoria Station (B.A. Gatwick Terminal). Tel: (071) 233 6661 (Monday–Friday 8.15am–11.30am; 12.30pm–3.45pm).

Money

Assuming the principle that one should respect adults as having responsibility for their own lives, it follows that people wanting to engage in expensive courses should be expected to accept the responsibility of earning the money themselves, and of paying off any debts that they incur. Furthermore, if people are prepared to devote their time to a movement so that they are unable to earn the money that they need for basic essentials, they ought to ensure that these are provided by the movement. They ought also to try to make sure that National Insurance contributions, or their equivalent, are paid.

Some of the movements do, however, put considerable pressure on members to obtain money from their relatives and friends on a number of pretexts. Parents are advised to take a hard line on this matter and *not* to provide their children with money unless they are certain that they know how it will be spent and they approve of the expenditure. Where possible, it could be prudent for parents and others who agree to a loan for a particular purpose to settle the expenditure directly, rather than sending cash, for medical expenses for example. It is also possible that parents might like to send 'care packages' containing clothes, or to buy their children shoes and other clothing when they visit home. Although some groups do pool clothing, it is likely that the recipient would be the chief beneficiary of such items – and it could be a not too expensive way of showing the member that the relative or friend cared and wanted to help them, if not the movement. This might be particularly relevant in the case of members who have young children whom grandparents would like to help.

There have been occasions when members of some NRMs, wanting to leave, or just wanting to visit home for a short time, have found themselves unable to do so because they did not have access to the money needed for the journey. If parents have reason to believe that this is a potential difficulty, they should try to ensure that their son or daughter either has the necessary amount hidden away or, if they think everything would be handed over to the movement, they should try to make sure that their child knows how to get money with as little difficulty as possible. The details concerning possible arrangements would depend on where and under what conditions the members are living, but they can at least be reminded that the police would be able to contact their parents, or that a local bank could be holding some money for an emergency. Such arrangements would, of course, have to be made with as much tact as possible, for it is unlikely in the kind of circumstances in which the need *would* arise that the convert would have been willing to admit to the parents or to him or herself that such an eventuality *could* arise.

It might be advisable to seek professional legal advice in some instances, such as when a child is likely to inherit either significant sums of money or possessions that the testators would not wish to be donated to the movement. It might also be advisable to ensure that, wherever possible, the originals of official documents (such as birth, insurance or examination certificates) are kept in a safe place, and that only copies are provided when requested. If the originals have to be sent, then copies should be kept.

One further remark might be made about money. Several members have commented that their parents have tried to bribe them to leave the movement by offering to pay for education, a house, a journey or nice clothes – but only if they leave. Although it is understandable that parents may well want to spend money on their child so long as he or she is not a member, the parents should be careful to make offers in such a way that they cannot be construed as being only for the purpose of persuading the member to leave. If such offers are seen in this way, they are likely to reinforce a belief that people in the 'outside' world are materialistic and manipulative – and, thus, reinforce the convert's resolve to stay in the movement.

❧ CHAPTER THIRTEEN ❧

Leaving a Movement

———◆··◆———

I
F THE DEPARTING member has kept in close touch with his or her parents, and is assured that there will be a genuine welcome without recrimination (this is no time for 'I told you so' – however true), the transition back to the 'outside world' will be easier. But it is still likely to take time and, unless the membership was of a peripheral nature or a short duration, the ex-member may need quite a lot of patient help and reassurance.

This is especially the case in situations where some time has been spent in one of the more close-knit, community-type movements in which major decisions will have been made for members. In some respects, adjusting to life outside may be similar to the difficulties that people are known to experience when they leave 'total institutions' such as a hospital, the army, a prison or even a boarding school.[46] It should, however, be recognised that there are also a number of crucial differences – not least of which is that decisions to leave will be far more likely to have been made by ex-members themselves than by patients, soldiers, prisoners, or even borders.[47] Another analogy that is sometimes applied to leaving an NRM is that it is like a divorce, or the end of a close relationship, when a huge gap and wound is left in the person's life.

The Hill Report to the Ontario Government stated that

> Only a small number of persons . . . related totally negative experiences. Most former members, even if strongly disenchanted with their movements on other grounds, were relatively healthy and admitted that their membership had some positive effects.

---

46. For the classic description of the characteristics of 'total institutions', see Erving Goffman *Asylums: Essays on the Social Situation of Mental Patients and Other Inmates*, Harmondsworth: Penguin, 1968.

47. For a discussion about the limitations in applying Goffman's concept of the total institution to a voluntary religious organisation, see Michael Hill *The Religious Order: A Study of Virtuoso Religion and its Legitimation in the Nineteenth Century Church of England*, London: Heinemann, 1973, pp. 72–82.

Most of those who became casualties or experienced substantial psychological difficulty short of breakdown seem to have undergone personal crises in their lives prior to joining their movements. A few clearly had been unstable.[48]

Frans Derks carried out a study of 31 ex-members of a number of different movements in the Netherlands. Over 80% (25 persons) had left voluntarily, 3 had been deprogrammed, 2 had been expelled and one had been both expelled and deprogrammed. Derks found that half his sample reported having had no psycho-social problems after leaving. About half the rest of the sample reported having had some such problems only in the period immediately following defection, but these problems had gone by the time of interview (on average, three and a half years after defection). Of the remaining eight, who reported still having had problems at the time of the interview, five also reported having had these problems before they had converted.[49] Although the numbers were too small to make reliable generalisations, the study suggests that around half those who leave an NRM may have some psycho-social problems (they may be 'rather emotional') just after they have left the movement, but the chances of their getting over this within a relatively short time are high, unless they had had such problems before they had ever joined the movement.

Ex-members will probably need time to think things through. Sometimes, however, they may lock themselves away from others for long periods and make little or no effort to take on new interests or to talk to others. If the ex-member seems to persist in bouts of 'difficult' behaviour, or seems to be seriously apathetic, withdrawn or disturbed in any other way, professional help should be sought.

Ex-members may feel very uncertain of their self-identity and future direction in life. Some will have become suspicious and, if they feel that they have been betrayed or let down, they may find it difficult to trust others. They may also, especially if they have been deprogrammed or expelled from the movement, find it difficult to trust themselves.

Some may seem less sophisticated or *au fait* with the 'ways of the world' than their peers, although it is quite possible that in some respects they will be more mature. While some, during long stints of evangelising and fundraising, will have developed skills in talking to almost anyone, they may find difficulty in relating to others in any depth. This may be particularly the case when meeting people of the opposite sex if the ex-member has been in a movement in which it was taken for granted either that a relationship with a non-relative will be purely platonic, or that virtually everyone is a potential sexual partner.

48. Hill (1980), p. 552.
49. Frans Derks "Uittreding uit Nieuwe Religieuze Bewegingen", Eindverslag van het Onderzoeksprojekt *Identiteitsverwarring bij Ex-Sekteleden*, Katholieke Universiteit Nijmegen, August 1983, pp. 115–6.

As was suggested in the Introduction, the term 'ex-member' may be misleading. It may, for example, imply that, rather like the popular image of ex-convicts, there is something rather dubious that lingers on and distinguishes ex-members from the rest of 'ordinary' society – they 'have a record'. On the other hand, it may suggest that while ex-members were once full-time, fully committed believers, they have now completely renounced their former beliefs and life-style.

In fact, neither of these descriptions need be the appropriate one. Although there certainly are cases where ex-members will have done a complete about-turn, or may still embrace a sectarian perspective on life, it is more likely that they will be 'normal' men and women who have undergone a particular type of experience that has not made them fundamentally different from their peers (who will themselves have undergone a variety of experiences).

People often make the mistake of thinking that, by defining the whole experience of involvement with the movement in negative terms, they are helping an ex-member. But, as has already been pointed out, it is rare for ex-members' memories of their time in the movement to be entirely negative. Ex-members may still accept many of the beliefs and practices that the movement taught them. For example, a woman who had left ISKCON was both offended and hurt when her mother assumed that, now that her daughter was out of the movement, she would be eager to eat meat. The reason for her distress was that her mother seemed unable to recognise that she had not become a vegetarian because the movement had forced her to, but that she had become a Krishna devotee because this involved accepting a set of beliefs and a way of life that she had believed and, in many respects, still believed to be right. And, to take another example, there are plenty of instances in which a couple continues to enjoy a happy marriage after they have decided to leave the movement in which they were married at the suggestion of the movement's leader.

It is, indeed, more than likely that people who leave one of the NRMs after some time as a member will have mixed feelings about the movement. In some cases, those who have rejected the beliefs will still miss the close comradeship that they enjoyed. In other cases, those who became disillusioned with the organisation or its members may still believe in some of the movement's tenets and they may well feel guilty about their defection. They may, rightly or wrongly, fear retribution from the movement, particularly if they know or suspect that they have been labelled as a dangerous enemy – a 'Suppressive Person' or 'the Beast of Blasphemy'.[50] Some may fear the supernatural retribution which, they were taught, always visits those who betray the movement. And there

---

50. See, for example, Wallis (1976), p. 144; Respondent's Brief In The Court of Appeal, State of California *Church Universal and Triumphant, Inc vs. Linda Witt* p. 9

are those who, while disillusioned with the corruption they observed in some of the members, still believe the leader to be an inspired or holy person to whom had been revealed (or who was revealing) an all-important truth.

One of Wright's interviewees described his ambivalence to his movement after four and a half years in the following words:

> You know, it's funny. I still have mixed feelings about the whole thing. It's just not that simple to say, well, it was all great, or it was all a bunch of shit. I'm sorry about what I put my parents through though. I know they went through hell, especially my mother. But there were also a lot of positive things that I experienced during that time in my life that I'm not going to forget.[51]

As was suggested earlier, the *manner* in which a person leaves a movement is likely to affect his or her attitude towards the movement. Wright asked voluntary defectors with no experience of 'exit treatment' "When you think about having been a member, how do you feel?" None responded with indifference; 7% said "angry", 9% felt that they had been duped or brainwashed, and 67% declared that they felt "wiser for the experience".[52]

In another study, James Lewis divided 154 ex-members of NRMs into three groups: (1) those who had left their movement voluntarily and had not been exposed to any form of 'anti-cult' counselling (what is sometimes referred to as 'exit counselling'), (2) those who had left voluntarily and then undergone some form of anti-cult counselling, and (3) those who had been forcibly deprogrammed. He asked the ex-members to evaluate the extent to which they believed that (a) they had been recruited deceptively, (b) they had been 'brainwashed', (c) their leader was insincere, and (d) the group's beliefs were spurious. He found that in all four of these matters the ex-members' attitudes were directly related to their "degree of contact with the anti-cult movement". In other words, the more contact that ex-members had had with the 'anti-cult movement', the more likely they were to interpret their movement in negative terms.[53]

Occasionally a person will have been expelled by an NRM. This could have been because he or she questioned authority and had become 'a disruptive influence', or, possibly, because of some illicit sexual relationship. Professional help may be needed when those who were expelled have been deeply dependent on the movement, or if they are suffering from strong feelings of guilt through believing that they have been justly

---

51. Wright (1987), p. 91.
52. Wright (1987), p. 87.
53. Lewis (n.d.), p. 15; James R. Lewis "Reconstructing the 'Cult' Experience: Post-Involvement Attitudes as a Function of Mode of Exit and Post-Involvement Socialization" *Sociological Analysis*, vol. 47, no. 2, 1986. Lewis' study replicated an earlier one by Trudy Solomon, reported in Robbins and Anthony (eds) (1981), pp. 275–294. See also Bromley (ed.) (1988), especially part III.

rejected because of something that they have done (or not done) that is contrary to teachings in which they still believe. Someone who has been expelled and still wants to return to the NRM may share some of the problems faced by those whose abrupt departure was precipitated by deprogramming. Such people are particularly likely to suffer from feelings of confusion, insecurity and lack of self-worth. They may also be experiencing some kind of identity crisis.

For ex-members to come to terms not only with their past lives but also with their present and future lives, there should be as little confusion as possible over understanding what was involved during the time spent in the movement: the ex-members should be given a fair hearing in contributing to an assessment of what was, after all, their own, personal experience.[54]

It is quite likely that ex-members will experience a number of potentially destructive emotions, such as anger and guilt, which they will need to 'work through'. They should be encouraged to express their anger, and to come to terms with themselves over things that they may now regret having done while they were in the movement, such as having persuaded others to join, having obtained money through deceptive practices or having treated their parents insensitively, or even cruelly.

But as well as learning from the more negative aspects, they should be encouraged to recognise without shame, and be able to benefit from, the positive aspects of their experience. They may need help in finding an alternative to the direction, motivation and answers to fundamental questions that the movement had offered them. Sometimes they will find the alternative in one of the mainstream religions; sometimes they need help in coming to terms with the fact that they may have to live without any very clear answers to such questions.

Because of their emotional involvement, parents may not always be the best people with whom someone who has recently left an NRM should stay. General confusion and possible recriminations on all sides could put an intolerable strain on the family relationships. In such circumstances, it is better if this is recognised and arrangements are made for ex-members to stay with other relatives or a sympathetic friend unless or until they are ready to cope on their own. In some countries there exist rehabilitation centres which, with varying degrees of success, assist ex-members of NRMs with their adjustment to 'the outside world'. There are, as yet, no such centres in Britain.

---

54. See Beckford (1985), chapters 4, 5 & 6, for a very helpful account of tensions that can arise when ex-members of an NRM define their experiences in terms that differ from those insisted upon by their friends and relatives. Although Beckford's research was confined mainly to ex-members of the Unification Church and their families, his observations are of a far wider applicability. See also James T. Richardson, Jan van der Lans and Frans Derks "Leaving and Labeling: Voluntary and coerced disaffiliation from religious social movements" *Research in Social Movements*, vol. 9, pp. 97–126.

Friends whom ex-members knew before becoming involved in the movement can play a valuable role by showing the ex-members that they care about them and that they accept them as they are *now*. Almost anyone who will lend a sympathetic ear might be able to help. Sometimes someone who has had professional training as a counsellor and who understands something about life in an NRM can be of particular assistance in helping ex-members to recognise their emotions and to assess their position. Talking to others who have gone through a similar experience can be helpful, not only because other ex-members will have shared experiences and understandings, but also because the relationship can be one of mutuality, rather than one in which it is assumed that it is the ex-member who is 'the one needing help'. INFORM may be able to help by putting enquirers in touch with counsellors and ex-members.

On leaving an NRM, at least some ex-members are likely to need more than emotional support. They may find themselves having to rebuild not only their private lives, but also the rest of their lives. They are likely to be facing a number of purely practical difficulties. Quite apart from the fact that they may have lost what worldly possessions they had, and may even be in debt, their peers are quite likely to have forged ahead of them in the job market, and they may feel that they have to conceal their past if they hope to obtain the sort of work that they would like. Whatever their experiences, it is improbable that membership of an NRM will have provided the ex-member with the sorts of credentials or training that the majority of employers would recognise immediately as exactly what they were looking for in a potential employee. Ex-members may, none the less, have developed a variety of useful skills (of, say, a practical or organisational nature) during their time in a movement.

While bearing in mind what was suggested in the earlier section about money, parents might like to consider being as generous as they can reasonably afford to be in helping their son or daughter to re-establish an independent position in society once he or she has left the movement. The expenditure may entail providing a grant for a previously abandoned course or just ensuring that the ex-member has enough money to be able to accept responsibility for making decisions about financial priorities. In some cases, parents may want to consider helping to pay off debts that have been incurred. Before paying off debts to the movement, it should be ascertained that the person really is legally liable to pay these. Members of some of the NRMs may believe that they are in debt or bound by some contract that has, in fact, no legal validity. Furthermore, few NRMs are likely to sue (with much hope of success) for debts incurred through a person's following their courses while he or she was an unpaid or low-paid worker for the movement.

By way of summary, relatives and friends should try not to have unrealistic expectations about what can be achieved immediately. At the same time, they should not assume that ex-members have ruined their lives and that there is no hope for their future. Ex-members should be encouraged, but not pushed. Without being patronising, small achievements should be recognised and applauded. By being patient and understanding, by giving ex-members time, love and friendship, parents and friends can play an important role in helping them to adjust to a new way of life.

There are by now plenty of examples of ex-members who have not merely 'recovered' from time spent in an NRM to become fully integrated members of the community, but who have beneficially drawn upon the (albeit somewhat unconventional) responsibilities, challenges and experiences that they encountered within the movement and gone on to lead full and rewarding lives in the 'outside world'.

❧ CHAPTER FOURTEEN ❧

A Wider Awareness

Art critic Harold Rosenberg once defined intellectuals as those who turn answers into questions. Those who have a passion for doing the opposite soon forget they had questions in the first place. The problem is not that so many are constantly looking for enlightenment, but that so many are constantly finding it.[55]

ALTHOUGH MOST PARENTS, teachers and ministers of religion have not spent much time thinking about NRMs until they have learned about an actual case of someone joining one of the movements, there is a growing awareness of the existence of the new religions and the fact that they seem to attract people who would not previously have been thought of as likely candidates for life in an NRM. And, although this book has been written mainly about the situation once a particular individual has joined an NRM, rather than about NRMs as a wider, social phenomenon, it may be helpful to end with a few comments about how people might consider reacting at a more general level to the existence of the movements.

Blanket warnings about the 'evils of the cults' are of little value. What is needed is a far better understanding of what it is that the movements seem to be offering, and some of the ways in which people might be made more aware of some of the potential difficulties that can arise out of membership of some of them.

It is also important that there should be a greater awareness of the differences between the movements. Sometimes people have joined a movement because, having discovered that some of the things that have been said about it are patently untrue, they assume that *everything* they have heard about it must be untrue and are ready to accept the movement's definitions of truth and reality more readily than they might otherwise have done.

Teachers, parents and clergy might want to be more aware of the anxieties of young people who have been looking for answers to questions

---

55. Rosen (1975), p. 230.

and problems which they have felt they had not had an opportunity to discuss seriously with anyone – until, that is, they met an NRM which offered them such an opportunity. It is possible that teachers, ministers and others who are anxious to warn people about the dangers of the movements could, through an awareness of what the NRMs seem to offer, learn something that could be of help to those who might otherwise join a movement. But it is also possible that they could learn something that could be of help to a far greater number of people who share the feelings of dissatisfaction, uncertainty or loneliness that those who join the movements may be experiencing. This book is not the place to go into such possibilities in detail, but three brief examples might help to make the point.

Loneliness

The proselytising member of an NRM might seem to be the only person who is ready to listen to potential converts' hopes and fears, or the only person ready to accept the converts 'as they really are'. It may be that the movement seems to provide the only friendly, caring, serious-minded, responsible and moral – or the only exciting, forward-looking and innovative – environment available to the seeker. Perhaps an examination of the apparent *absence* of such enviroments could be discussed with young, and elderly, people who are experiencing loneliness or, which is not quite the same thing, aloneness. This is not an easy proposal to put into action, and it certainly is not a new idea – there are plenty of examples of people and organisations that have tried, and several are succeeding in their efforts to help those who feel cut off from mainstream society in one way or another. All that is being suggested is that the NRMs might provide further clues as to some of the unfilled gaps.

The opportunity to discuss religious questions

In an earlier section, it was mentioned that religious seekers have frequently remarked that they have had difficulty in finding the opportunity to discuss questions such as "What is the meaning of life?" "What am I here for?" "Why is there so much suffering in the world?" There are those who have had an experience of a religious nature that has been of significant importance to them, yet they feel that to mention it to anyone would be to run the risk of being thought a 'bit peculiar'.[56]

Ministers can seem to religious seekers to be either remote and unapproachable, or else so 'trendy' that God would seem to be the last topic that they would choose to discuss.[57] Religious Education can sometimes appear to concentrate on 'comparative religious studies' that provide

---

56. See David Hay *Exploring Inner Space: Is God still possible in the twentieth century?* Harmondsworth: Penguin, 1982; and Barker (1984), pp. 216–220.

57. See Eileen Barker "A Moonie Challenge to the Churches" in Dan Cohn Sherbok (ed.) *Tradition and Unity: Sermons Published in Honour of Robert Runcie*, London: Bellew, 1991, pp. 237–242.

little beyond descriptions of colourful festivals and some very basic information about 'other faiths'. Alternatively, R.E. may focus almost exclusively on moral questions such as whether people should sleep together before they are married.

Some young people who have been brought up with an unquestioning belief in the absolute truth of one religion may find their belief shattered when they find that they can no longer accept the faith in the way it had been presented to them. The child who had believed in the literal truth of the first Book of Genesis, that God created every living thing "after his kind" within six 24-hour days, may become suspicious of the whole of Christianity when he or she is taught about evolution.[58] The child who believed that all priests were representatives of God may become disillusioned with the whole Church when he or she learns of the corruption or misdemeanours of an individual priest.

Other children, brought up without any religious background, may become aware of the sorts of questions that religions have traditionally asked and have only the vaguest of ideas about what kinds of answer a religion might give to such questions. Children such as these could, to some extent, have been 'prepared' to accept a ready-made set of answers when these are offered by an NRM.[59] One, somewhat embittered, ex-member, regretting the time that he had spent believing almost whatever he had been told while in an NRM, told me in a letter:

> The difficulty with coming from a non-religious upbringing is that you're *groundless* – I had no theological experience – no grounded experience to judge anything by. If I could have read William James or someone and had understood the dynamics, I wouldn't have gone to [the movement] – but it was all so powerful, coming in like that when there was nothing else. . . X scared the shit out of me, because I'd never had that experience before – of a religious fanatic declaring God's will – and so that I was part of it – part of God's game – wow!

It may well be that the set of answers that potential converts are offered by an NRM would have satisfied them even if they had previously had the opportunity to discuss such questions. It might be the case, however, that they would have questioned some of the answers that the movement offered a little more closely if they had already been more aware of alternative answers and of some of the complexities of the issues involved.

---

58. Eileen Barker "Science as Theology: The Theological Functioning of Western Science" in Arthur R. Peacocke (ed.) *The Sciences and Theology in the Twentieth Century*, London: Oriel Press and University of Notre Dame Press, Indiana, 1981, p. 265.

59. Edwin Cox suggests an approach to R.E. that would form an excellent basis for discussing the theological content of NRMs in his book *Problems and Possibilities for Religious Education*, London: Hodder & Stoughton, 1983.

The opportunity to improve things

An awareness of complexity might also be helpful for those who are searching for a way in which they can improve things – whether they want to improve their own achievement in their career or in personal relations, or they want to make the world a better place. If an analysis of the issues and questions for which the NRMs might be offering answers were to *precede* an analysis of potential answers, it could help to prepare young people to assess the ready-made answers they may be offered.

Perhaps those who are willing to learn from the NRMs could become more aware of the desire of many young people to have the opportunity to *give*. In a world of specialisation, bureaucracy and social welfare, it is not always easy for young people with idealism to know how to expend their undirected energy for the good of others. Some churches, some schools and some community centres do tap this energy. So do some NRMs.

★   ★   ★

In short, while it is certainly advisable that the public should become more generally educated about NRMs, and that potential converts should be aware of the problems that have been mentioned in this book, not everything that the NRMs offer should be assessed in negative terms. It is equally possible, and perhaps more constructive, to look upon them as a positive challenge to society.[60]

---

60. To a certain extent, this approach is already being adopted by some of the mainstream Churches. See, for example, Brockway and Rajashekar (eds) (1987) for a World Council of Churches' response; *Sects or New Religious Movements: Pastoral Challenge*, a paper prepared by the Vatican Secretariat for Promoting Christian Unity, Rome, May 3, 1986; and John A. Saliba, "The Christian Church and the New Religious Movements: towards theological understanding" *Theological Studies*, 1981, 43(3): pp. 468–485 for a sensitive discussion by a Jesuit scholar.

Concluding Remarks

A brief summary

1. One of the main assumptions of this book has been that there are few simple or easy answers to the questions that have been raised by the existence of NRMs in contemporary Western society.

2. Some commonly observed characteristics of some NRMs arise from the fact that the movements are, for the most part, both *new* and (using the word rather widely) *religious*, and that, unlike earlier waves of NRMs in the West, many have emerged from traditions that are still alien to most Westerners.

3. None the less, the differences between the movements are enormous in every area of belief and practice, and it should never be assumed that the characteristics of some movements apply to others.

4. The vast majority of those who become involved in an NRM suffer no serious damage as a result of their involvement. Many will testify that they gain considerable benefit.

5. It is, however, also true that serious problems do arise in a small minority of cases, and less serious, but none the less disturbing, situations can arise in further cases. Among the *potentially* dangerous situations to which the reader has been alerted, are:

   (i) A movement cutting itself off (either geographically or socially) from the rest of society.

   (ii) A convert becoming increasingly dependent on the movement for definitions and the testing of 'reality'.

   (iii) A movement drawing sharp, unnegotiable boundaries between 'them' and 'us', 'godly' and 'satanic', 'good' and 'bad' – and so on.

   (iv) Important decisions about converts' lives being made for them by others.

   (v) Leaders claiming divine authority for their actions and their demands.

   (vi) Leaders or movements pursuing a single goal in a single-minded manner.

6. It is not always easy to distinguish between individuals who have decided to lead their lives in a way others might find incomprehensible or unattractive, and those who have, for some reason or other, abrogated responsibility. It is an assumption of this book that those who allow others to 'show them the way' are not necessarily being irresponsible. At the same time, it is assumed that each individual should, unless clearly suffering from some kind of mental incapacity, be held responsible, and accept responsibility, for every action that he or she takes.

7. A number of suggestions have been made. Some of these arise from the beliefs that:

(i) An awareness both of the diversity and of the more frequently recurring features of NRMs can alert us not only to some of the causes for worry to which they give rise, but also to some of the attractions that the movements undoubtedly hold for certain people in modern society.

(ii) The indisputable evidence that the vast majority of people leave NRMs voluntarily suggests that we have to look beyond the movements' evangelising processes if we want to understand why a particular person does *not* leave.

(iii) Forcible deprogramming is unethical, illegal, and based on an assumption about mind control that has been severely undermined by a considerable body of scholarly research. It is also likely to result in more problems than it solves.

(iv) It could be unwise to adopt a *laissez faire* attitude before any particular case has been carefully investigated.

(v) But deprogramming and *laissez faire* are by no means the only options.

(vi) Parents and friends of those who join a new religious movement should make every possible effort to keep in touch and to foster a good relationship with the convert.

(vii) Those who want to help should try to get as much accurate and unbiased information as possible about both the movement and the convert in order to decide how best to act in any particular case.

(viii) They should also encourage the convert to assess *practically* (rather than just theoretically or to rehearse as a matter of faith) his or her movement in the light of factual information and in the light of general principles such as honesty, respect for others and personal responsibility for one's own actions.

(ix) It should never be forgotten that, in Western democracies, adult human beings have the right to enjoy religious liberty.

8. INFORM has been set up to try to help either directly or indirectly through its network of contacts.

A final, personal statement

It is, perhaps, a truism that people and their experiences of life differ, but one important consequence of this simple fact is that people will interpret situations in different ways – and as a society becomes more diversified, life can come increasingly to have different meanings for different people. But modern society is one of mutual interdependence: 'No man is an island entire of itself'. Whether we like it or not, we live together and have to take account of each other to a greater or lesser extent. Some misunderstandings can be resolved through factual inquiry and dialogue, but there will always be differences in perspective that can be neither dissolved nor resolved. Some members of some NRMs and some of their opponents would prefer our society to have more control over what people may choose to believe or to do with their lives; there are others who believe that there should be no control over people, whatever they do. I believe that if we wish to protect our liberties we need, very firmly, to maintain a very delicate balance. We have to recognise each individual's rights while making sure that they do not erode the rights of others. We cannot afford to make the mistake of assuming either that all difficulties can be resolved by coercion or that if they are ignored they will go away.

Although I have tried to be as objective and balanced as possible in my presentation of 'the facts', this has been a personal account. Perhaps I could conclude with one further personal statement. I do not accept that individual perfection is possible nor do I accept that a society that is not the best of all possible worlds is necessarily one that is the worst of all possible worlds. I do, however, believe that individuals behave better (with more honesty, responsibility and respect for the feelings and welfare of others) in some situations than they do in others.

I also believe that the attempt to create perfect individuals or societies (rather than an attempt to improve them or pursue the even more modest, but perhaps more attainable, goal of minimising suffering), can result in both individuals and societies becoming worse (displaying less honesty, less responsibility, less respect for others and becoming more authoritarian and totalitarian).[61] This, I believe, is a risk that both some new religious movements and some 'anti-cultists' run in their more absolutist pronouncements about right and wrong, and good and evil. It is not that I wish to deny or even to relativise the difference between good and bad – far from it. But many values (individualism or community; justice or equality; personal freedom or social order) can be realised only at the expense of other values when they are pursued to an extreme. History has shown the tragedies that can result when leaders, their followers and their equally absolutist opponents have taken *a* truth, *a* value, or *a* way and proclaimed it to be The Truth, The Value or The Way, neglecting other truths, other values or other ways that may need to be weighed in the balance. The price of a pluralistic democracy that permits the existence of pockets of extremism, and a price that many of us are prepared to pay when we consider the alternatives, is that of eternal vigilance.[62]

---

61. Eileen Barker *Armageddon and Aquarius: New Religions in Contemporary Christendom*, Manchester University Press, forthcoming.

62. Eileen Barker "New Lines in the Supra-Market: How much can we buy?" in Ian Hamnett (ed.) *Religious Pluralism and Unbelief: Studies Critical and Comparative*, London & New York: Routledge, 1990, chapter 3, pp. 31–42.

❧ APPENDIX I ❧

INFORM
Information Network Focus
on Religious Movements

———————▶••◀———————

INFORM is an incorporated charity,[1] which has a formal link with the London School of Economics. It was started in 1988 with funding from the Home Office and further resources from the Church of England and other mainstream Churches.

INFORM's *primary aims* are to conduct research into new religious movements (as defined in *Appendix II*) and to provide information about the movements that is as objective, balanced and up-to-date as possible.

INFORM's *research* includes the collection, analysis and publication of information about the diverse beliefs, practices, membership and organisation of the NRMs, and the consequences of their existence both for their members and for the rest of society.

Among *those who contact INFORM* for help are the relatives and friends of people who have become involved in one or other of the movements, ex-members, Churches and affiliated bodies, secular agencies, academics, students, schools, government departments and agencies, the media and other members of the general public.

INFORM helps enquirers by giving them *information* either directly or by putting them in touch with its extensive national and international *network* of people with specialist knowledge and experience which has been accumulated both from scholarship and from handling problems that have arisen as a result of the existence of the movements. This network of contacts includes academics and organisations engaged in research, the friends and relatives of members of the movements, current members and ex-members of the movements, a number of professional bodies and individuals, and various other people who have acquired information about a movement through direct or indirect means.

---

1. Registration number 801729.

While willing to offer help with information and suggestions INFORM does not offer a professional *counselling* service. It is, however, training a small group of professional counsellors to deal with NRM-related problems. If enquirers are experiencing difficulties because of their own or someone else's involvement with one of the movements, INFORM may be able to put them in touch with individuals or organisations that can offer various kinds of help. This help might be purely practical, or it could be sympathetic support from someone with personal experience or understanding of the situation; it might be pastoral care from a member of the clergy, or the assistance of a professional counsellor.

INFORM organises day-long *Seminars* for counsellors, clergy, social workers and others who want the opportunity to gain and exchange information that could be of practical use. Smaller groups of (a) relatives and friends of members of NRMs and (b) ex-members of NRMs meet on a regular basis. INFORM also provides *speakers* for schools, universities, seminaries, churches and other groups of institutions.

INFORM's *Board of Governors* is responsible for formalising its *policy* and for overviewing the work of the staff. A representative from the Home Office is present as an Observer at all meetings of the Board. The Board's members include parents of members of NRMs, ministers of religion, academics and counsellors; three mainstream Christian traditions and a professional organisation nominate four of the Governors. (See the end of this section for the list of Governors.)

INFORM is *non-political* and *non-sectarian*. Although, obviously enough, the individual members of its Board of Governors have their own personal beliefs. INFORM, as a body, is not prepared to enter into debate about the truth or falsity of particular theological or philosophical positions. INFORM does not, and will not, have a member of any new religious movement as a Governor or as a member of staff, and it has a policy of not accepting money from any of the new religious movements or any organisation that might wish to prejudge the outcome of its research.

While an examination of the practices of some NRMs (and some of their opponents) may lead to the conclusion that *new legislation* needs to be introduced, INFORM does not believe that legislation should be applied selectively; it believes that the laws of the land should apply equally to everyone, whatever his or her beliefs.

INFORM has a policy of fostering *direct contact with NRMs* that are willing to co-operate. This is in order to obtain information (although INFORM's research does not rely solely or even primarily upon information supplied by the movements); and to give the movements the opportunity to respond to statements made about them.

Although it recognises that there will always be problems to which there is no apparent solution, INFORM's experience has shown that, in some instances, direct contact with a movement can make a positive contribution toward resolving a variety of difficulties, especially, but not exclusively, those that have arisen between parents and their children. INFORM would never reveal to an NRM (or, indeed, to anyone) that an enquiry has been received concerning any identifiable person unless the enquirer were to make an explicit request for this to be done.

INFORM's policy of maintaining, wherever possible, direct contact with new religions does not imply that INFORM agrees with or approves of any of the movements in question.

INFORM stresses the importance of recognising that *generalisations* can be both misleading and dangerous, and urges that *each case should be considered unique*. It does, however, recognise that many of the problems that arise have a number of common elements, whatever the movement or individuals involved.

INFORM's *network* is conceived as very much a *two-way process*, with information going out from its headquarters and coming in from the wide network of contacts. Anyone who has either a query or information concerning the new religions is invited to become part of this network by getting in touch with INFORM. In other words, INFORM hopes that people will contribute to, as well as benefit from, its network. New movements are continually appearing on the scene; those that have been around for several years are constantly undergoing change. One way in which INFORM can keep abreast of what is happening, and can assess its information and the helpfulness of those with whom it puts enquirers in touch, is for those who seek information to be willing to provide feed-back and further information. *Confidentiality* is, of course, respected where individual cases are concerned.

In conclusion, INFORM has no illusions that it can perform miracles, but experience has shown that its approach is capable of helping a large number of people in a great variety of situations. It welcomes enquiries from anyone seeking, or willing to provide, information or help in the general area of new religious movements.

*   *   *

Enquirers can write, telephone or make an appointment to visit INFORM's offices in central London. When no one is in the office, messages may be left on an answer-phone, which is checked at regular intervals. Further details can be obtained from INFORM's headquarters at

Houghton Street,
London WC2A 2AE
England
Telephone (071) 955 7654.
Facsimile line (071) 242 0392 – please state clearly that the communication is intended for INFORM.

❧ APPENDIX II ❧

New Religious Movements: Definitions, Variety and Numbers

Problems with definitions

Most of the movements referred to as part of the current wave of new religious movements are *new* in that they have become visible in their present form since the Second World War; and most are *religious* in the sense that either they offer a religious or philosophical world-view, or they claim to provide the means by which some higher goal such as transcendent knowledge, spiritual enlightenment, self-realisation or 'true' development may be obtained. The term is, thus, used to cover groups that might provide their members with ultimate answers to fundamental questions (such as the meaning of life or one's place in the nature of things).[2]

There is, however, no general agreement over precisely what constitutes a religion. Some definitions, by referring to belief in a god, could exclude Buddhism; others are so all-encompassing that they could include ideologies such as Marxism.[3] Even more disagreement surrounds definitions of 'new religious movements' or 'cults'. In an attempt to address the question as to whether or not the Church of Scientology is a religion, Bryan Wilson listed 20 different characteristics, some, but not all, of which would have to be present for a movement to qualify as a religion. He found 11 of these clearly present in Scientology, 5 clearly absent, and the presence of the remaining 4 characteristics arguable.[4]

---

2. See McGuire (1989).
3. For a discussion about the range of definitions of religion, and the consequences of using one definition rather than another, see Meredith McGuire, *Religion: The Social Context*, Belmont CA: Wadsworth, 1992, 3rd edition, chapter 1.
4. "Scientology: A Secularized Religion?" in Bryan R. Wilson *The Social Dimensions of Sectarianism*, Oxford: Oxford University Press, 1990, chapter 13.

Those who object to the term 'new religious movement' frequently do so on the grounds that NRMs are not *real* religions, the assumption often being that religions are seen as 'good', so movements such as ISKCON (the International Society for Krishna Consciousness, popularly known as the Hare Krishna movement) or the Unification Church (popularly known as the Moonies), both of which, by *any* dictionary definition, would be religions, may be denied the label by their opponents. On the other hand, some of the NRMs see religion in negative terms as either a divisive or a lifeless institution, and they do not, therefore, wish to be associated with the term – even if their movement would be covered by most definitions of religion.

There are, moreover, numerous vested interests, both religious and secular, that make any drawing of precise boundaries a contentious and risky exercise. The disagreements over usage of these terms often lead to sterile arguments, in which different groups merely assert their definition in order to make a particular point because of the associations, benefits or restrictions implied by their own or others' understanding of the term. For example, being defined as a religion may mean that an NRM can claim tax exemption; but it may also mean that it is not allowed to be taught in American public schools as a consequence of the First Amendment to the United States' Constitution.[5]

The Church of Scientology has fought in the courts (successfully in Australia) to be registered as a religion for the purposes of taxation. Transcendental Meditation (TM) has fought in a New Jersey court in an (unsuccessful) attempt to prove that it is *not* a religion but, rather, a technique which might be taught in the state schools. TM describes itself as "a technique for deep relaxation and revitalisation which develops the inner potential of energy and intelligence that forms the basis of all success in life", and it points out that one can belong to any or to no religion and still practise TM (See p. 77 above). The Brahma Kumaris provide another example of a movement that would rather not be labelled a religion; they prefer to be seen as a spiritual or educational movement. Ananda Marga, which is against all religions in so far as these are seen as artificial barriers that divide humanity, describes itself as a socio-spiritual organisation. Graduates of the Forum or Exegesis are likely to insist that these are not religious organisations, but that they transcend or go beyond religion in so far as religion is associated with dogma and empty ritual. Raëlians have referred to their movement as an atheistic religion.

Some of the movements will deny that they are 'new' when their novelty is rooted in a traditional religion. For example, ISKCON devotees

---

5. "Congress shall make no law respecting an establishment of religion, or prohibiting the free exercise thereof; or abridging the freedom of speech, or of the press; or the right of the people peaceably to assemble, and to petition the Government for a redress of grievances."

consider theirs to be an ancient and a traditional religion. So far as their vedic beliefs and ritual practices are concerned, this is undoubtedly true. None the less, the *organisation*, set up in the West by Srila Prabhupada, is a new organisation that has exhibited several of the characteristics of an NRM since its inception.

Sometimes controversy arises over whether or not one should include groups that have, generally speaking, come to be considered 'respectable', but about which anxious enquiries are, none the less, made to an organisation such as INFORM. Should one, as is sometimes done, label Freemasons, or the numerous professional people (teachers, journalists, lawyers, and writers) who are involved in secret Gurdjieffian groups, cultists or members of NRMs? It has been pointed out that the United Reformed Church (which was formed in 1972 as a union between the Presbyterian Church of England and the Congregational Union of England and Wales) could be called a new religious movement – although few would dream of doing so. And, although most Westerners would consider *Western* Krishna devotees to be members of an NRM, they might be less certain whether to label as 'cultists' the far larger number of worshippers in ISKCON temples in Britain who are drawn from the Asian community and are regarded as little more or less than members of one Hindu tradition among many by most of their fellow Asians. ISKCON is, indeed, a respected member of the National Council of Hindu Temples.[6] The point at issue here is that, explicitly or implicitly, *respectability* or 'cause for concern' are sometimes drawn into the *definition* of what constitutes an NRM (or 'cult'). This is discussed in more detail in the next section.

Among the better-known of the movements that fall slightly less ambiguously into the general category under consideration are the Bhagwan Rajneesh movement, the Children of God (Family of Love, Heaven's Magic), the Divine Light Mission (Elan Vital), Jews for Jesus, Sahaja Yoga, the Summit Lighthouse and the Unification Church (the 'Moonies'). Then there is the New Age movement, which, when broadly defined, includes at its 'psycho-spiritual' wing, the Human Potential movement. Paul Heelas has termed many of the groups to be found in such categories the 'self-religions' in that they see the self as the ultimate locus of the Ultimate, and the ego, or some equivalent, as standing in the way of realising the self's true potential.[7] These groups may draw from a number of diverse sources such as the teachings of Jung, Gurdjieff, Alan Watts and, more recently, L. Ron Hubbard, as well as from various traditions of the East (certain kinds of Buddhism in particular). Examples of these very different groups would be Arica, the Emin, Emissaries of Divine

---

6. National Council of Hindu Temples (U.K.), 150 Penn Road, Wolverhampton, WV3 0EH, UK.
7. Paul Heelas "Californian Self-Religions and Socialising the Subjective" in Barker (ed.) (1982), p. 69ff.

Light, Exegesis (which no longer offers seminars to the public but has developed into Programmes Ltd.), The Findhorn Foundation, the Forum (a later development of *est*), Insight/MSIA, Primal Therapy, Psychosynthesis, some versions of Rebirthing, the School of Ecomonic Science, Self Transformation (now referred to as the Bellin Partnership), Silva Mind Control, TOPY and a great variety of 'growth centres', encounter, therapeutic, self-development and holistic healing groups.[8]

There are numerous Witches' covens, and pagan, occult and 'magick' movements. Satanism, while itself not exactly a new religion, has been viewed as a cult in recent years, and there are a few satanic NRMs. There are, futhermore, several groups or organisations that, although still linked to one or other of the mainstream religions, have been thought to exhibit certain sectarian or 'cult-like' characteristics; several Christian groups (Protestant and Roman Catholic) fall into this last category, especially some of those of a more fundamentalist nature that place the winning of converts high among their priorities.

But while attempts to define too precisely what is or is not an NRM are undoubtedly foolhardy, the term should be used within common-sense boundaries. It would clearly be unhelpful to consider Jainism, The Society of Friends, Friends of the Earth or the Wimbledon Pigeon Fanciers Association to be either a 'cult' or an NRM. Those who wish to know more about a mainstream religion, such as Jainism, Islam or Zoroastrianism, that has long been established in other societies but is relatively new to Westerners, might seek further information from the religion's own representatives, or from The Inter Faith Network.[9]

Numbers of movements

The actual number of NRMs in Britain depends upon the definition used (see the previous section), but a figure of around six hundred is not unreasonable. Claims have been made that there are up to 5,000 'cults' in North America, but no one has produced a list of these movements, and anyone who tried to do so would undoubtedly be using a very broad definition – a figure somewhere between between 1,500 and 2,000 might be more realistic.

---

8. See Robert Adams (compiler) *The New Times Network: Groups and Centres for Personal Growth*, London: Routledge and Kegan Paul, 1982; Guy Claxton (ed.) *Beyond Therapy: The Impact of Psychological Theory and Practice*, London: Wisdom, 1986; Marilyn Ferguson *The Aquarian Conspiracy: Personal and Social Transformation in the 1980s*, London, Toronto, Sydney & New York: Granada, 1982; Jean Hardy *A Psychology with a Soul: Psychosynthesis in Evolutionary Context*, London: Routledge and Kegan Paul, 1987; Hounam and Hogg (1984); Leonard Orr and Sondra Ray *Rebirthing in the New Age*, Berkeley: Celestial Arts, 1977 & 1983; Roszak (1976); Rosen (1975); John Rowan and Windy Dryden *Inovative Therapy in Britain*, Oxford University Press, 1988; Aland Watts *In My Own Way: An Autobiography*, New York: Random Haouse, 1972.

9. The Inter Faith Network for the United Kingdom, 5–7 Tavistock Place, London WC1H 9SS, Telephone: (071) 388 0008.

The Institute for the Study of American Religion, which houses one of the most comprehensive collections of data on American religion, has knowledge of a total of 1,667 different religious groups in North America; of these, 836 are classified as 'nonconventional religions'. The Institute does *not* include movements which do not fall under the definition of religion used by the Institute, but which are sometimes called 'cults'. Examples would be *est*, Primal Therapy or Rebirthing. Of the nonconventional movements recognised as such by the Institute, around 500 were founded between 1950 and 1988.[10]

If one turns to countries other than those in the West, a task not attempted in this book, the numbers of movements do, of course, increase enormously. Harold Turner has estimated that there could be over 10,000 new religious movements in Africa alone;[11] and several hundred, if not several thousand, more could be added to the list if one were to include the movements in Asia (particularly Japan and Korea), the sub-continent of India, the Pacific Islands, South America and the West Indies.[12]

There are around thirty new religious movements in the West about which a considerable amount of systematically researched information is available; there exists a growing collection of somewhat fragmentary information about a further two hundred or so of the movements; but there is, as yet, only the scantiest of information available to any but their members about the rest of the movements. The literature is extremely variable in content, but the total number of books and articles written on the subject during the past twenty years must be well into five figures – Peter Clarke and Elizabeth Arweck have, so far, collected 8,000 entries for an annotated bibliography that they are preparing at the Centre for New Religious Movements at King's College, London;[13] John Saliba cites nearly 2,000 books and papers written from a psychological perspective, and 2219 from a social science perspective;[14] and Michael Mickler has compiled a list of 1,826 pieces of literature produced by or about the Unification Church alone.[15]

---

10. See Melton (1989); and J. Gordon Melton *Testing the Truisms about the "Cults": Toward a New Perspective on Nonconventional Religion*, paper presented to the American Academy of Religion meeting in Chicago, November 19–22, 1988, revised December 1988.
11. Entry on "New Religious Movements in Primal Societies" in *The Penguin Dictionary of Religions*, edited by John R. Hinnells, Harmondsworth: Penguin, 1984.
12. For a global introduction to the NRMs, see the appropriate entries in *The Encyclopedia of Religion*, vol. 10, Mircea Eliade (ed.), New York: Free Press, 1987.
13. Peter Clarke and Elizabeth Arweck *An Annotated Bibliography of New Religions in Western Europe*, Westport CT & London, Greenwood Press, forthcoming.
14. Saliba (1987); Saliba (1990).
15. Michael L. Mickler *The Unification Church in America: A Bibliography and Research Guide*, New York & London: Garland, 1987. [Choquette (1985) cites 738 books and articles.]

Counting members in Britain

An obvious problem, which is related to that discussed in the previous sections, arises when one tries to estimate the total numbers of people involved in NRMs: a decision has to have been made as to what constitutes an NRM. Furthermore, even when one is attempting to count the number of members of a particular NRM, it is important to recognise the enormous diversity in the degree and type of membership that the movements may demand of their followers.

Most NRMs (like most mainstream Churches) have different 'layers' of membership, ranging from full-time service (equivalent to a priest-hood), to active followers (similar to devout lay members of a congregation), with yet others who may be classified as constituting a mildly involved band of sympathisers. Another complication is that some people, especially those who have pursued a course with more than one of the self-religions, are quite likely to be counted several times as they move from one path to another. Bearing these problems in mind, what follows can be no more than a tentative attempt to give some idea of the membership of the movements in so far as such information is available.

In Britain, it is unlikely that any of the NRMs has succeeded, at any one time, in accumulating more than a few hundred members who devote their whole lives to working for their movement. It is impossible to estimate the number of people who, while living in their own homes and employed in an 'outside' job are deeply committed, and devote almost all of their spare time to a particular group or movement – rather like, in some ways, the elders or those who organise or devotedly attend the functions of their local church. If, however, an estimate were to be made, it would be likely to be somewhere in the tens of thousands. A greater number of people maintain a more peripheral relationship, which may, none the less, be of considerable importance in their lives. An even greater number will have come into contact with one or other of the movements for a short, transitory period. It is not impossible for members to change the level of their involvement according to their personal circumstances – for example, student (CARP) members of the Unification Church could become either full-time or associate members upon completing their studies.

There could be a million or so people who have, minimally, 'dabbled in' or 'flirted with' one or other of the movements in Britain at some time during the past quarter century. If one were to accept the claim that there is "a conservative estimated population of over 250,000 Witches/Pagans throughout the UK and many more hundreds of thousands of people with a serious interest in Astrology, Alternative Healing Techniques and Psychic Powers",[16] and if one were to count such people as

---

16. *The Occult Census: Statistical Analysis and Results*, Leeds: The Sorcerer's Apprentice Press, 1989, p. 3.

members of NRMs, the total could be considerably greater.

Perhaps half a million have gone so far as to participate in a seminar, course or workshop or to spend at least several hours investigating an NRM. Half of these people could, however, be accounted for by their having taken part in no more than a short course with either Transcendental Meditation or the Church of Scientology. A spokesman for Elan Vital (previously the Divine Light Mission) has said that around 20,000 persons have 'received the Knowledge' in Britain; *est* claims to have had 8,000 'graduates' during its time in Britain – an equal number may now have graduated from its successor, the Forum, and other related seminars – and it is estimated that around 7,000 persons went through the Exegesis seminar; other movements such as Insight/MSIA, Psychosynthesis, the Rajneesh Foundation, Rebirthing, the School of Economic Science and Self-Transformation Seminars have possibly had 4–7,000 doing one of their courses.[17]

The Unification Church has about 350 full-time 'Core' members in Britain (roughly two-thirds of whom are British); a further 100 or so 'Practising' members, while not working full-time for the movement, accept the teachings and attend services and donate money on a regular basis; and about 8,000 people have signed an 'Associate membership' form – although less than one in ten of these have any continuing contact with the movement. The number of British Unificationists world-wide is unknown, but it does not exceed 600, and may be well under 500.

In Britain, around 1,000 'students' practise Raja Yoga with the Brahma Kumaris, but only about eight work for the movement on a full-time basis. Nichiren Shoshu Buddhism has four thousand members who have received their Gohonzon, but less than ten full-time staff members. Between 1,200 to 1,400 people are said to practise the 'latihan' twice a week with fellow members of Subud. There are about 300 names on the Raëlians' mailing list, but reportedly only a dozen or so are committed followers.[18]

Other movements with probably more than a hundred, but less than a thousand, fully committed members in Britain include the Aetherius Society, the Children of God (Family of Love), ECKANKAR, the Emin Foundation, Friends of the Western Buddhist Order, and Sahaja Yoga. The Ananda Marga has a large following in India, but only a few hundred associated members and no more than 30 or so full-time Margiis in Britain. The Jesus Fellowship has 950 members, 600 of whom live in

17. These estimates owe much to discussions with Dr Paul Heelas, of the University of Lancaster, who has studied the 'self-religions' for several years. Peter Clarke has estimated membership figures for several of the movements in both Britain and the rest of Europe in the first chapter of Clarke (ed.) (1987). See also Stark and Bainbridge (1985) for further discussion about NRM statistics in North America and Western Europe.

18. Alan Yeo "Is There Anybody Out There?" *Midweek*, 28 July 1988.

one or other of their residential communities. There are about 150
Emissaries of Divine Light, 60 of whom live in their Cotswold community. ISKCON (the 'Hare Krishna' movement) has several tens of
thousands of members of the Asian community associated with it,[19] but
only about 300 full-time devotees. There could be 10,000 or so followers
of Sathya Sai Baba, the overwhelming majority belonging to the Asian
community.[20]

Perhaps the confusion that sometimes arises about what exactly is
meant by membership and, consequently, about the numbers of people
'involved' in the movements can be further illustrated by looking in a
bit more detail at the different kinds of involvement that exist in two
movements that have had a relatively large number of people associated
with them at some point: Transcendental Meditation and the Church of
Scientology.

TM's Office of Information and Inspiration says that about 150,000
people in Britain have learned TM during a 4-day course, with about
6,000 more people currently taking the course every year. A total of
around 2,500 have proceeded to the advanced 'TM-Sidhi Programme'.
Most of these people have continued to lead 'ordinary lives' in that they
neither work for nor reside with the movement, although an unknown
number of them devote some time to meditation each day. However,
some of those who practise the advanced TM-Sidhi Programme will,
while remaining in outside jobs, have moved to live in the movement's
'Ideal Village' in Skelmersdale, Lancashire, which now has around 400
residents and a day school for about 80 of the residents' children. About
350 Meditators have pursued the techniques to train as TM teachers; of
these, about 40 have a full-time career as TM teachers and a further 60
or so will teach on a part-time basis. About 40 people are engaged in
various projects at Mentmore Towers, a further 8 or so are 'working for
charity' at the movement's residential academy in Kent. Altogether there
are around 100 people working full-time for TM in Britain.

The Church of Scientology says that, since it started offering courses
in Britain in the early 1950s, around one hundred thousand people have
paid for at least one of their introductory courses, which normally take
place over a weekend. Only a very small proportion of these people will
end up devoting their lives to the movement; at the time of writing, the
movement has about 250 full-time staff members at its headquarters in
East Grinstead, and about the same number of staff members spread
around other centres throughout the country.

The point to be stressed is that, although some hundreds of thousands
of individuals may have been classified as a 'member' of an NRM at

---

19. One estimate is of 50,000 in 1987: the *UK Christian Handbook 1989/90 Edition*,
Peter Brierley (ed.), Bromley: Marc Europe; London: Evangelical Alliance; and Swindon:
Bible Society, 1989, p. 176.
    20. Bowen (1988).

some time during the past quarter of a century, the number of people whose involvement in an NRM results in their having greatly reduced contact with the rest of the world because they are living in a centre or working full-time for a movement is very small. In 1985, Beckford estimated that there had never been more than 15,000 committed members in Britain at any point in the previous decade.[21]

The relevance of these figures, so far as this book is concerned, lies in the fact that it is the actions of the fully committed members, and the effect that full commitment can have on an individual's life, that give rise to most of the worries that have been expressed in relation to the NRMs. As suggested earlier, worries are seldom expressed about the tens of thousands of people of Asian origin who are associated with the Hare Krishna movement and who attend the movement's Temples for worship. The parents who become anxious are those whose sons or daughters become one of the few hundred Anglo-Saxon devotees who have dedicated their entire lives to Krishna Consciousness. Similarly, it is not the 8,000 or so people who have signed a Unification membership form who are going to change their lives in any significant way, but the 300 or so 'Core' members residing in Britain who will be significantly affected by their Unification membership.

A few further points ought to be made about the interpretation (or, more often, misinterpretation) of statistics when attempts to discern trends are made by the unwary – or by those who are overly eager to make a particular point. First, a *relative rate* of change in membership will be affected by the *absolute number* from which calculation starts (that is, how far the starting number is from zero). Secondly, the direction and strength of a trend will be affected by the *dates* that are chosen (for example, a closer look at a number of different points over a long period may reveal a cyclical pattern, a long-term trend that is not the same as a short-term trend, or a previous trend that has been reversed). Thirdly, when assessing the rate of *growth* of a movement, it is necessary to take account not only of conversion, but also of *defection*. Fourthly, care needs to be taken that one is measuring the same phenomenon when comparing change over time. Suppose, for example, the British membership of a movement were to be counted by itself to produce a statistic, then, at a later date, both the British and the Japanese membership of the movement were taken together to produce a second statistic. The fact that the second statistic was greater than the first could not be taken to indicate that either the British membership or the movement as a whole had increased in size. Fifthly, it is necessary to make sure that the statistics from which any inference about trends is being made are accurate.

All these rather obvious, but perhaps somewhat abstract, pitfalls can be illustrated in a more practical way by reference simply to one recent

---

21. Beckford (1985), p. 244.

television programme which was introduced with the statement that
fringe religions are steadily increasing their membership. As 'evidence',
it went on to report that:

> The growth rate of the cults is phenomenal. According to the Christian
> Handbook, in 1970 the Moonies had just 50 followers in Britain; today
> they have 500. At the same time, the Scientologists had 10,000
> followers; today they have 50,000. . .[22]

As the Unification Church had only just started up in Britain in 1970,
almost any increase would be bound to seem enormous when presented
as it was on the programme by a histogram (a column representing 50
in 1970 was compared with one representing 450 in 1989) – while a
similar addition of 450 members to the 516,739 recorded Methodists, or
even the 107,767 Jehovah's Witnesses, would be quite undetectable.
Turning to the trend, or pattern of the statistics, the number of Unificationists in Britain actually reached a peak of over a thousand (well under
half of whom were British) in 1978 when several hundred members of
the 'International One World Crusade' were sent to Britain on an
evangelising mission. With the departure of the Crusade in 1981, it is
hardly surprising that the number of Unificationists in Britain dropped;
and the number continued to fall as British members were sent on
overseas missions. However, the number of members actually joining in
Britain has since then been matched by the number leaving the movement.
This has meant that, throughout the 1980s, there has been a fairly stable
situation so far as the 'British Family' is concerned – the 'British Family'
being those who join the Unification Church in Britain – whatever their
nationality. It might also be mentioned (although the programme did not
do so) that the figure of 500 is given in the Handbook as an editorial
estimate. The grounds for such an estimate is not immediately obvious
as the Handbook's table reports a fall in membership from 570 in 1980
to 350 in 1985.[23]

So far as the Scientology statistics are concerned, the way in which
the movement's membership figures are recorded can, by itself, account
for the increase. This is because, generally speaking, 'turn-over' does not
affect the figures – anyone who has proceeded beyond a basic introductory
course is counted as a member and is unlikely ever to be removed from
the count. This means that even if, in any one year, 100 people ceased
being associated with the movement and 10 people were to start being
associated, the figures would give the misleading impression that there
had been an increase rather than a fall in membership.

22. *Thames Report*, 3 July 1989.
23. Peter Brierley (ed.) *The UK Christian Handbook* 1989/90 Edition, Bromley: Marc
Europe; London: Evangelical Alliance; and Swindon: Bible Society, 1988 p. 174. See also
my comments concerning the interpretation of membership statistics in the 1983 edition
of the Handbook, pp. 5–9.

Of course, small, even declining, membership figures do not imply that new religious movements are socially insignificant – other sections of society are indirectly affected by their beliefs and practices.[24] Nor, indeed, do such figures mean that the movements are not of fundamental concern to certain categories of people who, although themselves not members of a movement, have become affected through, for example, the involvement of a relative or friend. The small numbers of fully involved persons should, none the less, be borne in mind when considering the place of the movements in British society.

24. See Barker (ed.) (1982).

❧ APPENDIX III ❧

Unsuccessful Deprogramming: Some Testimonies

————◆••◀—————

IT IS NOT DIFFICULT to find accounts of how people have been 'successfully rescued' from an NRM.[25] Such reports may describe the anguish that both the parents and their children had suffered, but how, after a series of desperado cloak-and-dagger incidents, the story eventually came to a happy ending with the reunited family in full agreement about the villainy of the NRM in question. The cases that are cited in this Appendix tell a different story. The anguish is there, but there is no happy ending.

No claim is being made that these stories are typical – there is no such thing as a typical deprogramming. They are told by four women and one man. all of whom are, at the time this book goes to press, still members of their respective movements. The ages that are given refer to the time of the deprogramming. Their sworn statements were all written within a few weeks of the attempted deprogramming. Each of them has given permission for their statements to be reproduced here. The four different British deprogrammers involved are referred to as W, X, Y and Z.

Case Number I concerns a 32 year-old French woman who had been a member of her movement for 9 years. She had been working as a secretary in London, but had planned to marry her fiancé in a civil ceremony in her parents' home town on July 11th, 1981. She arrived in

25. Erica Heftmann *Dark Side of the Moonies: A powerful warning of the spread of the bizarre cults in modern society*, Harmondsworth: Penguin, 1983; Susan and Anne Swatland *Escape from the Moonies*, London: New English Library, 1982; Barbara & Betty Underwood *Hostage to Heaven: Four Years in the Unification Church by an Ex Moonie and the mother who fought to free her*, New York: Clarkson N. Potter, 1979; Morris Yanoff *Where is Joey? Lost among the Hare Krishna*, Chicago: Swallow Press, 1981; and Patrick (1976).

France on July 5th, expecting to go straight to her parents' house, but was met by her two brothers and her brother-in-law at the station and told that they would go to a house in the country where the wedding reception was to take place. When they arrived at the house she was met by W and some other people whom she soon realised were deprogrammers.

> I was held there from July 5th to July 17th. . . The window had been covered over in the room where I stayed, and the door could not be closed. The toilet and the bathroom doors had been removed for surveillance, giving me no privacy. The outside door in the adjoining corridor was locked and guarded at all times. . .
>
> I was subjected to physical threats of violence when they took my rings – a gold ring with the emblem of my church and my engagement ring. W forced them off while M [a French woman assisting with the deprogramming attempt] smiled cynically. Because of the pressure they put on me, including depriving me of sleep and food, I began to feel drained both physically and morally. The insults, humiliations, and the psychological strain from my torturers increased my anguish. . .

On July 17th, the deprogrammers drove her to Spain, and she managed to throw a letter she had written to her fiancé into another car. W found out what she had done when her fiancé started to make enquiries.

> That made W even more brutal and cruel. He threatened to punish my fiancé with physical violence and even death if they met. . . On 29th July . . . I found myself totally alone, at the mercy of W. Switching back and forth from kindness to violence, he tried to break my resistance and destroy my self-respect by forcing me into a sexual relationship (which I desperately refused), and deliberately surprising me when I was naked.
>
> By the 8th of August I was broken and confused. . . W took me back to Paris to the house of B [who] knew that the police were looking for me. . . . [Later] W struck me on the face twice. By this time I had no strength left. . .
>
> [In Paris] I was encouraged to speak to journalists and to write articles against my church. Knowing that a blunt refusal would lead to renewed violence, I delayed doing so. . .
>
> From the 25th of August to the 8th of September, very much thinner and psychologically dependent, I was returned to my parents [who] were not convinced I was completely deprogrammed and took me back to Paris. . .
>
> [On 11th September] in a state of complete mental confusion, I found myself then in a house . . . which W said he bought for the rehabilitation of his clients. . .
>
> From the 30th September to the 2nd of October I was again held in Paris . . . where I finally met my fiancé. After a final blackmail attempt on October 1st, we managed to escape.
>
> I came through this ordeal, which I can only call psychic rape, utterly exhausted, and morally degraded by the actions of my captor and his conspirators. They almost succeeded in turning me into a puppet which they could manipulate as they pleased . . . They made

me feel guilty and live in fear. I came to doubt my own goals because of the insecurity and fear that I would not be able to retain my own will. They also tried to destroy my personality and moral values by humiliating me.

I had to consult a psychiatrist in order to recover. On October 24th, 1981 a medical certificate was issued stating a total temporary disability to work for one month.

I have been hesitant to sue my parents and brothers and sisters because I believe they were motivated by love. However, I totally deplore the actions of the mercenaries, professionals at psychic torture, who cheated them of an estimated £6,000. The only result has been an even greater distance between my family and myself.

Since then, I have been subjected to the strain of a possible second kidnapping, and must hide to avoid W. . .[26]

Case Number II concerns a 28 year-old British woman who had been a member of her movement for 4 years. She had been with the movement in the United States, but, with two other members, she had been arrested by U.S. Immigration officials and deported to England, arriving on March 18th, 1982. On April 6th, she accepted an invitation to a friend's house for tea. This proved to have been a ruse by which she could be kidnapped and submitted to an attempted deprogramming by W and another British deprogrammer.

> . . . as I was leaving the house, I was greeted by three men who walked towards me singing 'Happy Birthday' (a common ruse to confuse unsuspecting bystanders). To my astonishment, they then suddenly grabbed hold of me and threw me into the back of a padded van. . .
>
> My parents were in the room with us initially and I was trying to assure them of my love for them, while all the time W was trying to convince them that I thought they were evil and satanic . . . In this way the 'deprogrammers' came between myself and my parents. I felt that if I could only speak to my parents away from . . . the influence of the 'deprogrammers', then I could make them see sense, but from that point on, I was never alone with my parents.
>
> Having someone right on your back every second of the day and night, even when you have a bath or go to the toilet, watching you stand up, sit down, breathe, *everything*, is enough to drive you crazy.
>
> . . . They made me feel guilty by saying that I had pushed my parents into arranging for the kidnapping and that I had caused them to spend so much money – as if the money was lining my pockets not theirs. Also that I had worried them and made them sick. When they saw I was worn down by their accusations, they would say then that it was not really my fault at all, that it was [the movement] that had made me like that.
>
> Unless one is able to see the way in which 'deprogrammers' use natural feelings like love and concern to produce guilt and self-accusation, one can be put under great strain by these tactics, and even though I myself could see that they were trying to blame me for the

---

26. Extracts taken from Complaint submitted to the Senior Judge at the Superior Court of Justice in Paris, signed 23 November 1981 (unofficial translation).

situation that they, and other people had created, it was still very stressful to be accused so constantly. . .

Over the next two months, with a continuation of this psychological harassment and emotional manipulation, the 'deprogrammers' tried ceaselessly to break my faith by eroding my integrity and self-respect.

They tried to make me feel abnormal so I would lose confidence in myself and feel that I was a freak. They criticised every aspect of my character, appearance and manner which they felt had changed since I had been working for the church . . . They tried to make me feel that the reason I could not agree with them was because of a fault in my own character and not that we just had a difference of opinion. They said I had an arrogant nature which prevented me from being objective – their standard of objectivity being when I agreed with them!

These tactics were being used to hit at any area of insecurity or weakness in my character, even though this was totally irrelevant to my beliefs. They were obviously trying to break me as a person so that I would lose confidence and turn to them. . .

They used every conceivable means of making me feel guilty, saying: "How could you possibly love your parents and allow this to happen?" They even went so far as to imply that if my father, who has poor health, had died during the Habeas Corpus court hearing, I would have had to live with this on my conscience for the rest of my life. . .

I was made to feel that if I *did* leave the church, I would want to work with them to help other people leave and realize the mistake they had made too.

By alienating me from the church and my life, it was plain they were trying to make me dependent on them for my support outside of the church, even though, *in words*, they insisted that they didn't want me to follow them. Also, despite their pretence at not wanting my gratitude, it was clear that they all thrived on the hero worship of the people they *had* managed to break down.

Eventually I was brought back to England from the continent and was allowed to call my parents. W didn't want me to go home in case members of the [movement] were still – after a period of two and a half months – hanging about ready to snatch me back. So I took my parents to Wales where we could be alone to talk. I broke the news to them that my desire was still very much to return to the church. This shocked them more than I had expected because, apparently, W had more or less told them that I was 'deprogrammed' . . . Naturally my parents were still anxious, but I said that after a week I would come back again to spend the weekend with them and they trusted me on this. . .

. . . after such an extreme experience of being exploited, my trust in people has been very deeply affected. I am one of the lucky ones; I have good friends in the church who I am able to trust and talk to, but those who do not rejoin will be mentally scarred for life.

The trust between my parents and myself is now being restored. Of course they still do not understand or agree with everything I am doing, but they are willing to listen to me. I go home very frequently to see them and spent three weeks there over Christmas. . .[27]

27. *New Tomorrow*, no. 46, February 1983, pp. 5ff.

Case Number III concerns a 23 year-old man, anxious to repudiate a report in the *Daily Mail* of 4 November 1985. As in Cases number I and II, the person attempting the deprogramming was W.

> During the days that this attempted deprogramming occurred R, a reporter from the *Daily Mail* was present. It was not until about half way through the second day that I was informed that he was a reporter.
>
> I was brought to a cottage under false pretences and when I came into the cottage I was met by W. I told him that I wanted to leave several times on that evening, but W told me that I could not go. . .
>
> At no point did W . . . succeed in making me change my mind or belief in the teachings . . . The only times I "broke down" were:
> a) after I became aware that there was a reporter of the *Daily Mail* present. I felt this was an invasion of my privacy and I stated categorically that there was no way I wanted to be splashed all over a rag like the *Daily Mail*. I felt that the *Daily Mail* would not represent my point of view and would sensationalize the story. I felt this because I noticed [the reporter] was diligently noting what W said but ignoring a large part of what I said. . .
> b) after W had been haranguing and continually harassing me for about 10 hours on the second day . . . I broke down for reasons of exhaustion and because of his constant pressure to alter my views.[28]

Case Number IV concerns a 24 year-old British woman who had been involved with her movement for about a year. On Friday July 19th, 1986 she left London, having agreed to nurse her mother for the weekend. She was met off the coach by her sister, S, and she was told that they would have a meal at the sister's cottage before she went on to her parent's home.

> On arrival at [the cottage], S told me that Z, my sister M and her husband N were waiting for me. I told S I did not wish to speak to Z and that I wanted to leave. S knew that I was the subject of an attempted deprogramming by Z in November 1985 when I had managed to escape from my parents' home and she had come to my rescue and helped me to get away. S and her boyfriend said that I had no choice about speaking to Z. . .
>
> Z made it plain to me that I had no choice but to listen . . . they would keep me there for as long as it took.

After an abortive attempt to escape and being driven to M's cottage

> I said I would like some sleep, but they said I was not going to have any . . . Z, S and M continued attacking me verbally about [the movement]. Z went to bed about 6 am, after which my sisters continued. . .
>
> At about 10 am, Z came down again . . . Again I asked if I could have some sleep as I was exhausted but my request was denied. S, M and Z continued harassing and haranguing me. . . At about 3.30 pm I said I wanted some sleep and they allowed me to go and rest on M's bed. I was woken one hour later. . .

---

28. Extracted from a Statutory Declaration, signed 6 December 1985.

N told me that I had shown definite signs of schizophrenia and that he could have me sectioned. I asked him what he meant. He explained that he knew someone who would examine me and could easily have me committed in a mental institution for a minimum of three days . . . N is a consultant at K Hospital and I knew he was in a position to carry out that threat. I was petrified.

All of them in turn continued verbally attacking me and blaming me for my mother's illness [reportedly cancer]. . .

At 3 am [on Sunday morning] I was left with R [a third sister] and Z, who continued the verbal battering.

At about 10 am . . . M told me that they were going to break me and to do it, I would have to cry. They sat directly in front of me, almost nose to nose, and chanted, "Cry" "Cry", for approximately 5 minutes. . . [After this] I took out a picture of F [her boyfriend] and as soon as I saw him, I burst into tears. . . Z said that F was the fly in the ointment. S then . . . said that I was never going back to London and would never see F again and I had to face up to it. At this point, I realised that if I did not show some cooperation, they would probably carry out their threat of committing me to a mental institution so I started to show agreement with their belief. . . They seemed pleased and let me have a bath and some sleep.

I slept for 3 hours. At approximately 5 pm on Sunday I was woken up. . . [later] I had a full night's sleep.

[On Monday morning a policeman arrived to get details about a stolen video] I interrupted and told him that I was being held against my will . . . He began to laugh and said your family wouldn't hold you against your will. N immediately intervened and explained to the policeman that I was under a lot of stress. . . The policeman knew that N is a doctor. N then asked the policeman if he could detain me for 3 days. The policeman said not. . . Z began talking to the policeman against [the movement] and during this time, M asked N if he could ring his friend in order to have me committed. N stated that he could ring his friend but did not think he could have me committed. . .

After several other ordeals, she managed to return to London on Sunday 3rd August.

The days I was held against my will by my family and Z were the roughest days of my life. It was like a nightmare I shall never forget and I would not wish anyone to be subjected to a similar experience from members of one's own family. I am still in constant fear of further measures my family might take to get me out of [the movement] and I feel they would not stop at anything as it seems they have no respect for the law.[29]

Case Number V concerns a 28-year-old British woman who had been a member of her movement for 9 years. She had been studying with the movement in the United States, but was on a visit to England, staying in her parents' house with her fiancé for a few days. She had felt that the visit was going well, until, on Sunday, 21 August 1988, she returned from seeing her fiancé off at the bus station.

29. Extracts from a Statutory Declaration, signed 5 August 1986

... my father opened the door and he said "There is someone to see you"... I was very surprised to see X especially as I had heard that she had left the Church some time ago... [After] a short time I realised that her purpose in speaking to me was to persuade me to leave the [movement]... After a little while I got up and tried to call my father as I wasn't sure if my father knew that she was trying to keep me in the room. Then he came ... and then he told me that all the doors and windows were locked and that what they wanted to do was talk to me. So I found out then that I was actually imprisoned in my own home...

There was always somebody with me ... and all the time they were asking me questions about my beliefs, about [the movement] basically accusing me of all kinds of horrendous things – hating my parents, lying to them, deceiving them and doing all sorts of filthy and vile things... I was even threatened with being locked up in a mental institution, being certified insane, all kinds of things I was threatened with...

... and then I realised that my parents had no intention of keeping their promise [to let me go, and] that the only way I would get out of this was ... when I decided to leave the [movement]... I basically made up my mind that the only way I was going to get out of this was basically to pretend to be deprogrammed...

X was very abusive, very insulting, very accusing but I could see that this other deprogrammer, Y, was much more ... professional ... He basically explained that he would get progressively worse if I didn't respond to him. In other words he would speak to me quietly in the beginning, if I didn't respond he would start yelling at me. Then if I didn't respond he would start throwing things at me and so on. So at first I was guaranteed by my family and by X that no violence would take place, but from the arrival of Y, then I saw that if he did get progressively worse, then there was no telling actually what would happen, and I believe that X did say, "Of course, we wouldn't like to use violence, but if it comes to that, then maybe it will be". So I realised that things could get a lot worse...

I really couldn't use the language that he used but I have never, never, in my life been spoken to like that... he was kind of helpful in a way because he explained what happens when somebody finally snaps or cracks and just lets go and actually comes out of their cult or whatever it is. So I had a pretty good idea that when I supposedly snapped, I should scream and cry a lot... what they expected me to do over the next days or weeks was to sleep a lot... and basically be quite unstable emotionally or mentally, so I was quite happy to oblige them...

[On September 5th she managed to telephone the movement and asked them] to have a plane ticket ready for me so that I could [get away] as fast as possible. At that point I said to [a person in the movement] that I really don't care what my parents think at this point, I can give them any sort of bogus call to keep them off the track, even give them a suicide call or something. I was just concerned to just get out as soon as possible before they even realised what had happened... [On September 8th she managed to catch a train to London.] Tonight [September 8th?] at about 7.30, I did call X and basically fed them a false story to lead them on the wrong track away from me... by the time they realise what's happened, I will be well away...

I'm sure that X did a lot to persuade my parents to actually do this. By themselves, I don't really know if they would have done it.[30]

---

30. Extracts from a Notarised Statement, sworn 4 March 1989. [The statement was originally made in the first half of September 1988, and sworn (without its having been altered) on the later date.]

❧ APPENDIX IV ❧

New Religious Movements: Some Examples

H AVING DECIDED to include this Appendix (see the section on *Contents* in the Introduction to the text), a decision had to be made about which of the 600 or so groups or movements in Britain should be selected for inclusion. Two main criteria were used. The first was that all those selected should be among the 150 or so organisations about which INFORM has received enquiries. The second was diversity, so that, taken together, the entries would indicate something of the extent to which the 'lumping together' of groups and movements that have been called cults or new religious movements can produce some very strange bed-fellows.

The quotations that appear at the beginning of the entries are all taken from the movements' own literature. Information that is given in the main text, and the statistics that are given in *Appendix II*, are not necessarily repeated in these entries, so a reader interested in a particular movement might like to check the index. When available, an address in the UK and the USA is given for each of the movements in the notes.

AETHERIUS SOCIETY[31]

> The crux of the Aetherius Society is direct co-operation with Higher Cosmic Forces, elevated Spiritual Beings Who have the welfare of mankind at heart and Who are directly assisting him at this crucial time, as indeed they have through history.[32]
>
> The Teachings of THE AETHERIUS SOCIETY are received from Cosmic Masters from other Planets through . . . His Eminence Sir George King, while he is in positive Yogic Samadhic trance.[33]

---

31. *European Headquarters*: 757 Fulham Road, London SW6 5UU, UK.
American Headquarters: 6202 Afton Place, Hollywood, CA 90028, USA.
32. Richard Lawrence *The Theology of Aetherius*, London: The Aetherius Society, 1987, p. 18.
33. *The Aetherius Society: Some Basic Principles included in its Teachings*, leaflet, 1988.

The Founder and President of The Aetherius Society, "An International Spiritual Brotherhood", is the Metropolitan Archbishop, His Eminence Sir George King (1919-), O.S.P., Ph.D., Th.D., D.D. His Eminence reports that, on 8 May 1954, he received the command "Prepare yourself! You are to become the voice of Interplanetary Parliament".[34] There followed a series of exchanges between Sir George and a number of Cosmic Beings (some of whom have come in UFOs or flying saucers). Of special importance have been a Cosmic Master from Venus who is known as Aetherius, from whom Sir George claims to have channelled many messages to this planet.

The Aetherius Society was founded in London in 1955, and is registered as a Church. Services, including marriage ceremonies, are conducted by the Society's ministers. There are branches in a number of other countries. Members pay an annual fee of £22, which entitles them to a subscription of the journal *Cosmic Voice*, mailouts, and a reduction for seminars, courses and lectures. They may also donate to the public service Cosmic Missions that the Society performs.

It is claimed that Sir George "was consecrated as an Archbishop in 1980 by an Archbishop from the Liberal Catholic Church and permitted, under ecclesiastical law, to establish his own Church as Metropolitan Archbishop".[35] However, the Liberal Catholic Church points out that it does not have Archbishops and says that it is unaware of the existence of George King. Sir George has invented Spiritual Energy Radiators through which, it is claimed, a giant spacecraft can beam thousands of Prayer Hours of spiritual energy. In another of Sir George's inventions, the Spiritual Energy Battery, energy invoked through Buddhist Mantra and Christian prayer is stored so that it can be sent out where and when it is most needed.[36]

Members of the Society believe that they "become part of a team of terrestrial co-operators with Cosmic Forces, playing an essential role in the Cosmic Plan at this vital stage in its unfoldment prior to the New Age upon Earth".[37] This, it is believed, is done mainly through co-operating with Cosmic Sources and The Great White Brotherhood to direct spiritual energy to help save the planet from disaster. We are told that during Operation Starlight (1958–61), 19 mountains around the world were charged with Cosmic Power and made forever Holy. Pilgrimages to the Holy Mountains are undertaken by the members.

---

34. *The Aetherius Society: A Brief Introduction*, leaflet, 1984. See also Roy Wallis "The Aetherius Society: A Case Study in the Formation of a Mystagogic Congregation" in Roy Wallis (ed.) *Sectarianism: Analyses of Religious and Non-Religious Sects*, London: Peter Owen, 1975, pp. 17–34.
35. Lawrence, op cit, p. 22.
36. Ibid, p. 21.
37. Ibid, p. 25.

ANANDA MARGA[38]

>   ANANDA MARGA (Path of Bliss) ... is a synthesis of traditional
>   tantric and yogic practices with a social aspect which includes social
>   service and social reform.[39]
>   As long as one harbours thoughts, or does actions with the
>   intention to harm or exploit others, one's progress towards peace and
>   understanding is hindered. ... In some circumstances it may be necess-
>   ary to use force to preserve human lives and liberties ... However,
>   our actions must never be undertaken with the thought of hatred or
>   anger.[40]
>   Human civilisation now faces the final moment of a critical
>   juncture. The dawn of a glorious new era is on one side and a worn
>   out skeleton of the past is on the other. Man has to adopt either of
>   the two.[41]

The movement was founded in Bihar, India in 1955 by Shrii Shrii
Anandamurti, whose 'secular name' was Prabhat Rainjan Sarkar
(1921–1990). It is described by its members not as a religion, but as a
way of life, attached to a philosophy or a socio-spiritual organisation.

The movement is highly structured, the 'London Diocese' being part
of the 'Berlin Sector'.[42] Affiliated organisations include Ananda Marga
Pracaraka Samgha, Renaissance Universal (RU), and AMURT (the
Ananda Marga Universal Relief Team which has, for example, recently
helped Zambian flood victims).[43] There is a special Women's Welfare
Department with several sub-groups. PROUT (PROgressive Utilisation
Theory) Universalism is officially independent of Ananda Marga, but it
is based on Sarkar's political theories.[44]

World-wide, there could be several hundred thousand core members,
with many more being in touch with the movement. Membership falls
into three categories: (1) Margiis, who have been initiated into the
movement but have jobs outside the movement and may not keep up
the practices; (2) Local Full Time Workers (LFTs); and (3) Acharyas, fully
committed members who may be sent to work any where in the world.

New members may be introduced through friends, by contact made
through a health food shop or restaurant or one of the schools run by

---

38. *London Headquarters:* 1 Cazenove Rd., London N16 6PA, UK.
American Headquarters: 854 Pearl Street, Denver, CO 80203, USA.
Further Reading: Melton (1989), entry no. 1349.
    39. Shrii Shrii Anandamurti *16 Points for Individual and Social Development: a summary
of the Spiritual Practices of Ananda Marga,* Liverpool: Ananda Marga Publications, n.d., p. 3.
    40. Ibid, p. 25.
    41. Shrii Shrii Anandamurti *The Chorus of Humanity: Discourses on Social and Spiritual
Progress,* London: Ananda Marga Publications, n.d., p. 27.
    42. *Handbook of Ananda Marga Organization,* Berlin: Ananda Marga Sectorial Office,
n.d.
    43. *Sunday Times of Zambia,* 1 March 1989, 5 March 1989; *Zambia Daily Mail,* 20
February 1989.
    44. Acharya Raghunath Prasad *PROUT-GITA (Pocket Book),* New Delhi: Ananda
Printing Press, 1978.

the movement, or by becoming involved with one of its many projects, or by attending lectures or courses in meditation and yoga. In Third World countries in particular, many make their first contact with the movement through one of its many social services (the movement runs schools, orphanages and programmes for rural poor). Potential converts will attend a few classes; they may then be initiated through the personal instruction of an Acharya and proceed to learn the special Ananda Marga techniques of tantric yoga.

The chant that is used "to focus the mind on the Supreme Consciousness" is BA'BA NA'M KEVALAM. Members are expected to practise meditation or yoga regularly each day, and to follow rules relating to cleanliness, food, fasting, conduct, posture, service and sex. Didis and Dadas (female and male Acharyas) wear special Indian dress; margiis cannot be distinguished by their clothes from other members of Western society. Committed members will be known by a Sanskrit or Hindu 'spiritual name'. There is a strict lacto-vegetarian diet and various foods, such as garlic and onions, are proscribed. The Dadas and Didis are celibate. Margiis are expected to have sexual relationships only within marriage.

Ananda Marga has been the subject of much controversy, being labelled by its opponents in India and other places as a violent terrorist organisation. The movement was banned under the state of emergency in India from 1975–1977 when over 400 of its schools in India were closed down, and several members were imprisoned. Anandamurti was himself imprisoned in India from 1971–1978, but was eventually acquitted of the charges of conspiracy to murder some of his former followers.[45] His followers protested strongly, insisting not only that the movement was being viciously and unfairly persecuted and that Anandamurti was innocent of all charges, but his life was in danger as there had been an attempt to poison him in prison.[46] Some followers felt the need to protest so strongly that they died by setting fire to themselves.

BRAHMA KUMARIS[47]

> Each of us has a THIRD EYE, often called the eye of wisdom or inner vision. And as the meditation gently opens this eye it brings rest and

45. David R. Telleen "The Rise and Fall of the Ananda Marga: A Modern Indian Morality Tale", 1977, MS lodged in the New Religions Research Collection, Graduate Theological Union, Berkeley, CA 94709; N. K. Singh "Ananda Marg's Lust for Blood", *The Illustrated Weekly of India*, 30 October 1977.

46. *The Persecution of Ananda Marga in India*, Liverpool: Ananda Printing, n.d.; *The Destruction of Democracy in India: The Case of Ananda Marga*, document published by the International Committee to Obtain Justice for Shrii Shrii Anandamurti, Liverpool, n.d.

47. *Raja Yoga Centre:* 98 Tennyson Rd, London NW6 7SB, UK.
USA address: c/o N.G.O. Offices, Church Centre, 777 UN Plaza, New York, NY10017, USA.
Further Reading: Melton (1989), entry no. 1356.

coolness to the mind, clarity to the intellect and complete self control. But above all there arises an overwhelming sense of peace. . . . You regain control of your own circumstances and the direction of your energies. This means you become much less open to stress and illness.[48]

Meditation as in Raja Yoga is not a rejection of the world, it is the preparation for life in the world. The detachment taught brings an objectivity that makes activity constantly positive.[49]

The Raja yoga which is practised by the Brahma Kumaris does not involve any mantras, special postures or breathing techniques; nor does it involve the worship of a guru. It is usually practised in a sitting position with the eyes open. The meditation is taught at the movement's centres or by Correspondence Course, with booklets and meditation cassettes. The student is taught "to understand the mind and then harness its hidden powers" and to grow in the realisation of the nature of the Supreme Being.

The Brahma Kumaris World Spiritual University (BKWSU) was founded in 1937 in Karachi by Dada Lekh Raj (1877–1969), a wealthy diamond merchant and a devout Hindu who was to take the spiritual name of Prajapita Brahma. At the age of 60, Dada Lehk Raj received a number of visions. It is reported that one day he was observed looking as though a light were shining through him, and a voice, that seemed as though it was another being speaking through him, was heard to say "I am the Blissful self, I am Shiva, I am Shiva; I am the Knowledgeful self, I am Shiva, I am Shiva; I am the Luminous self, I am Shiva, I am Shiva". The Brahma Kumaris believe that "Shiva, God the Supreme Soul, had entered the body of Dada . . . to begin the task of creation of a new world order."[50]

The BKWSU, which now has its headquarters on Mount Abu in Rajasthan, advertises itself as non-political, non-religious and non-sectarian.[51] Nearly all those in positions of spiritual authority are women (Kumari means unmarried woman). The movement's first branches were established in the West in 1971. Since 1980 the BKWSU has been affiliated with the United Nations as a Non-Governmental Organisation. The movement has sponsored a number of Congresses with academics and personalities concerned with Peace. In 1987 Brahma Kumari Prakashmani, the Administrative Head of the BKWSU, was presented with the United Nations International 'Peace Messenger' Award.

It is claimed that 200,000 people practise Raja Yoga every day throughout the world. Recently, the meditation has been taught to children in some of London's inner city schools, to prisoners, to police cadets and to members of the Houses of Parliament.

---

48. *How to Open your Third Eye*, Raja Yoga leaflet, n.d.
49. "What is Meditation?" leaflet published by the Raja Yoga Centre, London, n.d.
50. *Meditations & Jewels of Knowledge*, Mount Abu, India: BKWSU, p. 90; *Brahma: The Father of Humanity*, Mount Abu: BKWSU, n.d.
51. *A Profile of the University*, Mount Abu: BKWSU, p. 1.

A few Brahma Kumaris work full time for the movement, but the vast majority are employed in 'normal' jobs, maintaining daily contact with a centre – especially for the 6 a.m. meditation. The Brahma Kumaris' life-style is ascetic; fully committed members are celibate, they usually wear white, and are strictly vegetarian. Money comes from donations, and from the members handing over their personal wealth and their earnings.

Publications include *Brahma Kumaris WORLDWIDE*, the international newsletter of the BKWSU, and *Visions*, an international newsletter of the affiliated organisation, *Global Co-operation for a Better World*, which has its co-ordinating office in London.[52]

Like most NRMs, the Brahma Kumaris have their critics, some of the more vocal being the husbands of women who have become committed to the life style and, therefore, accepted a life of celibacy.[53]

CENTRAL LONDON CHURCH OF CHRIST See LONDON CHURCH OF CHRIST

CENTRES NETWORK, The[54]

> Your participation in the Forum takes you beyond a mere understanding of *being*, beyond even an occasional, unpredictable experience of *being*, and provides you with direct access to the domain of *being* itself. This is the magic of the Forum. . .
>
> Out of the Forum, you bring this magic to all areas of your life – to your relationships with your family, friends and associates, to your enjoyment of life, to your thinking, communicating and acting, to your recreation and to your work.[55]

Werner Erhard (1935–) gave the first Erhard Seminars Training (*est*) in California in 1971. The Centres Network organises the Forum (which has now replaced *est*) and a number of other courses, including Communication Courses and a series of Seminar Programmes on such subjects as Relationships, Empowerment and Productivity, that are available to Forum 'graduates'. Erhard is also recognised as a principal founder of other, legally independent, organisations such as the Education Network and the Hunger Project. The latter has been the focus of some controversy as the money is not spent on buying food; the point of the Hunger

---

52. Leaflet entitled WHO IS GOD?

53. See, for example, *The Sydney Morning Herald*, 1 August 1987. See also Vieda Skultans "The Brahma Kumaris and the Role of Women", and "The Brahma Kumaris", both mimeographed, undated papers, University of Bristol.

54. *Central Office:* Centres Network Great Britain, 10–14 Macklin Street, London WC2B 5NG, UK.
San Francisco Area Center: 765 California Street, San Francisco, CA 94108, USA.
Further Reading: Barclay, W.W. (III) *Werner Erhard: The Transformation of Jack Rosenberg*, New York: Clarendon Potter, 1978; Rhinehart (1976); Tipton (1984).

55. *The Forum*, booklet published by Werner Erhard and Associates, 1986.

Project is to effect an awareness that the necessary resources are already available and to try to mobilise these already existing resources and *thus* eliminate hunger.[56]

The Forum, which costs £325, takes place over two consecutive weekends (Saturday and Sunday 9am–11.30pm) and one 3-hour evening. Graduates are likely to insist that it is impossible to describe what happens in the Seminars – the only way to find out is to undergo the experience.

There are graduates of both *est* and the Forum who claim that the experience has revolutionised their lives, giving them 'communication skills' that make them more effective. Concern has, however, been expressed over the pressure which has been put on people who attend 'guest' evenings in an attempt to persuade them to put down a £50 non-returnable deposit for the next programme. Furthermore, the intensity of the seminars may be severely disturbing for a few people, and the Centres Network has suggested that those who are undergoing therapy should get their therapist's permission before going on a course.

CHILDREN OF GOD[57]

> *YE CANNOT BELONG TO BOTH THE SYSTEM AND THE REVOLUTION*, the forces of reaction *and* the forces of change! It's impossible; as Jesus said, you'll *either hate* the *one*, and *love* the *other*; or *hold to* the *one* and *despise* the *other*. You'll *either stay* in the *System* or *drop out*. There's no such thing as hanging somewhere in between, suspended between Heaven and Hell in some kind of compromiser's limbo![58]
> ENJOY YOURSELF AND SEX AND WHAT GOD HAS GIVEN YOU TO ENJOY, WITHOUT FEAR OR CONDEM-NATION! . . . **Cut loose** from those old foolish fancies . . . still taught by some churches and parents! **Let yourself go in the bosom of God and let God do it to you in an orgasm of the Spirit till you're free! You're His wife!--Sock it to him! Hallelujah, I am free--**Jesus gives us **liberty!**--Amen?--Now try it!--You'll **like** it!--And **thank God for** it! Amen? It's a **Revolution!**--For **Jesus! Power** to the **People!--Sex** power!--**God's** power!--Can be **your** power! Amen?--**Be a sex revolutionist for Jesus!--Wow!**--There we **go** again! **Hallelujah!**--Are you **comin'?**[59]

---

56. See Marilyn Ferguson *The Aquarian Conspiracy: Personal and Social Transformation in the 1980's*, London, New York: Granada, 1982, pp. 453-7.

57. *UK postal address:* BM Box 8440, London WC1N 3XX, UK. No American address available.

Further Reading: Van Zandt (1991); Beckford (1985) 33–42; Davis (1984); Rex Davis and James T. Richardson "The Organization and Functioning of the Children of God" *Sociological Analysis,* 37/4, 1976; Una McManus *Not for a Million Dollars*, Nashville TN; Impact Books, 1980; James T. Richardson and Rex Davis "Experiential Fundamentalism: Revisions of Orthodoxy in the Jesus Movement" *Journal of the American Academy of Religion*, LI/3, 1983; Roy Wallis "Yesterday's Children: Cultural and Structural Change in a New Religious Movement" in Wilson (ed.) (1981); Royal Wallis "Charisma, Commitment and Control in a New Religious Movement" in *Millennialism and Charisma*, Belfast: The Queen's University, 1982.

58. From MO Letter no. 330.

59. From MO Letter no. 258.

David Brandt Berg (1919–) was a minister in the Christian and Missionary Alliance Church, a conservative Holiness denomination, when he became involved in work with hippies in the California of the late 1960s. A small community calling themselves Teens for Christ was formed as part of the Jesus Revolution of the time. Berg became known as Moses David, Mo, Father David or 'Dad'; his movement became known as the Children of God – and was renamed the Family of Love at the end of the 1970s. It has also been referred to by other names, such as the Local Area Fellowship, Heaven's Magic and, like many other movements, The Family.

Total commitment to the movement is expected. On joining, members adopt Biblical names and may move into a 'colony'; later, they may operate as part of a small family unit. There is a hierarchical authority structure with ultimate power resting with Berg and his immediate family. Contact with non-members tends to be confined to obtaining money and evangelising. Children of God can be seen on the streets of Britain at the present time (early 1990s), but they are unlikely to disclose their identity. Although members may keep in touch and visit their family, their family may not know where they live. Many Western members have moved to Third World countries – Latin America, India, Japan, Australasia, Thailand, Hong Kong, Macao and mainland China being among the places where the movement is or has been active. Numbers are unknown, but there appears to be both a high defection rate and a steady conversion rate (although the movement appears to have had very little success in Britain in recent years). A significant number of children have been born into the movement. It is unlikely that there are as many as 10,000 members world-wide; there may be less than half that number.

The tracts (True Comix/Komix) and coloured Disney-style posters that are handed out on the streets (with requests for donations – possibly 'for children in need') are typically full of statements about Jesus and love, and contain numerous exclamation marks, with typographical emphases. They may bear the name 'World Services', with a Zurich box number. The internal MO Letters are also produced with comic-strip drawings, but the content is by no means as bland as the public literature. Other publications include *New Nation News* and *Family News International*.

Berg declares himself to be an 'end-time prophet' who has received a number of special revelations. Although frequent references are made to the Bible, and to Jesus in particular, Christian critics have considered his writings not only offensive, but also blasphemous. Although Berg's pronouncements are constantly changing, two themes emerge clearly: first, we are living in the 'last days'; we are to expect the destruction of capitalism and communism, leading to a godly socialism and control by third world countries – it has been predicted that the Battle of Armageddon will occur in 1993.[60] Secondly, Berg's apparently insatiable interest

60. Beckford (1985), p. 35.

in sex has coloured not only his writings, but also the manner in which the movement has developed – particularly with respect to the involvement of children and 'flirty fishing' (see the main text), although the fear of AIDS has meant that sexual 'sharing' has tended to be confined to the movement in recent years.

The authoritarian leadership and the control it has over its followers (many of whom are undoubtedly sincere in their belief that they are dedicating their lives to God), the secret nature and exclusivity of the movement, the employment of sex for what outsiders interpret as purely manipulative purposes, and the style and content of many of the MO letters has led to feelings of outrage and revulsion by most non-members learning about Berg and his movement. It was, indeed, the Children of God who were the subject of what was probably the first group of parents who organised themselves in opposition to a contemporary NRM to form the Parents' Committee to Free Our Sons and Daughters from the Children of God (FREECOG) in the early 1970s.

CHURCH OF SCIENTOLOGY[61]

> Scientology is a study of . . . the very basic knowledge about man and about life that is vital for each person to have if he is to be happy and accomplish those things he sets out to do. . . . The application of Scientology principles can improve a person's confidence, intelligence, abilities and skills . . . Scientology steers the individual out of the problems and seeming restrictions of everyday life, to a point where he can gain higher levels of spiritual freedom.[62]

Dianetics: The Modern Science of Mental Health by L. Ron Hubbard (1911–1986) was first published in 1950. This book, which is still a best seller, describes the basic philosophy behind the techniques of 'dianetic therapy' during which an 'auditor', sometimes using an E-meter, is believed to help people who are being audited to erase 'engrams' that have been recorded onto part of their minds in the past and which are currently interfering with the optimal functioning of their mind and their body. A 'Clear' is "the optimum individual; no longer possessed of any engrams"[63]

The Church of Scientology was founded in 1954. Although the movement's chapel in Britain has been refused registration as a Place of Worship, the High Court of Australia ruled that the movement was, for the purposes of taxation, a religion because:

61. *UK HQ*: Saint Hill Manor, East Grinstead, Sussex. RH19 4JY, UK.
Church of Scientology International: 4751 Fountain Avenue, Los Angeles, CA 90029, USA.
Further Reading: Atck, Jon *A Piece of Blue Sky: Scientology, Dianetics and L. Ron Hubbard exposed*, New York: Carol, (1990); Beckford (1985), pp. 51–60; Melton (1986), pp. 128–134; Wallis (1976)

62. *Scientology: What is it?* booklet published by The Church of Scientology International, Los Angeles, 1985.

63. L. Ron Hubbard *Dianetics: The Modern Science of Mental Health*, Copenhagen: New Era Publications, 1950, p. 421.

> the essence of Scientology is a belief in reincarnation and concern with the passage of the 'thetan' or the spirit or soul of man through eight 'dynamics' and the ultimate release of the 'thetan' from the bondage of the body.[64]

The movement adopts an aggressive stance on a number of issues: it campaigns against the use of certain drugs, electro-convulsive therapy and psycho-surgery, and it has accused the United States Central Intelligence Agency of a number of illicit activities.

The numerous organisations that are associated with the movement include: Author Services Incorporated; AOSH UK (Advanced Organization Saint Hill); Bridge Publications (Los Angeles); Concerned Businessmen's Association of the UK; Narconon; New Era Publications (Copenhagen); Saint Hill Foundation; Sea Org; Way to Happiness Campaign. Periodicals include: *Advance; Auditor; Crusader; Freedom.*

In 1968, the Government imposed restrictions on foreigners entering the UK to study, or work for, Scientology. Following the Foster Report, these were lifted in 1980. Currently, the Church is appealing against the award of $30 million to an ex-member for "intentional and negligent infliction of emotional distress". A frequent complaint concerns the money that Scientologists pay for their courses. Clients have found themselves running up debts of thousands of pounds. There have also been accusations of brainwashing and undue coercion by the movement.

CHURCH UNIVERSAL AND TRIUMPHANT See SUMMIT LIGHTHOUSE

DIANETICS See CHURCH OF SCIENTOLOGY

DIVINE LIGHT MISSION See ELAN VITAL

ECKANKAR[65]

> Membership in ECKANKAR is for those whose goals are Self-Realization and God-Realization in this lifetime... ECKANKAR is a secret science known to a select few throughout the ages and brought to the modern world by Sri Paul Twitchell, the great ECK Master and modern-day founded of ECKANKAR.[66]
>
> ECKANKAR is a way of life. It is the most ancient way known to man and is based upon individual experience with the ECK (Spirit) – that divine essence of God within each of us.[67]

---

64. *The Church of the New Faith v. The Commissioner for Payroll Tax*, High Court of Australia, 27 October 1983, p. 58 of typed transcript.

65. *ECKANKAR Book Shop:* 8 Thackeray Street, London W8 5ET, UK.
ECKANKAR: Box 27300, Minneapolis, MN 55427, USA.
Further Reading: Melton (1986), pp. 146–153; Melton (1989), entry no. 1444.

66. *Membership in ECKANKAR*, leaflet, 1982.

67. *ECKANKAR A Way of Life: Book Catalog*, ECKANKAR, P.O.Box 3100, Menlo Park, CA 94025, USA, June 1982.

> The ECK Masters carry the message of Spirit and emphasize the necessity of the individual linking-up with Spirit which is achieved through the spiritual exercises of ECKANKAR.[68]

Before he declared himself the living ECK Master in 1965 and incorporated his own movement, ECKANKAR, in Las Vegas, John Paul Twitchell (1908/12?-1971) was associated with a number of other movements, such as Carpal (Kirpal) Singh's Ruhani Satsang and L. Ron Hubbard's Church of Scientology – he was, indeed, among the first of those to achieve the status of a 'Clear'.[69]

The teachings of ECKANKAR are said to have been handed down through an unbroken line of ECK Masters of whom Twitchell was the 971st; when he 'translated' (died), Sri Darwin Gross was pronounced the 972nd ECK Master, but his leadership was controversial. In 1984, the present leader, Sri Harold Klemp (also known by the spiritual name of Wah Z, whom Gross had declared the 973rd Living ECK Master in 1981) pronounced that Gross was no longer recognised as an ECK Master.[70]

The teaching is considered to be an advanced form of surat shabda Yoga, which concentrates on physical techniques and spiritual exercises that enable the soul to travel beyond the physical limitations of the body to the higher spiritual realms of the 'Sugmad' – defined as the formless, All-embracing, impersonal and infinite, the Ocean of Love and Mercy, from which flows all of life, the equivalent of God in theistic religions.[71]

Special courses are available for children under the age of 18, starting with an ECK Teenie series for those aged 4–6. Members pay an annual subscription which, in 1989, started at $80, increasing to $100 for the second year and $120 per annum thereafter (family membership is also available). Membership entitles people to a series of 12 ECK discourses and further monthly mailings. Members do not live in communities. No hard and fast rules for behaviour are laid down, although moderation in life-style is encouraged. Various 20-minute Spiritual Exercises are practised daily at home by the individual student (who is called a chela). Studies may also be carried out in an ECK Satsang class at a local centre. International seminars at which Sri Harold Klemp is "the featured speaker" are held for three days, four times a year.

The First Initiation in ECKANKAR does not involve any formal, outer ceremony – "it takes place in the invisible, inner realms. [It] often comes in the dream state." After two years of membership, one is eligible for the Second Initiation which "links the individual with Spirit, freeing him from the necessity of further incarnations in this physical world."[72]

---

68. *ECK London: News and Events*, December 1982.
69. Melton (1986), p. 146.
70. David Christopher Lane (ed.) *Understanding Cults and Spiritual Movements*, vol. 2, no. 1, 1987, pp. 1–6; vol. 2, nos 2/3, 1987, pp. 1–13.
71. Melton (1986), p. 148.
72. *ECKANKAR: How to Know Yourself as Soul*, Minneapolis MN: ECKANKAR, 1988, p. 10.

Those committing themselves to ECK by the Second Initiation "receive a secret word which is all their own".[73]

David Christopher Lane, who started to investigate ECKANKAR for a student project, has accused Twitchell of plagiarism and of dishonesty in his book *The Making of a Spiritual Movement*. Lane reported that the world-wide membership was estimated between 40,000 and 60,000 in the early 1980s.[74]

ELAN VITAL[75]

> We can be happy in this life. You don't have to wait. There can be that joy, there can be that love, there can be that experience. It's not a way of life. It's not a way of thinking. It's not a philosophy... I'm talking about an experience that's continually happening. That true enjoyment of just being a human being – you can enjoy that simple fact now.[76]
>
> To know how to appreciate Knowledge, you need to know how to appreciate life... Nobody is playing a game with us in life, except with our own selves... But you don't have to lose every hand... There is a quality to this life, which all you have to do is simply uncover. You don't have to do anything... All you have to do is take a brush and undust it...
>
> Everywhere, everywhere in this world people receive this Knowledge and their first question is, "How come I didn't know about this before?" "How come it's so simple?" It is simple because life is simple, very very simple.[77]

The Divine Light Mission (DLM) was founded in the 1930s by Shri Hans Ji Maharaj. His youngest son, Prem Pal Singh Rawat (1957–), later known as Guru Maharaj Ji, and then as Maharaji, to his followers, became the Satguru or Perfect Master at the age of eight, when his father died in 1966. In 1971, at the age of 13, Maharaji came to England; soon afterwards, he established his base in the United States.

Although there are transcripts, audio cassettes and videos of Maharaji's speeches, the movement has never produced a body of literature about its beliefs and practices in the way that other movements, such as the Church of Scientology, ISKCON, or the Unification Church have done. A central belief held by members is that the key to self-understanding and self-realisation lies in practising the 'Knowledge". While the

---

73. Ibid.

74. David Christopher Lane *The Making of a Spiritual Movement: the untold story of Paul Twitchell and Eckankar*, Del Mar, CA: Del Mar Press, 1983, p. 47.

75. *Elan Vital*: P.O.Box 131, Hove, Sussex, BN3 1JA, UK.
USA Address: Box 6130, Malibu, CA 90264, USA.
Further Reading: Downton (1979); Maeve Price "The Divine Light Mission as a Social Organisation", *The Sociological Review*, vol. 27, no. 2, May 1979, pp. 279–296.

76. Maharaji quoted in a leaflet handed out at a Royal Albert Hall, London, meeting 12 October 1981.

77. Maharaji in Stockholm, 5 September 1985, printed in leaflet entitled *Painting a Perfect Picture*, distributed by Elan Vital, Sussex, n.d.

Knowledge is within each individual, it is said that it can only be practised after it has been revealed by Maharaji or one of his appointed initiators. The Knowledge consists of four techniques which enable initiates to turn their senses within and to perceive what were described in the early 1970s as Divine Light, Music, Nectar, and the 'primordial vibration' or 'Holy Name'.

Those who take the Knowledge are asked to promise not to reveal the techniques; they explain that taking the Knowledge cannot be described because, in an important, fundamental way, it can only be subjectively experienced. None the less, a number of accounts of the external, physical aspects, and some of the feelings they have experienced, have been given by ex-members.[78]

In its early days, the movement grew quickly, and by the summer of 1973, it claimed to have 8,000 devotees or 'premies' (who were drawn largely from the young, white, middle-class hippie culture) and about 40 ashrams (designated premie households) in Britain.[79] By about the same time, an estimated 50,000 in the United States had 'received the Knowledge'', although the number of committed followers was considerably smaller – about 500 were sufficiently dedicated to live in one of the 24 American DLM ashrams.[80]

The movement, which was run largely by Maharaji's mother, Mata Ji, with the help of his older brother, soon ran into difficulties, however. A financial crisis followed a gathering in 1973 at the Houston Astrodome;[81] and, in 1974, Maharaji's marriage to his American secretary, Marolyn, precipitated a power struggle within his family.[82] This resulted in Maharaji taking sole control of the movement in the West.

The general character of the movement changed. Maharaji rejected many aspects that had been associated with Indian traditions, and focused on the essence of his teaching. The name Elan Vital was adopted in the early 1980s; Maharaji insisted that he was not to be worshipped as a God; the ashrams were dissolved; the term 'premie' was dropped; and initiators came to be called instructors, not mahatmas. Although those who had received the Knowledge might still meet together, *satsang* (holy discourse) ceased to be a regular part of their lives; and although many have continued to work for the promotion of Maharaji's work, they are no longer expected to 'do service' as they once were. As part of a policy of adopting a low profile, the media and others who had not received the Knowledge found it increasingly difficult to obtain information.

---

78. See Enroth (1977), pp. 137–8; Melton (1989), entry 1445, p. 901; and Melton (1976), p. 143. See also Downton (1979), chapter 10; and Jeanne Messer "Guru Maharaj Ji and the Divine Light Mission" in Glock and Bellah (1976), p. 54.
79. Price, op cit, p. 281.
80. Downton (1979), p. 4.
81. Downton (1979), p. 189; Messer, op cit, p. 67; Price, op cit, p. 282.
82. Price, op cit; Downton, op cit, chapter 1.

During the past few years, however, the movement has become more open to outside enquires.

Until recently, donations to Maharaji's work had been unpredictable, but recently the movement in the UK has made an attempt to 'rationalize' its financial situation by asking people to contribute a small sum (perhaps £5) on a monthly basis. By April 1989, there were, according to Elan Vital's internal UK newsletter, *Newsline*, 1,420 'subscribers' to the scheme.[83] There are about 5,000 persons on the UK's mailing list, and perhaps 7,000 (15,000 in the USA) who still practise the Knowledge on a more or less regular basis. Although the number of new people receiving the Knowledge is nothing like as high as it was in the early 1970s, about 100 persons in the UK received it during the past year, and, at the time of writing, there are evidently about 150 aspirants waiting to receive it from one of Maharaji's instructors – a 4-day long Instructor-Training Conference was held for almost 200 candidates from the UK and north Europe in 1989; three similar courses had already been held in the USA and two more were to be held in Italy and Australia.[84]

During its early years in the West, the Divine Light Mission was the subject of considerable controversy. Maharaji himself was constantly derided as the 'boy-guru' by the media; accusations were made of brainwashing and of premies becoming 'spaced out' on the Knowledge. In recent years, partly because of conscious efforts to maintain a low profile, and partly because most of those who practise the Knowledge lead relatively 'normal' lives, there has been less public controversy.

EMISSARIES OF DIVINE LIGHT[85]

> The Emissaries are an association of individuals of many countries whose primary interest is to co-ordinate accurately with the way life works in all aspects of daily experience. . .
> The premise is that self-discovery is only possible in the context of a greater whole and is known through giving whatever is practical, helpful and balanced in any situation.[86]

The Emissaries of Divine Light, initiated in the 1930s in the United States by Lloyd Meeker (who wrote under the name, Uranda), was established at Sunrise Ranch in Colorado in 1945. Lord Martin Cecil (1909–1988), the late Marquess of Exeter, founded a community in Canada in 1948 and it was he who "provided a spiritual focus for the

---

83. *Newsline*, June 1989, p. 7.
84. Ibid, p. 3.
85. *UK Headquarters:* Mickleton House, Mickleton, Gloucestershire, GL55 6RY, UK. *Emissaries of Divine Light*: 5569 North County Road 29, Loveland, CO 80537, USA.
86. *Introducing The Emissaries*, leaflet published by The Emissaries, Loveland, CO, USA, n.d.

Emissaries from 1954 to 1988".[87] His son, Michael Exeter, took over the leadership on his father's death.

There are 12 communities and somewhere between 2–3,000 Emissaries world-wide. In Britain there about 150 Emissaries, around 60 of whom live in the community that was established in the Cotswolds in 1979. Seminars on a number of topics are held there and elsewhere; for example, a seminar on *The Art of Living* lasted five days and cost £225.

Associated with The Emissary Foundation International, which publishes the magazine *Integrity*, are a number of organisations such as Renaissance Educational Associates, which publishes *The Renaissance Educator*, Renaissance Business Associates, The Stewardship Community, The Whole Health Institute and The Association for Responsible Communication.

FLAME FOUNDATION[88]

> THE ETERNAL FLAME is a group of physically immortal people from various parts of the world who have come together from an inner responding to the Founders' words for the purpose of revealing and establishing physical immortality amongst themselves and to all who desire to live. . .
>
> Death of the physical body is an imposition of limitation no longer acceptable to those of us who have awakened to physical immortality.[89]
>
> Physical immortality is the condition that exists in the human form when all traces of death have been removed. Put another way, it is the condition of total physical aliveness![90]
>
> Do you still think that you can be saved from your sins by another's death? In that case, let's all die and save everybody else from their sins! We are still going to be sacrificing ourselves. We cannot sacrifice one to save others. Nobody benefits from death![91]

Charles Paul Brown (*c.*1933–), BernaDeane Brown (*c.*1934–) and James Russell Strole (*c.*1949–) are the "architects" and the "ministers" of physical immortality. Charles Brown describes how he underwent a tremendous supernatural experience in 1960 when he realised that Jesus spoke of *physical* immortality, and he (Brown) felt a completely New Intelligence operating in his body.[92] The basic theory underlying this revelation is that physical immortality is dormant within the cellular structure of the human body. Once we accept that we are physically immortal, immortal cells multiply to strengthen the immune system and

---

87. *A Conversation About Emissaries and the 100 Mile Lodge Community, Canadian Headquarters for the International Emissary program*, booklet published by the Emissary Foundation International, Canada, n.d.

88. *Together Forever:* 47 Richmond Ave, Wimbledon Chase, London SW20 8LA. *Flame Foundation:* P.O. Box 1954, Scottsdale, Arizona 85252, USA.

89. *Physical Immortality: The Eternal Flame Foundation*, leaflet, n.d.

90. *Questions and Answers About THE ETERNAL FLAME FOUNDATION*, Scottsdale, AZ, n.d., p. 1.

91. James Russell Strole "Immortal Integration", *The Eternal Flame*, May 1989, p. 13.

92. *The Eternal Flame*, January 1979, p. 2.

eliminate death enzymes in the DNA, and 'death-oriented programs', which have been genetically and culturally encoded to destroy the body, reveal themselves so that we can rid ourselves of them and "BUILD one another until the true expanded, creative, joyful self triumphs".[93] The Foundation's magazine, *The Eternal Flame*, is full of references to New Age ideas, the Bible and scientific discoveries that are taken to be relevant to the movement's understanding of the biological warfare that is being fought in our bodies.

As it is believed that physical immortality must be experienced 'cellularly', and that it cannot be learned except through contact with other immortal bodies, importance is attached to regular get-togethers in which the immortals explore their immortal existence. These meetings evoke 'passion, intensity and intimacy') and, sometimes, 'sorrow, anger and hatred'. Thus, it is claimed, the immortals may fully experience parts of themselves which they had previously denied through fear of rejection.

The Immortals from Arizona started to expand their activities in Europe and Israel in the late 1980s – BernaDeane "wanted the planet Earth to be covered by bodies like us".[94] A tour of the UK and Eire in 1989 was planned to reach its climax in Glastonbury at Pentecost.[95] In June 1989, the 9-day 22nd Annual International Physical Immortality Convergence in Scottsdale offered spontaneous open forums 'facilitated' by the Browns and Strole, intensive and spontaneous in-depth experiences, workshops and a Mexican Fiesta – for $1,095 with a private room.[96]

There are said to be about 200 immortals in Scottsdale, some of whom have moved there from Britain in order to be near the "dynamic trio".[97] Immortals are encouraged to tithe at least 10% of their income to the Foundation. The Foundation has produced audiotapes (such as "Body Dynamics and Physical Immortality", $20 + p&p) and video tapes (such as "Physical Immortality, a cellular awakening", $50 + p&p in the UK), as well as a growing body of literature.

HUMAN POTENTIAL MOVEMENT and TRANSPERSONAL PSYCHOLOGY[98]

(See also entries on the CENTRES NETWORK; INSIGHT; the NEW AGE   MOVEMENT;   OCCULTISM,   NEO-PAGANISM,

---

93. Ibid; and May 1989. Quotation taken from undated leaflet.

94. *The Eternal Flame*, Spring 1988, p. 3.

95. See K. Alan Yeo "Do You Want to Live Forever?" *Midweek*, 1 December 1988 for an account, with interesting comments, of an introductory meeting in London.

96. *Eternal Flame*, May 1989, pp. 7–8.

97. Personal communication from Alan Yeo.

98. *Human Potential Research Group*: Department of Educational Studies, University of Surrey, Guildford, Surrey GU2 5XH, UK.
The Centre for Transpersonal Psychology: The Studio Flat, 8 Elsworthy Terrace, Hampstead, London NW3 3DR, UK.
Esalen Institute, Big Sur, CA 93920, USA.

WITCHCRAFT, SHAMANISM and SATANISM; and TRANSCEN-
DENTAL MEDITATION.)

The Human Potential Research Project was set up at the University of
Surrey in November 1970. It is now the longest established centre for
humanistic and transpersonal education in Europe. Its main aims are
to:-

> encourage the extension of higher and continuing education
> into the dimensions of professional and personal development
> promote holistic forms of practice, education and research.[99]

Transpersonal psychology is an umbrella name. While its formal establishment is very recent (1969) its roots lie in the far distant past. The
religions of the world with their systems of spiritual training; mystery
schools and esoteric movements; symbolic systems of alchemy, tarot
and the I Ching; all have been custodians of the approach to the self. . .

The real dividing line between what is transpersonal and what is
not [is] *an acceptance of the reality of the self.* In the beginning was the
self, in potentia.

At the end there is also the *self,* realized and actualized. . .

Transpersonal psychology *is a perspective, not a system or doctrine. . .*
Our experience in therapy is that *the image of the person that matters is
the one that is most meaningful and creative for the client.*[100]

HUMANISTIC PSYCHOLOGY emphasises personal responsibility and co-operation. It recognises the spiritual dimension to life
without encouraging dependence on authoritarian gurus or rigid organisations. Mind and body are assumed to have an underlying unity and
Human Beings a natural tendency to growth, health and good feelings.
Trust, respect and acceptance of ourselves and others are an important
aspect of this approach.[101]

Many of the ideas and sources of the Human Potential movement (HPM)
are shared with those to be found within the New Age movement (see
separate entry) and, for some, the HPM is part of the New Age
movement. Others, however, draw a distinction between the two by
saying that while the New Age movement tends to look 'out there'
for new forms of relating to the environment, the HPM (including
Transpersonal Psychology) is more concerned to look *inside* the self by
using psychotherapy (in its very broadest sense) to develop people's
potential. Transpersonal psychology transcends the ego. This may be
done by helping individuals to get in touch with their feelings and
become emotionally competent – able, that is, to discharge feelings in an

---

99. *Human Potential Research Project 1986-87* (now *Research Group*), Programme, University of Surrey, p. 1.
100. Ian Gordon-Brown and Barbara Somers "Transpersonal Psychotherapy" in John
Rowan and Windy Dryden (eds) *Innovative Therapy in Britain*, Milton Keynes: Open
University Press, 1988, pp. 224, 227, 228.
101. David Jones, leaflet advertising courses in Humanistic Psychology, 1989.

effective and 'appropriate' way. This can involve a restructuring of people's own relationship with their own feelings and their own experience through some sort of reorganisation of their concepts.

Among the better-known methods, therapies and techniques, one can find Alexander Lowen's Bioenergetics; David Boadella's Biosynthesis; Harvey Jackin's Co-counselling; Encounter Groups; Fritz Perls' Gestalt Therapy; Guided Fantasy; Humanistic Psychology; Sondra Ray's LRT (Loving Relationship Training); Arthur Janov's Primal Therapy; Psychodrama; Rebirthing; Roberto Assagioli's Psychosynthesis; and Eric Berne's Transactional Analysis. One of the general tenets of Humanistic Psychology is that individuals are 'guided' and encouraged to work things out for themselves, rather than being educated by an expert.

The main text indicates some of the controversies that surround some of these groups (which largely overlap with what Heelas has called the 'self religions', and mostly fall into Wallis' category of 'world-affirming religions). The divers groups and therapies cannot be explored here in further detail, but the many references in the notes here and elsewhere in the text will enable those interested in the area to explore the literature further.[102]

INSIGHT and MSIA [103]

> Insight provides tools to help you create:
>   Greater self confidence
>   Increased self-esteem
>   Improved communication and listening skills
>   Increased motivation and enthusiasm
>   Higher productivity
>   Improved relationships[104]
>   In Insight we work with the heartfelt energies; **Awakening the Heart.** The way you can experience more of the heartfelt energy is by

102. *The London Guide to Mind Body Spirit: comprehensive and easy to use listings of psychotherapy, alternative health and spiritual centres in the capital*, compiled by Kate Brady and Mike Considine, London: Brainwave, 1988; *The New Times Network: Groups and Centres for Personal Growth*, compiled by Robert Adams, London & Boston: Routledge and Kegan Paul, 1982; J. Rowan *A Guide to Humanistic Psychology*, London: Association for Humanistic Psychology in Britain, 1987.
For examples of, respectively, critical, sympathetic-systematic, and sympathetic-personal accounts of some of the movements, see: Rosen (1975); John Rowan and Windy Dryden (eds) *Innovative Therapy in Britain*, Milton Keynes: Open University Press, 1988; John St John *Travels in Inner Space: One man's exploration of Encounter Groups, Meditation, and Altered States of Consciousness*, London: Gollancz, 1977.
103. *Insight Seminars*: 9 Spring Street, London W2 3RA, UK. *MSIA*: 1 Harcourt Street, London W1H 1DS. *International Headquarters*: 2101 Wilshire Boulevard, Santa Monica, CA 90403, USA. *Further Reading*: Melton (1986) pp. 150–3; Melton (1989), entry no. 1447.
104. *The Insight Seminar: A Seminar to Enhance Your Personal and Professional Life*, Leaflet distributed by the British Insight Seminars, n.d.

becoming more involved and more active in your life. . . This energy will move past your mind, emotions and ego until it comes to the very center that we call Love, or God, or Heart, or Spirit, or whatever term you want to call it.

In awakening the heartfelt energies, you can't help but **discover your own self-worth, your own self-love, your own magnificence.**[105]

You don't have to die to discover the Christ. You can move into that which is your own spiritual inner awareness and move upwards through the levels of your own consciousness until you find that which is the Christ within you. . .

The indwelling Christ sings a beautiful song. That is the sound of God, the audible Light Stream, the current of energy that is flowing upward to God. . . and the only way to God is by that invisible route.[106]

John-Roger Hinkins (1934–), who had been an early ECKANKAR student (see separate entry), founded his own Church of the Movement of Spiritual Inner Awareness (MSIA – pronounced Messiah) "about 1963". Over the years, his interests grew. Among his ventures have been the establishment of the Prana (Purple Rose Ashram of the New Age) Theological Seminary and College of Philosophy in Los Angeles, the Baraka Holistic Center for Therapy and Research and the KOH-E-NOR University (both in Santa Monica), the latter being the international headquarters of the Insight Transformational Seminars, founded in 1978. John-Roger's private life, his spiritual integrity and his running of 'the Movement' have become the subject of controversy in the past few years.[107]

The Insight Seminars became popular in Britain in 1979, largely through the effort of Arianna Stassinopoulos Huffington, who persuaded many of her friends to participate. Two full-time staff now run Insight from a London office. They are helped by enthusiastic volunteers, some of whom will be donating their time out of commitment to 'the cause', and because they enjoy each other's company; some may be wanting to do further Seminars but would otherwise be unable to afford to do so. As participants are frequently middle-class professionals who are not expected to stop working on account of their involvement with Insight, courses are usually scheduled for weekday evenings and weekends.

---

105. John-Roger in *The Awakening Heart Seminar*, booklet distributed by Insight Transformational Seminars, California, n.d.

106. John-Roger "Awakening to the Christ", *The Movement*, published monthly by the Church of the Movement of Spiritual Inner Awareness, Los Angeles, CA., vol. 12, issue 12, December 1987, p. 16.

107. David Christopher Lane "The J.R. Controversy: A Critical Analysis of John-Roger and M.S.I.A." *Understanding Cults and Spiritual Movements*, vol. 1, no. 1; David Christopher Lane "The Criminal Activities of John-Roger Hinkins" *Understanding Cults and Spiritual Movements*, vol. 2, no. 2, 1986; Bob Sipchen and David Johnson "John-Roger: Remarkable Journey from Rosemead Teacher to Spiritual Leader of a New Age Empire", *Los Angeles Times* (First of 2 parts) 14 August 1988.

Most of those who attend one of the free Introductory evenings do so because a friend who has taken the Seminar has invited them. Insight Seminar I costs £300 and takes place in a hotel room over a period of 50 hours spread over six days. There are likely to be between 150 and 200 people participating in the seminar, which is led by a 'facilitator', assisted by around 20 volunteers. Many of those who have taken the Seminar declare that it has radically altered their life, making them more confident, better able to communicate with others and, in general, more fulfilled in their lives. People who are in therapy are advised to consult with their therapist before embarking on the course.

INTERNATIONAL SOCIETY FOR KRISHNA CONSCIOUSNESS (ISKCON)[108]

ISKCON is a worldwide community of devotees practising *bhakti-yoga*, the eternal science of loving service to God. The Society was founded in 1966 by His Divine Grace A. C. Bhaktivedanta Swami Prabhupada, a pure devotee of God representing an unbroken chain of spiritual masters originating with Lord Krishna Himself.[109]

The theology of the Hare Krishna movement is in the tradition of Vaishnava Hinduism, tracing its roots through the sixteenth century monk, Chaitanya Mahaprabhu. The Bhagavad-Gita is its central scripture.

Shortly after Prabhupada (1896–1977) had arrived in the United States, ISKCON was to become one of the most visible NRMs, its devotees, with their shaven heads and brightly coloured Indian dress, dancing and chanting their mantra *Hare Krishna, Hare Krishna, Krishna Krishna, Hare Hare, Hare Rama, Hare Rama, Rama Rama, Hare Hare* in the streets of the major cities of the West.

Devotees are expected to lead strictly ascetic lives. They may not take meat, drugs or alcohol and they must remain celibate except for the procreation of children within marriage. They rise about 3.00 a.m. to start the morning by worshipping the deities in the Temple. They spend about two hours each day chanting *japa* – that is, chanting 16 rounds of the Hare Krishna mantra on their string of 108 beads. Devotees also fulfil a variety of more secular duties, some working within the community, some distributing Krishna-consciousness literature in the streets

---

108. *UK Headquarters:* Bhaktivedanta Manor, Letchmore Heath, Hertfordshire, WD2 8EP, UK.
ISKCON International Ministry of Public Affairs: 1030 Grand Avenue, San Diego, CA 92109, USA.
Further Reading: David G. Bromley and Larry D. Shinn (ed.s) *Krishna Consciousness in the West*, Lewisburg: Bucknell University Press, 1989; Kim Knott *My Sweet Lord: The Hare Krishna Movement*, Wellingborough: Aquarian Press, 1986; Rochford (1985); Larry D. Shinn *The Dark Lord: Cult Images and the Hare Krishnas in America*, Philadelphia: Westminster Press, 1987.
109. *Back to Godhead*, vol. 10, no. 10, p. 29.

and other public places, and, to an increasing extent, some working in 'outside' employment.

Many members of the Hindu community in the West (and, indeed, in India) accept ISKCON as an authentic strand within their tradition. ISKCON is, for example, involved fully in the work of the National Council for Hindu Temples in Britain, and of the European Council of Hindu Organisations.

By the time Prabhupada died, ISKCON had a Governing Body Commission with 22 members responsible for the general administration of the Society. To some extent overlapping in membership, there were 11 initiating gurus whom Prabhupada had charged with responsibility for the spiritual standards of the movement. Within 10 years of Prabhupada's death, about half the original gurus (including two who had been responsible for Britain) had left or been expelled from the movement.

Criticism has been levied at ISKCON on a number of fronts, including accusations of brainwashing and deceptive fundraising activities. Some devotees, shocked by the behaviour of some of their erstwhile leaders, have left ISKCON, while still espousing Krishna consciousness; others have tried to keep the movement in order by remaining inside.

JESUS FELLOWSHIP CHURCH (BAPTIST)[110]

> This Church upholds the full historic, biblical Christian Faith, being Reformed, Evangelical and Charismatic. In particular, it upholds the doctrine of the Trinity and the full divinity of the Lord Jesus Christ.[111]

Under the leadership of Noel Stanton (1928?-), the Church's 'Senior Pastor', the Jesus Fellowship has grown from small beginnings in 1969, when members of the Bugbrooke Baptist Church were "filled with the Holy Spirit". The *New Creation Christian Community* consists of the 600 members who live in 50 or so community houses. The life-style of these members is simple and hard-working, the week being closely ordered with special times set aside for communal worship, prayer, and Bible study in addition to daily work. An important feature of the Community's structure has been 'shepherding', with the Church being split into Shepherding Groups (now called Households) in which members are cared for by their own Pastor-Elder. Although the Community has many married couples with children, others of the members have committed themselves to leading celibate lives. Property is shared, with wages being contributed to the common purse. The Church's 350 non-residential members do not participate in the disciplines of community living.

---

110. *Central Office*: New Creation Farmhouse, Nether Heyford, Northants NN7 3LB, UK.
Further Reading: William Dalrymple "The Jesus People", *The Independent Magazine*, 8 April 1989, pp. 24–8.
111. Printed on official notepaper.

Apart from the farming of over 400 acres, there are a number of other Community-owned businesses. These include *House of Goodness Ltd., Towcester Building Supplies Ltd.*, and a building and vehicle repair operation called *Skaino Services Ltd.* Publications include the *Jesus Army Newspaper*, and magazines: *Jesus Lifestyle* and *Heartcry*.

In 1986 the Church withdrew from the Evangelical Alliance and then its membership with the Baptist Union of Great Britain was terminated on the grounds that the Fellowship's nation-wide organisation and its form of government could no longer be recognised as a local Baptist Church. Adverse publicity in the media has centred mainly on the discipline and rigours of the community life, and the movement's aggressive evangelism. The *Jesus Army*, with its slogan 'Love, Power & Sacrifice' and its promise to fight for YOU, was inaugurated in 1987. Its members, wearing combat-style uniforms, can be seen travelling around the country in converted double-decker buses and taking part in marches, festivals, residential camps and 'Eat, Drink and Pray' Campaigns of all-night evangelism in Central London. A recent innovation is the setting up of a 'Jesus Phone network'.[112]

LONDON CHURCH OF CHRIST and BIRMINGHAM CHURCH OF CHRIST[113]

> In each zone there will be exciting and relevant messages to which we will invite the hundreds of thousands we meet during the door-knocking, 'tubing', and 'blitzing' by which we will assail this great stronghold of Satan, London. These messages will be designed to awaken a desire in non-Christian visitors to seek God's will for their lives – and to become involved in personal Bible studies.[114]
>
> The Central London Church of Christ has tried to model itself on the great Antioch church. Just as the Antioch church was sent out from Jerusalem, the London church was sent out from Boston, in July 1982. Now London has sent out its own church planting in Sydney, Australia in February 1987, and is on the verge of sending teams to Singapore; Bangalore, India; and Birmingham, England in the coming months. To God be the glory![115]

The Central London Church of Christ (CLCOC) was founded in 1982 by Douglas Arthur and James Lloyd with some other missionaries who came to Britain from the Boston Church of Christ, which is part of the controversial 'Crossroads Movement'.[116] The movement has also been

---

112. *Jesus Army Newspaper*, no. 15, 1989, p. 8.
113. *London Church of Christ Office*: 2 Park Place, Acton, London W3 8JY, UK. *Boston Church of Christ*: P.O.Box 144, Lexington MA 02173, USA.
114. 'The Evangelists' "Going up into Canaan", *A Light to London*, vol. 5, no. 7, July 1986, p. 1.
115. Douglas Arthur "The London Family" *A Light to London*, vol. 6, no. 10, October 1987, p. 1.
116. *Boston Globe Magazine*, 8 June 1986; "Some charge 'true religion' a cult" *Middlesex News* (Massachusetts), 28 June 1987; Melton (1989) entry 625; Robert Nelson *Understanding the Crossroads Controversy*, Fort Worth TX: Star Bible Publications, 1986.

known as the International Church of Christ and the Multiplying Ministry Movement. It is currently known in London as the London Church
of Christ (LCC) and in Birmingham as the Birmingham Church of
Christ. Plans are in hand to start Edinburgh and Manchester Churches
of Christ. One of the movement's Evangelists has indicated that the
Central London congregation could be seen as a renewal movement for
the Churches of Christ which started in England in the 17th century.[117]
Longer-established Churches of Christ have, however, explicitly denied
any connection with the CLCOC.[118]

Many of the movement's beliefs are similar to those of conservative
evangelicals, but in 1986 the Universities and Colleges Christian Fellowship of Evangelical Unions (UCCF) issued a statement to the effect that
the CLCOC was distinctive in that it holds both that a person cannot
be a Christian unless he or she is baptised as a believing adult by
immersion, and that it is possible to lose one's salvation.[119] The statement,
which was read out at Christian Union (CU) meetings in London,
declared: "The activities of CLCOC have nothing to do with the CU
or UCCF."[120]

The movement has a hierarchical authority structure. Leaders do not
wear a dog collar or any distinctive dress. Britain is led by a few
Evangelists, who, "as in the Bible", are male; then there are 'Mission
Evangelists' (also men) and the 'Women's Counsellors' who deal exclusively with women members. Training for a leadership position, which
may take between two and eight years, is an apprenticeship, rather than
a formal course. An important feature of the movement is its practice of
discipleship – members all have a 'discipler' who is 'older in the Lord'
and is expected to help them to learn how to become better Christians
by discussing details of their daily lives and offering advice.

Discipline is another important feature. Members are expected to
spend time in prayer and Bible study each day, and there are several
services and meetings to be attended throughout the week. These are
enthusiastic in style – no musical instrument accompanies the singing.
Premarital sex is forbidden. Divorce is not an option unless the partner
has committed adultery. Sometimes fasting for periods of several days is
encouraged. Members are expected to donate around £5–£10 a week,
but they will also be asked for 'love offerings' and other special contributions. There are about 1,100 members in London and a further 160 in
Birmingham at the present time, many of whom live in community flats.

---

117. Douglas Jacoby "Are You an American Church?" *A Light to London*, vol. 5, no.
8, p. 3.
118. See, for example, a leaflet entitled *Allow us to Introduce Ourselves*, distributed by
the Church of Christ in Wembley. The leaflet also says: "We use the term church of Christ
not as a title, but to describe to whom we belong. We are Christ's Church. . ."
119. UCCF International Office "Statement on Central London Church of Christ",
May 1986.
120. Ibid.

The majority of members are under thirty. Despite strong pressure to stay in the movement, the figures suggest that about half of those who have joined in Britain have subsequently left.

The movement places a special emphasis on conversion. Unlike most evangelical groups, which, it claims, have only a small core of people spreading the message, *everyone* in the CLCOC is expected to evangelise as part of being a Christian. In its early days, members would stop people in public places, trying to persuade them to come to a service – 'tubing' is the expression used for witnessing to people on London's Underground Transport system. This practice continues, but there has recently been a move towards 'friendship evangelism', with approaches being made to friends and work colleagues who are invited to barbecues or to take part in a sporting event and have 'fun in the sun' in order to get to know individual members.

The movement's aggressive evangelism has become a subject of considerable concern, especially in universities and colleges. A number of Students' Unions (including those of the London School of Economics and Birmingham University) have banned the movement, and student newspapers have issued warnings about the CLCOC.[121] The movement puts the opposition it has received down to misinformation and their uncompromising stand on the Bible, discipline and evangelism. Allegations that students have to spend so much time in Bible study and evangelism that their studies suffer are dismissed with the rejoinder that the discipline they are taught helps them to study.

NEO-PAGANISM See OCULTISM, NEO-PAGANISM, WITCHCRAFT, SHAMANISM and SATANISM

NEW AGE MOVEMENT[122]
(See also the HUMAN POTENTIAL MOVEMENT and OCCULTISM, NEO-PAGANISM, WITCHCRAFT, SHAMANISM AND SATANISM)

> A leaderless but powerful network is working to bring about radical change in the United States. Its members have broken with certain key elements of Western thought, and they may even have broken continuity with history. This network is the Aquarian Conspiracy. It is a conspiracy without a political doctrine. Without a manifesto.[123]
> ...the Aquarian Conspiracy is a different kind of revolution, with different revolutionaries. It looks to the turnabout in consciousness of

---

121. See, for example, *London Student*, 2 February and 9 March, 1989.
122. *Alternatives:* St James's Church, 197 Piccadilly, London W1V 9LF, UK. For a list of some networks and organisations in both the USA and the UK, see Marilyn Ferguson *The Aquarian Conspiracy: Personal and Social Transformation in the 1980s*, London, Toronto, Sydney, New York: Granada, 1982. Appendix B, pp. 465–471.
123. Marilyn Ferguson op cit, p. 23. See also Michael York *A Sociological Profile on the New Age and Neo-pagan Movements*, unpublished Ph.D. thesis, King's College, University of London, 1991.

a critical number of individuals, enough to bring about a renewal of society.[124]

Ask and it will be given to you; seek and you will find; knock and the door will be opened to you. For everyone who asks receives; he who seeks finds; and to him who knocks, the door will be opened.[125]

The New Age 'label' has been applied relatively indiscriminately both by those for whom it is a proud affirmation, and by those for whom it is a term of abuse. In fact, the 'movement' is not so much *a* movement as a number of groups and individuals that have a number of beliefs and orientations that have what the philosopher Ludwig Wittgenstein has called a 'family resemblance' – two members of the family may bear almost no resemblance to each other, although they both resemble a third member. Some commentators would include groups that can be found in this Appendix under the headings of the Human Potential movement or Occultism, Neo-Paganism, Witchcraft, Shamanism and Satanism. The distinctions in the Appendix are made merely in order to try to provide an initial orientation in a highly amorphous and confusing area.

Most people connected with the New Age would see themselves as seekers who are exploring new and exciting frontiers. Several individuals belong to a number of different groups – some will also belong to a more traditional religious group, but be wanting to open themselves up to new ideas and experiences; others are 'New Age' through having rejected traditional religious and philosophical options as bankrupt.

There is no central organisation. In the UK, a central meeting place is *Alternatives* at St James's Church, Piccadilly. Other groups that form part of the network include the Teilhard Centre,[126] Turning Points,[127] World Goodwill,[128] and the Wrekin Trust.[129] There are several 'guides' to New Age groups that indicate both the overlap and the autonomy of the miscellany.[130] During the past quarter century, there have mushroomed numerous 'resource centres' specialising in books, cassettes, candles, crystals and a motley assortment of curiosities associated with New Age

---

124. Ibid, p. 26.
125. Matthew Chapter 7, verses 7–8, quoted in Gari Gold *Crystal Energy: Put the Power in the Palm of Your Hand*, Chicago & New York: Contemporary Books, 1987.
126. 23 Kensington Square, London W8 5HN, UK.
127. 120 The Vale, London W3 7JT, UK.
128. 3 Whitehall Court, Suite 54, London SW1A 2EF, UK.
129. Runnings Park, Croft Bank, West Malvern, WR14 4BP, UK.
130. For example: *Directory of New Age Resources (Southern California)*, compiled by Joshua Shapiro, Los Gatos CA: J & S Aquarian Networking, 1985; *A Pilgrim's Guide to Planet Earth: A traveler's handbook & New Age Directory*, London: Wildwood House, 1981; San Raphael CA: Spiritual Community Publications, 1981; *Spiritual Community Guide: The New Consciousness Source Book*, edited by Parmatma Singh Khalsa, San Raphael CA: Spiritual Community Publications (published annually).

thought.[131] In such centres, the seeker may spend hours browsing through stacks of New Age periodicals, full of advertisements and announcements of forthcoming events.[132] There are also a number of New Age 'markets' (the annual Festival for Mind-Body-Spirit is but one example) that can give the uninitiated an introduction to the scope of New Age ideas.

Also associated with, if not necessarily part of, the New Age movement is a wide range of alternative medicines. A glance at the *Journal of Alternative and Complementary Medicine*, for example, reveals advertisements for acupuncture, alchemy, the Alexander technique, aromatherapy, electro-crystal therapy, herbalism, homoeopathy, lymphatic irrigation therapy, radionics, reflextherapy and a hundred other cures and healing therapies, some as old as civilisation, others born, the advertisement seems to indicate, in the 21st century.

Although many of the ideas and groups identifiable with New Age thought go back hundreds, even thousands of years, the movement started to manifest itself in its present form in the 1960s. One belief commonly found among New Agers is that humanity is entering the dawn of a new form of consciousness: humanity is currently undergoing radical spiritual change; it has reached the Aquarian frontier.[133] Concepts such as exploration, spiritual awareness, cosmic consciousness and the (w)holistic approach are common in New Age thought. Evolution is important, but it is spiritual rather than material or technological evolution that is celebrated. Ecological issues take a high priority: one finds vegetarianism, 'back-to-the-earth' communes, organic farming, home-spun textiles, cottage industries, alternative technology – usually with

---

131. In Britain, for example: *Alternative Bookshop*, 3 Langley Court, Covent Garden, London WC2E 9JY; *Compendium*, 234 Camden High Street, London NW1 8QS; *Genesis Books*, 188 Old Street, London EC1V 9BP; *Merlin's Cave*, Bullens Courtyard, Mill Lane Mews, Ashby-de-la-Zouch, Leicestershire, LE6 5HP; *Mysteries*, London's Psychic Shop and New Age Centre, 9/11 Monmouth Street, Covent Garden, London WC2H 9DA; *Watkins Books*, 19 Cecil Court, London WC2N 4EZ.
And in California: *Bodhi Tree Bookstore*, 8585 Melrose Avenue, Los Angeles, California 90069, USA; *Controversial Books*, 3021 University, San Diego, CA 92105, USA.
132. For example: *Aquarian Arrow; Body Mind Spirit: your new age information resource; Communities: journal of cooperation; Creation: earthy spirituality for an evolving planet; Dawn: a quarterly publication devoted to yoga, meditation, philosophy, psychology and holistic living; Gnosis: a journal of the Western inner traditions; Internal Arts: the magazine for self development of mind and body; Life Times: forum for a new age; Kindred Spirit: in tune with the holistic vision; Magical Blend: a transformative journey; Meditation; New Age: exploring the new frontiers of body, mind and spirit; New Frontier: magazine of transformation; New Realities: oneness of self, mind and body; ReVision: the journal of consciousness and change; Search; Shaman's Drum: a journal of experimental shamanism; Shambhala; Sharing News: holistic journal; The Unexplained: explaining world's mysteries; Yoga Journal: the magazine for conscious living.*
133. See Theodore Roszak *Unfinished Animal: The Aquarian Frontier and the Evolution of Consciousness*, London: Faber, 1976 (first published in USA 1975).

the conviction that 'small-is-beautiful'.[134] The feminine is stressed; politics are decidedly Green.[135]

The Findhorn Foundation in the north of Scotland is one of the best-known of the New Age communities in Britain,[136] The Farm is one of the best-known in the United States.[137] But there are hundreds of others scattered around Europe and North America.[138] Sometimes the communes are in remote rural areas, but there are also numerous urban, middle-class communes.[139] Self expression through dance, drama, pottery or poetry is believed to promote creative energy – or enable the individual to tap into cosmic energy.

New Age ideas may be bound up with Christianity, but it is a Christianity that can absorb aspects of other faiths and philosophies. The life and works of Alan Watts (1915–1973) have been influential in introducing Zen Buddhism as a further thread in the New Age tapestry.[140] New Age beliefs may also embrace ancient Shamanistic and Pagan beliefs (see separate entry), and several varieties of Spiritualism. In recent years, 'Channelling' has become big business for certain New Age devotees. One of the most successful 'channels' is J. Z. Knight, a medium through which a 35,000 year old spirit called Ramtha speaks to paying customers.[141]

Generally speaking, New Agers are not aggressive proselytisers; only rarely will they find themselves under the control of an authoritarian leader, and the vast majority of New Age groups are unlikely to give rise to serious worries. Perhaps the most common controversies rest on

---

134. E. F. Schumacher *Small is Beautiful: A Study of Economics as if People Mattered*, London: Abacus, 1974.

135. For an example of a wholistic statement concerning the application of a green perspective to the global predicament, see Walter and Dorothy Schwarz *Breaking Through: Theory and Practice of Wholistic Living*, Bideford, Devon: Green Books, 1987.

136. *Findhorn Foundation*: Cluny Hill College, Forres, I36 ORD. See Paul Hawken *The Magic of Findhorn*, London: Harper & Row, 1975.

137. *The Farm*: 156 Drakes Lane, Summerton, TN 38483. See Corinne McLaughlin and Gordon Davidson *Builders of the Dawn: Community Lifestyles in a Changing World*, Shutesbury MA: Sirius, 1986, pp. 199–202; J. Hall *The Ways Out: Utopian Communal Groups in an Age of Babylon*, London: Routledge & Kegan Paul, 1978.

138. Philip Abrams and Andrew McCulloch *Communes, Sociology and Society*, Cambridge University Press, 1976; Karol Borowski *Attempting an Alternative Society: A Sociological Study of a Selected Communal-Revitalisation Movement in the United States*, Norwood PA: Norwood Editions, 1984; Rosabeth Moss Kantor *Communes, Creating and Managing the Collective Life*, New York: Harper and Row, 1975; Judson Jerome *Families of Eden: Communes and the New Anarchism*, New York: Seabury Press, 1974; McLaughlin and Davidson, op cit.

139. Lewis E. Durham "The Urban Middle-Class Communal Movement", *Communities: Journal of Cooperation*, Summer 1987, pp. 4–9.

140. Alan Watts *In My Own Way: An Autobiography*, New York: Random House, 1972; Monica Furlong *Zen Effects: the life of Alan Watts*, Boston: Houghton Mifflin, 1986.

141. Ramtha, with Douglas James Mahr, *Voyage to the New World*, Friday Harbour WA: Masterworks, 1985.

theological grounds, particularly on the part of some evangelical Christians who consider their syncretistic approach dangerous,[142] because they remove Christ from the centre.[143] (The "Aquarian Christ" can, indeed, be found playing some very unusual roles.)[144] Some conservative Christians have condemned the writings of people such as Shirley MacLaine[145] as satanic.[146] Rational sceptics are worried that New Age thought means the decline of rational, scientific thought and, as such, ought to be exposed as "*bunk, rubbish, idiocy, and nonsensical drivel*";[147] and the American Family Foundation has held a special symposium on 'Business and the New Age Movement' "to examine widespread allegations that some New Age programs employ damaging cultic techniques of persuasion and control".[148] This is, however, to include as part of the New Age movement elements that have been classified in this Appendix as part of the Human Potential movement (see separate entry).

NICHIREN SHOSHU BUDDHISM [149] *(SOKA GAKKAI)*

> If you wish to free yourself from the sufferings of birth and death you have endured through eternity and attain supreme enlightenment in this lifetime, you must awaken to the mystic truth which has always been within your life. This truth is Myoho-renge-kyo. Chanting Nam-myoho-renge-kyo will therefore enable you to grasp the mystic truth within you. Myoho-renge-kyo is the king of sutras, flawless in both letter and principle. Its words are the reality of life, and the reality of life is the mystic law (*myoho*). It is called the Mystic Law because it explains the mutually inclusive relationship of life and all phenomena. That is why this sutra is the wisdom of all Buddhas.[150]
>
> You must never seek any of Shakyamuni's teachings or the Buddhas and bodhisattvas of the universe outside yourself. Your mastery of the Buddhist teachings will not relieve you of mortal sufferings in the least unless you perceive the nature of your own life.

---

142. See editorial in "Enter the Apostate Church" in *Prophecy Today* vol. 5, no. 3, May/June, 1989.

143. Johannes Aargaard "Modern Syncretist Movements – A General Overview" *Update*, vol. V, issue 2, August 1981, p. 29.

144. Arild Romarheim "The Aquarian Christ" in Dyson and Barker (eds) (1988), pp. 197–207.

145. Shirley MacLaine *Out on a Limb*; *Dancing in the Light*, Toronto, New York, London, Sydney, Auckland: Bantam, 1983, 1985.

146. Fergus M. Bordewich "Colorado's Thriving Cults", *New York Times Magazine*, 1 May 1988.

147. Bob Sipchen "'New Age' Skeptics Have a Convergence All Their Own", *Los Angeles Times*, 13 November 1988.

148. AFF Report 1988.

149. *NSUK Centre*: Taplow Court, Taplow, Maidenhead, Berkshire SL6 0ER, UK. *Nichiren Shoshu of America (NSA)*: 525 Wilshire Boulevard, Santa Monica, CA 90401, USA. *Further Reading*: David A. Snow *The Nichiren Shoshu Buddhist Movement in America: A Sociological Evaluation of its Value Orientations, Recruitment Effort, and Spread,* unpublished Ph.D. thesis, University of California, Los Angeles, 1976.

150. Nichiren Shoshu *On Attaining Buddhahood. Major Writings of Nichiren Buddhism*, vol. 1, p. 3, quoted in Pat Allwright "The Meaning of Nam-Myoho-Renge-Kyo" *UK Express: An Introduction to Nichiren Shoshu Buddhism*, London, 1982, p. 5.

> If you seek enlightenment outside yourself, any discipline or good deed will be meaningless.[151]

In the 13th century, a new tradition of Japanese Buddhism was founded by a monk, Nichiren Daishonin (1222–1282), who believed that the *Lotus Sutra* contained the quintessence of the Buddha's message. Central to his teaching was the belief that the individual should chant (invoke) the phrase *Nam-myoho-renge-kyo* "I devote myself to the inexpressibly profound and wonderful truth – the law of life – expounded in the Lotus Sutra, which embodies the loftiest teachings of Buddhism". Unlike the Jewish, Christian and Islamic traditions, Buddhism is atheistic. Nichiren Shoshu Buddhism teaches that there is a universal Law of life that operates within each one of us and with which the chanter will be put in touch. Even if the chanter does not understand the meaning of the chant, the practice can still bring about benefits such as better health, improved relationships, promotion at work, or some kind of financial benefit.

What became known in 1913 as Nichiren Shoshu is one of several Nichiren sects.[152] The Soka Gakkai is the lay organisation associated with Nichiren Shoshu Buddhism and of which NSUK is a member. It was founded (under the name of Soka Kyoiku Gakkai) in 1930 by Tsunesaburo Makiguchi (1871–1944) and Josei Toda (1900-1958). In the post-war period, the movement has grown at a rapid rate in Japan – it was claiming over 16 million adherents by 1970,[153] and around 20 million in 115 countries by the late 1980s.[154] In late 1990, a rift developed between the priesthood of Nichiren Shoshu and the Soka Gakkai, with the vast majority of followers remaining loyal to Soka Gakkai.

Daisaku Ikeda, who founded Soka Gakkai International (SGI) in 1975, and is its current President, was awarded the United Nations peace award and medal in 1983. Among the movement's many ventures are Tokyo's Soka University, the monthly newsletter, *Soka Gakkai News*, and the daily paper *Seikyo Shimbun*. Legally distinct from, but closely associated with, SGI, is one of Japan's political parties: Komeito (Clean Government Party), which emerged in 1964.

Nichiren Shoshu in America (NSA) was established in 1960. The original members were nearly all Japanese brides of American G.I.s, but by the mid–1970s the movement claimed more than 200,000 adherents, over 90% of whom were occidental.[155] It was in 1974 that Nichiren

---

151. Nichiren Daishonin in *On Attaining Buddhahood*, quoted in Richard Causton *Nichiren Shoshu Buddhism: An Introduction*, London, Sydney, Auckland, Johannesburg: Rider, 1988, p. 27.

152. Hori Ichiro (ed.) *Japanese Religion: A Survey by the Agency for Cultural Affairs*, Tokyo, New York & San Francisco: Kodansha International, 1972, pp. 206–210.

153. Hori Ichiro (ed.), op cit, p. 208.

154. Causton, op cit, p. 269.

155. Snow, op cit; and David Snow and Richard Machalek "The Convert as a Social Type" in Randall Collins (ed.) *Sociological Theory*, San Francisco, Washington & London: Jossey-Bass, 1983, pp. 280–1.

Shoshu Buddhism became established in the UK when Richard Causton (1920-), an English businessman who had started 'to practise' while he was working in Japan, returned to England. Under his leadership, NSUK has grown to a membership of around 4,000.

Gongyo is the practice of chanting *Nam-myoho-renge-kyo* twice daily in front of the *Gohonzon* (a scroll inscribed with many Chinese and two Sanskrit characters, which is the object of devotion in Nichiren Shoshu Buddhism), and, as a 'supporting practice', reciting two chapters of the *Lotus Sutra*.[156] Joining the movement involves receiving one's own personal Gohonzon at a special Gohonzon ceremony at which the initiate promises to discard all other invocations, and other objects of worship. Until recently, pilgrimages were made by those who could afford it to the movement's head temple, which contains the *Dai-Gohonzon* (the original Gohonzon inscribed by Nichiren Daishonin), at Taiseki-ji at the foot of Mount Fuji, and was visited by thousands of people each day.

In Britain, all but the handful of NSUK members who are employed by the movement lead 'ordinary' lives, in ordinary (often middle-class) jobs. No special lifestyle is adopted, no special clothes are worn. Members can be found in all age-groups, but there would seem to be a preponderance of young adults. The movement has two centres where members can get together, but the monthly discussion meetings are held in members' homes throughout the country. Some activities are organised for 'Divisions' classified according to age and sex (such as the Young Women's Division), and there are special interest groups (for, for example, doctors, lawyers, teachers or nurses) which meet three or four times a year for discussions about their profession in the light of Buddhist ideas. NSUK also organises public lectures to promote their beliefs. Other public events have included a musical spectacular, *Alice*, which filled the Hammersmith Odeon in 1986 with songs containing lines such as: "It's here and now, Heaven is where you are; not far like some distant star".[157] The proceeds from the first night were donated to the United Nations and, for the second night, to an environmental project.[158] A monthly magazine, *UK Express*, carries reports of the movement's activities and numerous testimonies about the extraordinary changes that have been wrought in people's lives as a consequence of their chanting.

The movement in Japan has been subjected to severe criticism by its opponents.[159] It has also been attacked in the United States, where there is an association, ex-NSA, run by disaffected members who question the reverence that they say is accorded to President Ikeda, the pressure put

---

156. See Causton, op cit, especially chapters 3 and 4.

157. These may not be the precise words, but the message was clear enough.

158. The Commonwealth Human Ecology Council (CHEC).

159. See, for example, Noah S. Brannen *Sokagakkai: Japan's Militant Buddhists*, Richmond VA: John Knox Press, 1968; Hirotatsu Fujiwara *I Denounce Soka Gakkai*, translated from the Japanese by Worth C. Grant, Tokyo: Nisshen Hood, 1970.

on people to join, the 'addiction' of daily chanting, and various other 'damages' that are attributed to membership, such as fear of not chanting, fear of leaving NSA, and confusion about reality.[160] There has, however, been relatively little controversy surrounding the movement in the UK, where its character has been less aggressive than in some other countries.

OCCULTISM, NEO-PAGANISM, WITCHCRAFT, SHAMANISM and SATANISM[161]
(See also NEW AGE and HUMAN POTENTIAL MOVEMENT)

> The number of people with a serious and calculated interest in Mystical and magickal things is growing by leaps and bounds . . . Occultists are usually MORE successful and talented at what they do (because of their special training). . . Occultists believe that the refinement of life energies, talents and abilities through occult technology can rapidly assist the development of our society.[162]

The word '**occult**' means covered up, concealed, hidden, esoteric, or beyond the range of ordinary knowledge. Among the many 'ancient wisdoms' and religious traditions that have been fed into present-day occultism are Alchemy, Egyptian, Chinese, Greek, Roman and Celtic Mythology, the Norse legends, Druidism, Goddess Worship, Gnosticism,[163] Rosicruceanism,[164] Madame Blavatsky's Theosophy,[165] Alice Bailey's Arcane School[166] – and much else besides.[167] One possible introduction to the more publicly available aspects of Occultism, Paganism and Witchcraft is to attend some of the lectures and workshops at the annual *Predictions* Festival in London, and to inspect the numerous stalls offering wands, ritual swords, hand-carved runes, tarot, I Ching,

160. See, for example, *Ex-NSA Journal/Newsletter* vol. 2, no. 2, and vol. 4, no. 3, Spring 1989.

161. *The Neopantheist Society*: BCM-OPAL, London WC1N 3XX, UK.
The Centre for Pagan Studies: 34 Kinkaid Road, Peckham, London SE15, UK.
The Pagan Federation: BM Box 7097, London WC1N 3XX, U.K.
Eagle's Wing, Centre for Contemporary Shamanism: 58 Westbere Road, London NW2 3RU, UK. Further addresses may be found in, for example, *The Q Directory No. 4: Occult, Pagan and New Age Groups, Services and Publications*, London, the Neopantheist Society: Aquariana, n.d. For a listing of Pagan resources in the USA and UK, see Appendix III of Margot Adler's *Drawing Down the Moon: Witches, Goddess-Worshippers, and Other Pagans in America Today*, Boston: Beacon Press, second edition, 1986. See also Melton (1989).

162. Chris Bray *The Occult Census: Statistical Analyses and Results*, Leeds: Sorcerer's Apprentice, 1989, pp. 3 & 5.

163. Elaine Pagels *The Gnostic Gospels*, Harmondsworth, Penguin, 1982.

164. Frances A. Yates *The Rosicrucian Enlightenment*, St Albans: Granada, Paladin, 1975.

165. Charles J. Ryan *H. P. Blavatsky and the Theosophical Movement*, Pasadena CA: Theosophical University Press, 1974.

166. Peter Sapat *The Return of the Christ and Prophecy*, Philadelphia: Dorrance, 1978.

167. For an overview, see J. Gordon Melton *Magic, Witchcraft and Paganism in America: A bibliography*, New York & London: Garland, 1982; and Jeffrey Mishlove *The Roots of Consciousness: Psychic Liberation through History, Science and Experience*, New York: Random House & Berkeley CA: Bookworks, 1975.

runic readings, healing quartz, crystal balls, pyramids, incense, candle magick, spell kits and books on Do-It-Yourself Witchcraft (which contain warnings that neither the authors nor the publishers are to be held responsible for any event arising out of their content).[168]

Marcello Truzzi has made a distinction between three different kinds of occult interest:[169] first there are occultists who are interested in anomalies, whether these be UFOs,[170] the Loch Ness monster or a rain of 'blood'. The International Fortean Society or the Society for the Investigation of the Unexplained would provide examples of this type. Secondly, there are occultists who are concerned with some inexplicable relationship between events, both of which may themselves be 'normal'. A prophetic reading about a future event using a pack of tarot cards would be an example. Truzzi points out, however, that although most magical activity could be of this type, it is rarely viewed as such by the practitioners. Thus, the High Priest of the Church of Satan, Anton LaVey has stated:

> I don't believe that magic is supernatural, only that it is supernormal. That it works for reasons that science cannot yet understand. As a shaman or magician, I am concerned with obtaining *recipes*. As a scientist, you seek *formulas*.[171]

Truzzi's third level of occultism is concerned with belief systems, which may incorporate elements of the other two types and attempt to explain them. Witchcraft-Satanism is the example that Truzzi himself pursues, but there are many other examples of modern occultisms.

Some **Neo-Pagans** (Pagan literally means 'inhabitant of the land') consider themselves to be occultists, but others do not.[172] Paganism and Witchcraft are sometimes, but not always, seen as synonymous; Paganism is sometimes seen as the more religious aspect of Witchcraft. According to Margot Adler, Neo-Pagan groups differ between themselves with regard to tradition, scope, structure, organisation, ritual and the names by which they call their deities. They do, none the less, see themselves as part of a single religio-philosophical movement; they share certain values and communicate with each other through a network of newsletters and gatherings. There are few Neo-Pagan temples; meetings may be held

---

168. See also reference books such as Richard Cavendish (ed.) *Encyclopedia of the Unexplained: Magic Occultism and Parapsychology*, London: Routledge & Kegan Paul, 1974, for recognising further the scope of the subject.

169. Marcello Truzzi "Towards a Sociology of the Occult: Notes on Modern Witchcraft" in Zaretsky and Leone (1974), pp. 628–645.

170. See Shirley McIver *Ufology in Britain: A Sociological Study of Unidentified Flying Object Groups*, unpublished Ph.D., University of York, 1983. See also the movement's various publications, such as *UFO: an international forum on extraterrestial theories and phenomena*.

171. Tape recorded interview in the possession of Marcel Truzzi, 1968.

172. Margot Adler op cit, p. 13; see also David Burnett *Drawing of the Second Moon: An Investigation into the Rise of Western Paganism*, Eastbourne: Marc, 1991.

in woods or in houses. Stonehenge and Glastonbury are among those celebrated as sacred places. Neo-Pagans tend to lead 'ordinary' lives, and to be generally indistinguishable from the rest of society, apart from their religious beliefs.[173]

What, then, are these beliefs? Paganism is, above all, a religion of nature.

> Most Neo-Pagans sense an aliveness and 'presence' in nature. They are usually polytheists [believing in many gods] or animists [believing that natural phenomena possess souls] or pantheists [believing that God is everything and everything is God] or two or three of these things at once. They share the goal of living in harmony with nature and they tend to view humanity's 'advancement' and separation from nature as the prime source of alienation. They see *ritual* as a tool to end that alienation.[174]

It is through their rites that Neo-Pagans explore possibilities for acquiring power by establishing a 'right relationship' with the cosmos. "Participants in the **Witchcraft** revival generally use *Witch* to mean simply an initiate of the religion Wicca, also known as the Craft".[175] A Witch can be defined as a woman (or man) skilled in the craft of shaping, bending and changing reality. Tania Luhrmann has estimated that "a small number of occultists describe what they do as magic, and a smaller number, perhaps 2,000 in the UK, practise in organised groups".[176] While Neo-Pagans may engage in low-key recruitment efforts through advertising, Witches only rarely evangelise – the impetus to join a coven will commonly come from the prospective member.

Among the many influences on contemporary magic are two Britons: Aleister Crowley (1875–1947) and Gerald Gardner (1884–1960).[177] Crowley, well-known for his elaboration of sex-magick rituals, taught:

> Do what thou wilt shall be the whole of the Law. . .
> There is no law beyond Do what thou wilt.
> Love is the law, love under will.[178]

Further influences come from the hermetic tradition (mainly alchemy) and the Kabbalistic tradition which holds that the world can be symbolically represented through numbers and letters. Voodoo, the Haitian

---

173. J. Gordon Melton "Neo-Paganism: Report on the survey of an alternative religion", paper presented to the Society for the Scientific Study of Religion, Cincinnati, Ohio, 1980.

174. Adler, op cit, p. 4.

175. Ibid, p. 10.

176. Tania M. Luhrmann "Witchcraft, Morality and Magic in Contemporary London" *International Journal of Moral and Social Sciences*, vol. 1, no. 1, Spring 1986, p. 77.

177. For short biographies of these two men, see J. Gordon Melton *Biographical Dictionary of American Cult and Sect Leaders*, New York & London: Garland, 1986, pp. 59–61 & 96–7.

178. "Aiwass" [Aleister Crowley] *The Book of the Law*, York Beach ME: Samuel Weiser, 1976 (first dictated 1904), p. 50.

religion that owes its origins to West African tribal religion, is a further resource.[179]

In recent years there has been an upsurge of interest in **Shamanism**, 'the technique of ecstasy'.[180]

> A Shaman is a healer, visionary, artist, psychic and psychotherapist – a Doctor of the soul... Someone who can change consciousness to bring about a greater state of wholeness, which is the real meaning of holiness... Ordinary people live in a state of 'waking sleep' (said Gurdjieff) deeply hypnotised by the apparent reality of the world-out-there. The Shaman knows that that is only a reflection of the real world, the world-in-here.[181]

It is believed that, while in the trance state, a Shaman can visit other worlds, re-enact traditional journeys and have encounters with gods and demons. Modern anthropologists have drawn parallels between the roles of the Shaman and the psychoanalyst or psychotherapist.[182] Largely, although by no means entirely, as a result of the writings of Carlos Castaneda,[183] there has been a special interest in the Shamanistic practices of the North American Indians.

Pagans and 'White' Witches are continually concerned to point out that they should not be confused with 'Black Witches' or **Satanists**.[184] The 1989 Occult Census reported that only 4% of its respondents had a deeply committed belief in Satanism, 46% and 42% being, respectively, deeply committed to Paganism and Witchcraft (respondents could declare a committed belief in more than one subject).[185] A basic distinction that

---

179. For introductory essays on some of the influences and history of magick, see Melton (1982), op cit; and Melton (1989), chapter 18. See also Francis King *Ritual Magic: 1887 to the present day*, London: New English Library, Nel books, 1972; and James Webb *The Occult Underground* La Salle IL: Open Court, 1974.

180. See I. M. Lewis *Ecstatic Religion: An anthropological study of Spirit Possession and Shamanism*, Harmondsworth: Penguin, 1971.

181. An Eagle's Wing leaflet advertising a one-year course (1989/90) on *Elements of Shamanism*.

182. Claude Lévi-Strauss *Structural Anthropology*, New York: Basic Books, pp. 167–85 and 186–205; Kakar (1984) pp. 89 ff; and E. Fuller Torrey "Spiritualists and Shamans as Psychotherapists: An Account of Original Anthropological Sin" in Zaretsky and Leone (1974), pp. 330–337; James Dow "Symbols, Soul, and Magical Healing among the Otomí Indians" *Journal of Latin American Lore*, vol. 10, no. 1, 1984, pp. 3–12; James Dow "Universal Aspects of Symbolic Healing: A Theoretical Synthesis" *American Anthropologist*, no. 88, 1986, pp. 65–69.

183. Carlos Castaneda *The Teachings of Don Juan: A Yaqui Way of Knowing*, Berkeley: University of California Press, 1968; *A Separate Reality: Further Conversations with Don Juan*, London: Bodley Head, 1971. See also David Silverman *Reading Castaneda: A Prologue to the Social Sciences*, London: Routledge & Kegan Paul, 1975.

184. Margot Adler *Drawing Down the Moon: Witches, Druids, Goddess-Worshippers, and Other Pagans in America Today*, revised and expanded edition, Boston: Beacon Press, 1986, p. 99; J. Gordon Melton *Magic, Witchcraft and Paganism in America: A bibliography*, New York & London: Garland, 1982, p. ix; Melinda Huddleston "Pagans" *Arkansas Democratic*, 1 May 1988.

185. *The Occult Census: Statistical Analyses and Results*, Leeds: The Sorcerer's Apprentice Press, 1989, p. 17. See Joel Birico "The Occult Senseless", *Aquarian Arrow*, no. 28, pp. 14–5 for an objection to the questions asked by the Census.

is frequently drawn is that Witchcraft, unlike Satanism, is independent of Christianity. According to one report:

> Wiccans differ from Christians in that they don't believe in sin, nor do they accept the ideas of redemption from an outside power (God or Christ) or temptation from evil spirits (Satan).[186]

The Gnostic mass is described as a "positive affirmation of an integrated complex of aspirations and ideals" – unlike the Black mass of Satanists, which is a parody or a desecration of the Christian mass,[187] but, in fact, by no means all Satanism is of the 'Christian' variety; other forms, such as the Church of Satan, have been called Palladism or Luciferism.[188] Satanists do share some symbols and rituals with magical religions, but they also have some that are unique and distinctive: a 5-pointed star, with a single point down, and the horned goat-god are common examples.

An important distinction, that has already been suggested in the text, is made by Melton:

> As one studies the contemporary Satanist scene, two distinct realities emerge. On the one hand are what are frequently termed the "sickies." These are disconnected groups of occultists who employ Satan worship to cover a variety of sexual, sado-masochistic, clandestine, psychopathic, and illegal activities. . . These groups are characterised by lack of theology, disconnectedness and short life, and informality of meetings. Usually they are discovered only in the incident that destroys them.
> On the other hand are the public groups which take Satanism as a religion seriously. . . While, theologically, the Christian might find both reprehensible, their behaviour is drastically different and the groups should not be confused.[189]

Satanism is discussed further in the text (the relevant places can be found by reference to the index). Most of the controversies surrounding the other kinds of groups in this section have also been mentioned elsewhere. It might, however, be added that this is an area where some evangelical Christians see the battle with the movements as having to be fought on a very different level from that at which it is fought with most other NRMs. The Evangelical Alliance, for example, has explained that:

> Today, the Christian Church faces up to the fact that demons and evil spirits are not fables from the past. Throughout the country there are

---

186. Thomas Edwards "Believers explain what draws them to witchcraft", *Express-News, San Antonio*, 31 October 1988. See also Richardson et al (eds) (1991).

187. Quotation taken from a video of Aleister Crowley's version of the Gnostic Mass, *Ecclesiae Gnosticae Catholicae Cannon Missae*, released by the Neopantheist Society, London, Spring 1987.

188. For a discussion on this point, see Marcello Truzzi "Towards a Sociology of the Occult: Notes on Modern Witchcraft" in Zaretsky and Leone (eds) (1974), pp. 634–5.

189. Melton (1989), pp. 145–6. See also Marcello Truzzi "Towards a Sociology of the Occult: Notes on Modern Witchcraft" in Zaretsky and Leone (1974), pp. 628–645; and Edward J. Moody "Magical Therapy: An Anthropological Investigation of Contemporary Satanism" in Zaretsky and Leone (eds) (1974), pp. 355–382.

> trained clergymen who have experience in freeing people who are
> oppressed or possessed by evil spirits... [Rev John Banner says]
> "sometimes during an exorcism, the spirits of a possessed person will
> speak to him... Occasionally, a demon inside a person will even quote
> from the Bible... If you start messing about with the occult, Satan
> will court you by saying '...I will give you power you've never had
> before.' But when you invite the spirit of darkness into your heart,
> that is when you become possessed and a temple of evil."[190]

The booklet in which the above quotation appears also warns of dangers
of astrology and 'Horror-scopes', and of children's attending Hallowe'en
parties.[191]

PAGANISM See OCCULTISM, NEO-PAGANISM, WITCHCRAFT, SHAMANISM and SATANISM

RAËLIANS[192]

> On December 13 1973 an extraterrestial appeared to Claude Vorilhon
> in France and invited him to step into his craft. Once inside the little
> man explained that a long time ago, on a distant planet, a HUMANITY
> comparable to ours had reached a scientific and technological level
> equal to the one we will reach in years to come...
>
> Allowing one to deprogramme the Judeo-Christian inhibitions of
> guilt whilst at the same time not falling into the etherial mysticisms of
> the oriental teachings, the sensual meditation allows the human to
> discover his/her body and especially to learn how to use it to enjoy
> sounds, colours, smells, tastes, caresses and particularly a sexuality felt
> with all one's senses so as to experience the cosmic orgasm, infinite,
> absolute which illuminates the mind by linking the one who reaches it
> with the universes s/he is composed of and composes.[193]

We are told that the Elohim, "our fathers from space" renamed Claude
Vorilhon (1946–) as 'Raël', which means "the messenger of those who
come from the sky."[194] The messages that Raël has relayed explain that
we are in danger of annihilating the human race, and that the human
race was created in their own image by the Elohim who had, a long
time ago, accomplished a perfect mastery of DNA. The Elohim asked
Raël to create a movement so that he could pass on the messages and
build an Embassy (preferably near Jerusalem) so that they could come
and meet our political leaders on an official basis.[195]

---

190. *Doorways to Danger*, published by the Evangelical Alliance, 1987.
191. The Deo Gloria Trust is another evangelical organisation that has produced
literature warning of the power of Satan as part of their *Christian Response to the Occult*
programme.
192. *British Raëlian Movement:* BCM Minstrel, London WC1N 3XX, UK.
USA Raëlian Movement: c/o Griffith Station, P.O.Box 39488, Los Angeles, CA 90039, USA.
193. *Space Aliens took me to their Planet*, pamphlet published by the British Raëlian
Movement, n.d.
194. Ibid.
195. Claude Vorilhon "Raël" *The Message Given to Me by Extra-Terrestrials: They Took
Me To Their Planet*, Tokyo: AOM Corporation, 1986; Claude Vorilhon "Raël" *Let's Welcome
our Fathers from Space: They Created Humanity in their Laboratories*, Tokyo: AOM Corporation,
1987.

Believers are expected to practise Sensual Meditation each day. The Sensual Meditation programme is normally taught "as a course of awakening which lasts for one week and contains a total of a dozen exercises". There are a number of centres in Europe and North America where one can meditate alone or in a group. Some of the cassette recordings

> are disigned [*sic*] to be listened to when accompanied by a partner of complementary sex, and so those who are single can hope to meet up with another person . . . with whom they can be sure to find spiritual harmony . . . and with whom they can also hope to find physical harmony.[196]

Raëlians do not (as yet) live in communities. Many evidently feel that they must concentrate on their professional lives so that they can develop themselves and can contribute money to the Movement;[197] they are expected to tithe 10% of their income, 3% for the British Raëlian Movement and 7% for the International Movement.[198] Raëlians can recognise each other when they wear their special medallion which looks like a six-pointed star with a swastika in the centre, and which is said to be the symbol of infinity that is the emblem of our Creators. "Moreover, it functions as a psychic catalyst during the attempts of telepathic communication with the Elohim and contributes to the awakening of mind".[199]

RAJA YOGA See BRAHMA KUMARIS

RAJNEESHISM[200]

> This is the whole art of meditation: how to be deep in action, how to renounce thinking, and how to convert the energy that was moving into thinking into awareness.[201]

---

196. Claude Vorilhon "Raël" *Sensual Meditation: Awakening the Mind by Awakening the Body*, Tokyo: AOM Corporation, 1986, p. 95.
197. Angela Henderson "Nurturing the Infant Religion", *Newsletter 2 of Year 42 after HIROSHIMA*, distributed by the British Raëlian Movement.
198. *Scientists from Another Planet Created all Life on Earth using DNA*, booklet distributed by the Raëlian Movement, n.d., p. 7.
199. Raël *The Message*, p. 287.
200. *Purnima Rajneesh Centre for Meditation*: Spring House, Spring Place, Kentish Town, London NW5 3BH, UK.
Rajneesh Followers of Bhagwan: c/o Swami Anand Vibhaven, 13041 S. W. Knaus Road, Lake Oswego, OR 97034, USA.
Further Reading: Sally Belfrage *Flowers of Emptiness: Reflections on an Ashram*, New York: Dial Press, 1981; Fitzgerald (1986); Milne (1986); Bob Mullan *Life as Laughter: Following Bhagwan Shree Rajneesh*, London: Routledge and Kegan Paul, 1983; Judith Thompson and Paul Heelas *The Way of the Heart: The Rajneesh Movement*, Wellingborough: Aquarian Press, 1986; and the special issue of *Self and Society, European Journal of Humanistic Psychology*, Vol. XV, no. 5, September – October 1987: *Bhagwan: Trick or Treat*.
201. Bhagwan Shree Rajneesh *The Orange Book*, Rajneeshpuram, OR: Rajneesh Foundation International, 1983, 2nd edition, p. 23.

Meditation can bring you to your nature... It can make you intelligent, it can make you loving, it can make you spontaneous, it can make you responsible. It can make you a benediction to yourself and to existence. Except meditation there is no other method which can help. This is the key, the master key.[202]

Rajneesh International No-University will function in freedom ... It is not prepared to compromise its revolutionary approach to education in order to gain official recognition...

The No-University presents a totally new division in education and does not believe in competition, examination, or knowledge through memory. It is non-authoritarian, non-conventional, and non-traditional. According to the enlightened perspective of Bhagwan Shree Rajneesh, the old education system has failed. Not only has it failed, but it has proved a disaster to humanity. It functions in the services of the past and is against the future.[203]

Religion has hopped from the altars and come to boogie at the Body Centre.[204]

Wherever there is a sannyasin of mine, *I am there*.[205]

Bhagwan Shree Rajneesh (1931–1990) is said to have 'received enlightenment' in 1953 while at university. By 1960, he was lecturing in philosophy at the University of Jabalpur, but he left his academic post to travel round India, "lecturing to huge crowds with his uncompromising and radically outspoken views on religion, sex and politics".[206] In 1974, a community, Shree Rajneesh Ashram, was founded in Poona. Here thousands of visitors flocked from around the world. The permanent population grew to around 2,000. Bernard Levin was one of the many who went to listen and was "struck by enlightenment in Poona".[207] Other visitors returned with stories of frenzied sexual practices, drug trafficking, suicides and physical and mental injury resulting from some of the numerous programmes that were on offer.

In the summer of 1981, Bhagwan suddenly disappeared from Poona. Several weeks later a 64,000-acre estate in Oregon became the international centre for his followers, who laboured hard (spent time in 'worship') to build the vast complex that became known as Rajneeshpuram. By this time, there were around 300 Rajneesh Meditation Centres world-wide. In Britain the centres included Medina, a large country house near Bury St Edmunds, Kalptaru and, later, the Body Centre in North London. These offered Rajneeshees (or anyone who could pay)

202. Bhagwan Shree Rajneesh *Guida Spirituale*, quoted in "The Poona Program" enclosed in *The Rajneesh Times*, vol. 4, no. 22, 1 November 1987.

203. "No Compromise Declaration" issued from the Rajneesh Press office, Poona, 15 April 1981.

204. *Medina Rajneesh Body Centre Programme* no. 1, September – December 1983, p. 1.

205. Osho Rajneesh *Rajneesh Times*, vol. 2, no. 13, 16 July 1989, p. 14.

206. Kalptaru Rajneesh Books leaflet, London, Kalptaru Rajneesh Meditation Centre, n.d.

207. *The Times* 8, 9 and 10 April 1981.

evening, week-end, week or months-long courses; the one-year Foundation Course in Rajneesh Therapy 1982–3 cost £3,500, including food,
accommodation and VAT. The range of subjects was vast, including, for
example, Bioenergetics, Body Awareness, Bodywork, Carpentry and
Woodwork, Dehypnotherapy, Encounter, Energy Balancing, Intuitive
Massage, Neo-Tantric, Orgasmic Undoing, Pleasuring, Rebalancing,
Rebirthing, Regression and Hypnotherapy, Relationships, Relaxation and
Energy, Satori, Self Exploration, Tai Chi or Zencounter. At the end of
these courses, there would usually be the invitation to go to Rajneeshpuram – an experience that could cost several thousands of dollars.
Sannyasins in the UK in the early 1980s numbered 3–4,000; they
belonged to what was possibly the most fashionable and fastest-growing
alternative spiritual/religious movement in Britain.

To be a Rajneeshee Sannyasin (or Neo-Sannyasin) one was told that
all that was really necessary was to feel a desire to surrender to Bhagwan
and to become his disciple, to be as honest and open as possible, to enjoy
life and learn to love oneself. The outward signs of such a commitment
were (i) to wear clothing of an orange colour (which often looked more
like pink or purple) – hence the nickname 'the Orange People', (ii) to
accept a new name, and (iii) to wear a picture of Bhagwan on a mala (a
necklace made of 108 sandalwood beads).

Before taking sannyas, most of Bhagwan's followers will have
completed at least a weekend introduction to the 'chaotic breathing
technique' that he developed.

> In Rajneesh Dynamic Meditation, the meditator deliberately increases
> his or her stress factor to an acute level before letting go and relaxing.
> This is done by rapid, chaotic breathing through which repressed
> tension and emotion is contacted and brought to the surface. The
> repressed feelings are then released through catharsis – screaming,
> shouting, crying, laughing, or whatever form it happens to take. This
> is followed by a third stage in which the meditator jumps up and
> down, arms in the air, shouting "Hoo! Hoo! Hoo!" Only after these
> three active steps, each lasting ten minutes, does the meditator relax
> into silence and stillness.[208]

Sannyasins are also likely to practise Rajneesh Kundalini Meditation,
which involves the total shaking of the body "to dissipate body tensions",
and dancing "to allow the expression of our rediscovered, flowing
vitality", followed by two stages of silence.[209]

Stress is laid on the fact that being a Sannyasin is just meant to be
fun. It is not a heavy, serious religion. In the words of one Sannyasin,
"A Catholic who becomes a Sannyasin doesn't make a decision to stop
being a Catholic – it just becomes irrelevant."[210]

---

208. Swami Shunyo MD quoted in *Medina Rajneesh Body Centre Programme* no. 1,
September – December 1983, p. 6.
209. Ibid.
210. Personal communication.

Most Sannyasins are between the ages of 25 and 45. Most come from the middle classes; frequently they are associated with teaching, counselling or alternative healing. The majority have continued to live in their own homes and to work in outside jobs, but the more committed have lived in communes, such as Medina (which has now been sold), and, until 1985, the most committed migrated to Rajneeshpuram.

But for all its declared pursuit of freedom, Rajneeshpuram was becoming increasingly controlled and totalitarian (see the text).[211] September 1985 saw the hasty departure from Rajneeshpuram of Bhagwan's personal secretary, Ma Anand Sheela, who, to all intents and purposes, had been ruling Rajneeshpuram during and after the period from 1981–4 when Bhagwan kept silent.[212] She was eventually imprisoned for a number of offences.[213] Shortly after Sheela's departure, Bhagwan was caught trying to leave the USA. He was imprisoned and then expelled from the country for immigration offences. After being refused entry by a number of countries, he eventually returned to Poona where the movement, slightly altered, succeeded in attracting a new following to join those who had remained loyal. The Master himself was no longer called Bhagwan, but Osho Rajneesh. Sannyasins were no longer expected to wear their malas, or 'orange':

> Osho has suggested that when sitting with him in Buddha Hall people wear white meditation robes, which they wear only when they are sitting in His presence or meditating alone. . . He also suggested that during the 3-day monthly meditation camps all participants wear maroon clothes.[214]

After a period of uncertainty, and, indeed, since Osho's death, centres presenting Rajneesh's philosophy, and offering the full range of therapies and avenues to self-enlightenment, have started opening up again and, it would appear, reassembling in North America, Europe and the UK, Australia, New Zealand and other parts of the world. A number of disaffected Sannyasins who had left either just before or shortly after the events of 1985, still believing in Bhagwan's basic philosophy, started teaching some of his ideas under a new name, or even established new movements of their own – Paul Lowe's International Academy of Meditation being but one. There are also a number of semi-independent

---

211. See Fitzgerald (1987); Milne (1986); and Thompson and Heelas, op cit; for three further and very different perspectives, see also Charles Newman "Bhagwan Shree Rajneesh: A New Man for All Seasons", David Boadella "The Fall of the Light-Bearer", and Eileen Barker "Freedom to Surrender with Bhagwan", all in *Self and Society* Vol. XV, no. 5, September – October 1987.

212. Kalptaru Rajneesh Books leaflet, London, Kalptaru Rajneesh Meditation Centre, n.d.; and "Rajneesh Spiritual Therapy and Meditation leaflet, Rajneeshpuram, OR: Rajneesh Foundation International, 1984. See also "Bhagwan goes into silence" *Rajneesh Buddhafield*, no. 4.

213. See Fitzgerald (1987); Milne (1986).

214. Enclosure in *Rajneesh Times*, vol. 2, no. 13, 16 July 1989.

'strands' within the movement, one of these being the Humaniversity run by a long-time Sannyasin, Vereesh, in Holland. Out of this have grown a number of 'Misfit Cities' which concentrate more on therapy than meditation.

RASTAFARIANISM[215]

> *Charter of the Rastafarians:*
>   1. Members of the Rastafarian Movement are an inseparable part of the Black people of Jamaica (Every African is a Rasta!). . .
>   12. The Rastafarian Movement stands for Repatriation and power and for the fullest cooperation and intercourse between the Governments and people of Africa and a free and independent people of Jamaica. . .
>   17. Because we have no other aims but the legitimate aims of all Black people on this island, this movement is open to all Black people, irrespective of class, religion or financial standing.[216]
> Rasta is the totality of a life's experience. . . The life of a Rasta is reflected in history and projected into time. Rasta is the spiritual/ material foundation of 'livity' prophetic realisation. Rasta is the result of a search for cultural identity and racial security. . .
> For Rastas worshipping the Almighty Creator is a constant manifestation. There is no time set for rituals or worship. . . I n I know that in Jah sight all acts are 'I-qual'.
> Haile Selassie I, Emperor of Ethiopia, is I n I Messiah and Leader. Wherever he leads, I n I follow. . .
> Rastas want land in Africa for the building of Rasta society, here on earth. . . I n I want to achieve peace and love among all people: I n I also want to achieve justice and rights for all people![217]

Rastafarianism grew out of the Back to Africa movement, started in the early part of the century by the Jamaican-born Marcus Garvey (1887–1940). It is a movement with no single creed – in fact, the diversity of the ideas to be found within Rastafarianism makes it difficult to call it either a political party or a religious 'movement'. The Old Testament plays an important role; many Rastafarians believe that all men are equal and bound by the spirit of 'jah' or god – jah does, however, especially favour Blacks. A strongly held belief accepted by nearly all Rastafarians (and many others) is that, ever since the Whites came to Africa, Blacks have been oppressed not only by slavery, but also by the social system (Babylon) that has, at a more subtle level after emancipation, continued

215. *Rastafari Universal Zion*: Seven Sisters School, Roslyn Road, London N15, UK. *Further Reading:* Leonard Barrett *The Rastafarians: Sounds of Cultural Dissonance*, Boston: Beacon Press, 1977; Horace Campbell *Rasta and Resistance: From Marcus Garvey to Walter Rodney*, Trenton NJ: Africa World Press, 1987; Cashmore (1983); Peter Clarke *The Rastafarian Movement*, Wellingborough: Aquarian, 1986; K. M. Williams *The Rastafarians*, London: Ward Lock Educational, 1981.

216. Ras Sam Brown *Charter of the Rastafarians*, 1961, quoted in Barrett, op cit, pp. 148–50; and Williams, op cit, pp. 58–9 (see also p. 33).

217. Jah Bones *One Love: Rastafari: History, Doctrine and Livity*, London: Voice of Rasta Publishing House, 1985, pp. 1–2.

to deny Blacks their rights and to make them feel themselves to be inferior to the Whites in power.

The majority of Rastafarians have believed in the Divinity of Ras Tafari (1892–1975) since he was crowned the Ethiopian Emperor, Haile Selassie I, in 1930. This event, it was believed, would herald a prophesied return of Blacks to Africa. Many believe that Haile Selassie is still alive – that he has merely 'disappeared' – but interpretations and hopes concerning this matter differ.[218]

Rastafarianism first made an appearance in the UK in the late 1950s. It became particularly visible in the late 1970s and early 1980s among Black youth in Britain's inner city areas, and, indeed, in North America, parts of Europe, Australia and New Zealand (where it found a particular resonance among certain Aboriginal and Maori communities). Its growth was greatly stimulated by the increasing unemployment and poor material conditions of young Blacks, and by the popularity of Reggae music - in particular, the songs of Bob Marley (1945–1981) which carried Rastafarian messages around the world.

A number of organisations associated with Rastafarianism were formed. Among these were The Universal Black Improvement Organisation, The People's Democratic Party, The Twelve Tribes of Israel, and The Ethiopian World Federation. Because of the lack of any centralised organisation or leadership, it is difficult to know how many Rastafarians there are, but it has been estimated that the total membership would be in tens of thousands.[219]

Rastafarians are distinguishable by their 'dreadlocks' (coils of uncut hair),[220] which are sometimes covered by tams knitted in the Rastafarian colours of red (signifying the blood of martyrs of Jamaican history), black (the colour of Africans' skin), green (representing green vegetation and the hope of victory over oppression) and the gold of the Jamaican flag.[221] 'Strict' Rastafarians do not eat meat or drink alcohol, but there are those who do. Although Rastafarianism is a male-oriented and male-dominated religion, which has perpetuated the image of women as inferior to men, there are Rastafarian men and women who are concerned to improve the ways in which women are regarded and treated.[222]

While usually pacifist in outlook, violence has occasionally been used by disaffected Rastafarians. This, the wild appearance of the dreadlocks, the fact that many of them smoke 'ganga', and the suspicion that they were at least in part responsible for the Brixton riots in 1981 have

---

218. See, for example, article and Letters page of *Rastafari International News*, vol. 2, no. 3, July-August 1989.

219. Ernest Ellis Cashmore *The Rastafarians*, London: The Minority Rights Group, Report no. 64, 1984, p. 9.

220. Leviticus 21:5, "They shall not make baldness upon their head".

221. Barrett, op cit, p. 143; Williams, op cit, p. 16.

222. Campbell, op cit, pp. 199–200; Cashmore, 1984, op cit, pp. 8–9; Williams, op cit, p. 25.

contributed to Rastafarians not generally having had a 'good press'.[223] There are, however, members of the white establishment who have forcefully defended the movement: Lord Scarman has, on more than one occasion, urged greater understanding and sympathy from the British people;[224] and the Catholic Commission for Racial Justice has recommended that "Rastafarianism should be recognised as a valid religion" and that Rastafarians should be treated with respect and, wherever possible, helped by the Churches and secular organisation.[225]

SAHAJA YOGA [226]

Sahaja Yoga is different from the other yogas because it begins with Self realization instead of this being the unobtainable dream of a distant goal. Her Holiness Mataji Nirmala Devi makes this possible, for in being born Self realized, She is able to pass on Her gift of Divine Revelation to others. . . Self Realization is the key which unlocks the invisible barrier which blocks the life force of kundalini. . .[227]

. . . *you have to dedicate yourself completely to me; not to Sahaja Yoga, but to me. Sahaja Yoga is just one of my aspects. Leaving everything, you have to dedicate. Complete Dedication, . otherwise you cannot ascend any further. Without questioning, without arguing.*[228]

Sahaja Yoga is the Last Judgement. This is described in the Bible. You are judged only after you come to Sahaja Yoga. For that purpose you, however, have to surrender yourself completely after coming to Sahaja Yoga.[229]

. . . you must know that I am the Holy Ghost. I am the Adi Shakti. I am the one who has come on this earth for the first time in this form to do this tremendous task.[230]

Christ is Me, now, sitting before you.[231]

Her Holiness Mataji Nirmala Devi Srivastava (1923–), who is known as the Divine Mother to her followers, was born at Chindawara, central

223. See Campbell, op cit, especially pp. 181–206; and Cashmore, op cit.

224. See *The Brixton Disorders 10.12 April 1981: Report of an Inquiry by the Rt Hon The Lord Scarman, OBE,* HMSO Cmnd 8427; and Foreword to Cashmore *The Rastafarians,* London: The Minority Rights Group, Report no. 64, 1984, p. 3.

225. *Rastafarians in Jamaica and Britain,* London: Catholic Commission for Racial Justice, Notes and Reports, no. 10, January 1982, p. 11.

226. *UK Centre:* 44 Chelsham Road, London SW4.
USA contact: 17301 S. Maria, Cerritos, CA 90701, USA.
Further reading: Kakar (1984), chapter 7; Philippa Pullar *The Shortest Journey,* London: Unwin, 1984 (1st edition 1981), parts IV & V; P.T. Rajasekharan and R. Venkatesam *Divine Knowledge through Vibrations,* Singapore: Printworld, 1992.

227. John Gent, Introduction to *Sahaja Yoga: Book One,* by Her Holiness Mataji Shri Nirmala Devi, Delhi: Nirmala Yoga, 1982, p. 1.

228. Shri Mataji "Complete Dedication the Only Way", Cowley Manor Seminar, 31 July 1982, reported in *Nirmala Yoga,* vol. 4, no. 24, November–December 1984, p. 3. See also *Nirmala Yoga,* vol. 5, no. 29, September–October 1985, p. 36.

229. Shri Mataji speaking at Hinduja Auditorium, Bombay, 26 September 1979, reported in *Nirmala Yoga,* vol. 4, no. 24, November–December 1984, p. 34.

230. Shri Mataji speaking in Sydney at her Birthday Puja, 21 March 1983, reported in *Nirmala Yoga,* vol. 4, no. 20, March–April p. 5

231. Shri Mataji speaking during puja at Bordi, Maharashtra, 13 February 1984, reported in *Nirmala Yoga,* vol. 4, no. 20, March–April, p. 16.

India, into a Protestant family. Her husband was the Secretary General of the International Maritime Organisation of the United Nations. Following an experience in 1970,[232] she has been teaching Sahaja Yoga, a central tenet of which is that the means to spontaneous union with the divine is born within all of us – and, with Mataji's help, it can be awakened.

Those who are to be 'realized' without the physical presence of Mataji, sit with the palms upwards, facing her picture. It is said that Kundalini (a potential spiritual energy which lies sleeping at the base of the spine) is awakened and passes up the spinal cord, through six chakras. A cool breeze may be sensed, and people have expressed extreme happiness or deep peace as a result of this experience. Others who do not feel the breeze may feel heat, get a severe headache, or even faint – yet others may remain unaffected. In such cases, Mataji or her disciples will attempt to clear whatever they believe is obstructing the flow of energy, possibly with the help of a lighted candle.

'Realized souls' may also experience sensations (such as pain in a particular part of a particular finger) that alert them to trouble in others.[233] It is claimed, furthermore, that Mataji can pass on to her disciples the power to heal diseases, such as cancer, by 'vibration therapy'.[234] It is even said that the vibrations can affect organic matter and that agricultural yields have been far higher when irrigated by 'vibrated water'.[235]

Most Sahaja Yogis are aged between 20 and 45 and from middle-class backgrounds. In its early days, conversion was mainly through friendship networks; now new members are introduced by attending one of the weekly meetings where they can watch a video of Mataji and be given the opportunity of 'feeling the vibrations'. More established Sahaja Yogis will also attend a Sunday morning puja where there will be prayers and singing, the ritual washing of Shri Mataji's picture and some silent meditation.[236] After the puja, the participants will usually have a meal together. Fully committed Sahaja Yogis attend the international pujas over which Mataji herself presides. They may also apply for Mataji to choose a marriage partner with whom they will participate in a group wedding, possibly as the culmination of the annual 'India tour'.[237]

There is a fairly high turn-over rate at all levels of involvement. At present, there are at most 3,000 Sahaja Yogis outside India, with a further 1–2,000 in India who are fully committed and up to 100,000 having some loose association with the movement. In Britain there are about 2–400

232. *Introduction to Sahaja Yoga*, p. 6.
233. See, for example, Grégoire de Kalbermatten *The Advent*, Bombay: Life Eternal Trust Publishers, 1979, p. 33. See also Kakar (1984).
234. Ibid, p. 186.
235. Ibid.
236. For a discussion of what is involved in the meditation, see Yogi Mahajan *The Ascent*, New Delhi: Mahayog Centre, 1984, chapter XIII.
237. See, for example, Antoinette S. "A True Passage of India" *Nirmala Yoga*, vol. 4, no. 20 March-April 1984, pp. 40–1.

disciples, the minority of whom live in an ashram or 'co-operative' with other Sahaja Yogis. Members are encouraged to make donations on a regular basis towards Mataji's travel expenses and for international projects administered in the UK by 'The Life Eternal Trust'.[238] Mataji also receives expensive presents and substantial donations from her followers,[239] who have been exhorted to contribute to such ventures as the purchase of Shudy Camps Park House, near Cambridge[240] – although Mataji insists that it is not 'her' house.[241] *Life Eternal* and *Nirmala Yoga* are among periodicals that the movement has published in the past – and there have been plans to restart *Nirmala Yoga*, in a slightly different format.

In the initial stages (for, perhaps, the first year or so), Sahaja Yogis' lives may not be outwardly affected to any noticeable extent. As their commitment grows, however, they may find themselves becoming increasingly subject to the influence and wishes of Mataji, and increasingly cut off from former contacts. They may be separated from their partners and, perhaps, their children. Mataji has also expelled a number of disciples who, continuing to believe in her power, have found it difficult to give up the techniques that Mataji teaches, and to adjust to 'normal life'.

SATANISM See OCCULTISM, NEO-PAGANISM, WITCHCRAFT, SHAMANISM and SATANISM

SCIENTOLOGY See CHURCH OF SCIENTOLOGY

SHAMANISM See OCCULTISM, NEO-PAGANISM, WITCHCRAFT, SHAMANISM and SATANISM

SOKA GAKKAI See NICHIREN SHOSHU BUDDHISM

SRI CHINMOY[242]

> The goal of meditation is God-realisation, or *siddhi*, which means self-discovery in the highest sense of the term. At this time, one consciously realises his oneness with God.

---

238. Grégoire de Kalbermatten "Open letter to all the Sahaja Yoga Centres on the Financing of Sahaja Yoga Activities", *Nirmala Yoga*, vol. 4, no. 23, September–October 1984, pp. 45–6.
239. See "Protocol of Giving Money", n.d.
240. See "Foundations of the New Jerusalem – A Golden Opportunity", letter circulated to Sahaja Yogis of England, n.d.
241. See Puja-talk of Her Holiness Shri Mataji Nirmala Devi at Guru-Puja, 1987 in Shudy Camps Park House, 12 July 1987, p. 4 of transcript. See also *Cambridge Evening News*, 8 August 1986.
242. *Run and Become*: 42 Palmer Street, London SW1H OAB, UK.
The Sri Chinmoy Centre: P.O.Box 32433, Jamaica, NJ 11431, USA.
Further Reading: Annett (1976), pp. 58–60; Melton (1989), entry no. 1360.

> Meditation is not an escape. Meditation is the acceptance of life
> in its totality with a view to transforming it for the highest manifestation
> of the divine Truth here on earth.[243]
>   When I pray, I talk and God listens. When I meditate, God talks
> and I listen.[244]

Sri Chinmoy Kumar Ghose was born in Bengal, India, in 1931. At the
age of twelve he entered an ashram. In 1964, he went to the United
States "to offer his spiritual wealth at the feet of all truly aspiring
seekers".[245] He now conducts regular meditations at the United Nations
premises in New York, and is the leader of over 100 other meditation
centres around the world.

Sri Chinmoy's followers must meditate for fifteen minutes early in
the morning and in the evening. They are expected to contribute to work
at their local centre, but otherwise they continue with their normal lives.
Stress is laid on cleanliness and health. Disciples are expected to refrain
from indulging in drugs, alcohol, tobacco and meat. Physical fitness is
promoted through a number of organised athletic activities – weight-
lifting, swimming, tennis, cycling and track and field sports, *Run and
Become* being a popular motto of the movement. In 1989 a 'Peace Run'
was organised from Glasgow to Dover whence it would link with a
European Peace Run as part of a 31,000 mile global relay. Peace is also
a theme that recurs in other fields in which the movement takes an
interest – 'Peace Concerts' have been held around the world. Sri Chinmoy
has also had a prodigious output of paintings (it is claimed that within
one year he created over 100,000 works of art) and literature (he has
published over 700 books and written more than 30,000 poems – on
one occasion he is said to have completed 843 poems within 24 hours).[246]

Although Sri Chinmoy says that if one wants to take hundreds and
thousands of years to realise God, a spiritual Master is not necessary,[247]
it is clear that he takes his role as a spiritual Master seriously, and he
expects his disciples to take their commitment to his teachings seriously.

SUBUD[248]

> Subud is neither a kind of religion nor a teaching, but it is a spiritual
> experience awakened by the power of God leading to spiritual reality
> free from the influence of passions, heart and mind.[249]

---

243. Sri Chinmoy *Meditation*, leaflet published by the Sri Chinmoy Centre, Jamaica,
New York, n.d.

244. Sri Chinmoy, quoted in leaflet entitled *About Sri Chinmoy*, n.d.

245. Ibid.

246. *Sri Chinmoy: A Man of Peace*, leaflet published by the Sri Chinmoy Centre,
Jamaica, New York, n.d.

247. Sri Chinmoy *Meditation*, leaflet published by the Sri Chinmoy Centre, Jamaica,
New York, n.d.

248. *SUBUD BRITAIN*: Southdown House, Golden Cross, Hailsham, East Sussex,
UK.
USA contact:: c/o Chairman Locksin Thompson, 4 Pilot Road, Carmel, CA 93924, USA.
Further Reading: Annett (1976), pp. 78–81; Melton (1989), entry no. 1321.

249. Bapak Muhammad Subuh Sumohadiwidjojo *The Basis and Aim of Subud*, leaflet
published by Subud Publications International Ltd., Tunbridge Wells, 1969.

SUBUD [SUsila BUdhi Dharma] means to follow the Will of God with the help of the Divine Power that works both within us and without, by the way of surrendering oneself to the Will of Almighty God.[250]

Subud was founded in the 1930s in Indonesia by Muhammad Subuh Sumohadiwidjojo (1901–87), known to his followers as Bapak, who brought the movement to the West when he visited Britain in 1957.

The experience that lies at the heart of Subud is called the 'latihan', a practice that involves standing in a group. "Many people feel a vibration, most soon feel an impulse to move, to utter sounds, or to sing."[251] The latihan lasts for about half an hour and is practised twice a week with men and women being in separate rooms. Potential members usually have to wait three months before, with the assistance of 'helpers', they can do the latihan for the first time – an occasion known as 'being opened'.

Subud now claims about 10,000 members in over 70 countries, over a thousand being in the UK. Several members of the movement work in about 200 different businesses world-wide which are said to generate a turnover of $34,000,000 p.a., a proportion of their profits being donated to Subud.[252]

SUMMIT LIGHTHOUSE[253]

Today as never before people are asking questions and demanding answers: "Who am I? Why was I born? Where am I going in time and space? and What am I doing on earth?" . . . Once again God has sent his own sons and daughters, the ascended masters, to answer the calls of his children wandering in the twentieth century. He has sent his emissaries to speak to them out of that pillar of sacred fire, the I AM THAT I AM, and to lead them to the Promised Land of their own God consciousness.[254]

Mark and Elizabeth Prophet, trained by [the Ascended Master] El Morya, are dedicated servants of God's will appointed in these "last days" to proclaim the Word of the Lord. Since his ascension in 1973, Mark Prophet fulfills his role from 'above' as the Ascended Master Lanello, while Elizabeth continues as God's messenger to the people here 'below'.[255]

---

250. Harris Smart *Subud in the World*, leaflet distributed by Subud Publications International, 1985.

251. *A Brief Introduction to SUBUD*, leaflet distributed by Subud, n.d.

252. Harris Smart *Subud in the World*, leaflet distributed by Subud Publications International, 1985.

253. *Summit Lighthouse* 4 Herald's Place, Gilbert Rd., London. SE11 4NP.
Church Universal and Triumphant: Box A, Livingston, MT 59047, USA.
Further Reading: Melton (1986), pp. 135–40; Melton (1989), entry no. 1150; Jim Robbins "A Question of Good Neighbours", *The Boston Globe Magazine*, 9 August 1987.

254. *What is an Ascended Master Retreat?*, leaflet published by Church Universal and Triumphant, Malibu, 1979.

255. *A Pearl of Wisdom for You*, leaflet published by Church Universal and Triumphant, Malibu, 1978.

Mark L. Prophet (1918–1973) founded the Summit Lighthouse in Washington D.C. in 1958. Later he was to marry Elizabeth Clare Wulf (1940–), who took over as spiritual leader of the movement on Mark's death, incorporating it in 1974 as the Church Universal and Triumphant (CUT), and who is now known to her followers as Guru Ma.

Those who have attended a conference, lasting 4 days or so, during which they will have heard lectures and learned how to 'decree' (a kind of chanting that members are expected to practise regularly, sometimes for hours on end), will be invited to become a member of the Keepers of the Flame Fraternity, an order which, it is said, was established by the Ascended Master Saint Germain in 1962. They may then receive tuition for a series of 3-month quarters at the Summit University (established in 1971) – which could cost them around $2,100 for tuition, room and board. Communicants (full members) have to be members of the Fraternity, to subscribe to the CUT's 'Tenets', to be formally baptised, to abstain from drugs, alcohol and tobacco, and to tithe 10% of their income. Some communicants live in communities; the movement has sold its Californian estate, 'Camelot', and now owns the 33,000-acre Royal Teton Ranch, near Yellowstone Park, in Montana. Montessori International is a private school for children of fraternity members.

It is CUT policy not to release membership figures, but there must be several thousand Keepers of the Flame world wide: the annual Summer Conference at the Royal Teton Ranch is attended by around 5,000 Keepers, and there are perhaps somewhere between 50 and 150 Keepers in the UK. The Summit University Press has published more than 50 books as well as having an extensive library of cassette and video recordings. It distributes *Pearls of Wisdom*, a publication that conveys the Masters' weekly letters to anyone who is interested.

The movement expresses strong support for family life and for the defence of the United States; it has spoken out against abortion, communism and rock music. Critics, including ex-members, accuse the movement of brainwashing techniques, encouraging divorce, exploiting its members and getting huge sums of money from them – and of its practices constituting necromancy. At the time of writing, the movement is appealing against an award of more than $1,500,000 that was made to an ex-member in 1986.

TEMPLE OV PSYCHICK YOUTH (TOPY)[256]

> Thee methods ov thee Temple are designed to provoke and promote
> psychic growth; to increase thee scope ov what is possible; to bring
> thee individual into direct contact with thee magickal Self.[257]

---

256. *Address:* BM: T.O.P.Y., London WC1N 3XX, UK.
T.O.P.Y.U.S.: P.O.Box 18223, Denver, CO 80218, USA.
257. *World in Action*, News Bulletin, T.O.P.Y.U.K., 1988.

Thee Temple ov Psychick Youth's perception ov life and its sexuality is limitless, it cannot be fixed into any gender, religion, or any other grouping but its own.

Nothing is sacred in thee Temple, nothing is disregarded, ignored or ridiculed, only questioned, never doubted.[258]

TOPY came into existence in 1981, largely due to the efforts of the pop musician, Genesis P Orridge, who had started his own group, 'Psychic TV', around the same time. It has been through the music of Psychic TV (with numbers such as "A Message from the Temple") that many of the 'Collaborators' first came to hear about the movement. By February 1988 TOPY reported having established a network of 13 'Access Points' internationally – 9 of these were in England, two in the USA, one in Germany and one in Holland.[259] It has been estimated that several hundred people (mostly caucasians in their late teens or early twenties) subscribe to the Temple Bulletin which is published about twice a year at £5 p.a.

The movement's philosophy shows the influence of a number of thinkers and traditions, including the works of Aleister Crowley. The fundamental belief seems to be that individuals should take it upon themselves to accept responsibility for control of their own lives. It is stressed that one should not rely merely on outside sources of information (such as books and television) in order to understand things in 'the correct way'; we have to investigate ourselves by listening to our doubts, and by engaging in a number of techniques, including 'sex magick', if we are to realise our true Self. While Collaborators will try to induce 'altered states' through music, dancing or strobe lights, they are against the use of drugs.

TRANSCENDENTAL MEDITATION (TM)[260]

Transcendental Meditation is a technique for deep relaxation and revitalization which develops the inner potential of energy and intelligence that form the basis of all success in life. TM is practised for twenty minutes morning and evening whilst sitting comfortably in a chair with the eyes closed ... [TM] is practised by people of every age, education culture and religion. TM requires no belief or any great commitment. More than three million people all over the world practise TM.[261]

Maharishi Mahesh Yogi (1911–) graduated in physics from Allahabad University in 1940 before studying for thirteen years with his spiritual

---

258. *True Will, Intuition, and Survival: Chains ov thee mind*, Thee Temple Ov Psychic Youth booklet, 1988.

259. *News Bulletin*, 1988.

260. *Central Office*: Mentmore Towers, Mentmore, Nr. Leighton Buzzard, Beds, LU7 OQH, UK.
World Plan Executive Council: 17310 Sunset Boulevard, Pacific Palisades, CA 90272, USA.
Further Reading: Annett (1976), pp. 62–4; Melton (1986), pp. 187–192.

261. *Corporate Development Programme: An Introduction to Transcendental Meditation*, leaflet distributed by Maharishi Corporate Development International, London, n.d.

master, Guru Dev (1869–1953), who had rediscovered, from Hindu Scriptures, the technique that is known as transcendental meditation. In 1958 Maharishi brought TM to the West.

To be taught the basic technique, which involves concentration on a mantra, costs £165. This covers an introductory presentation, an hour-long personal instruction and three further instruction meetings that last one and a half hours. Those who go on to the more advanced TM-Sidhi course pay about £1,200 for a weekend course, two weeks of evening courses and, later, a two-week course at one of the movement's Academies, when they can be taught the widely publicised levitation or 'flying' technique during which the person, cross-legged, hops about and, if successful, manages to jump onto a pile of mattresses.

The movement produces an abundance of literature describing both the achievements of TM and Vedic Science "the science of life according to pure knowledge", and the movement's plans for implementing such ambitious projects as world peace, the reduction of world poverty and the achievement of perfect health.[262] Associated with TM are numerous other organisations promoting various ventures. Maharishi Corporate Development International provides not only courses for business executives, but also a number of in-company programmes. In the United States, Maharishi International University, founded in 1971, offers over a thousand students undergraduate, master's and doctoral programmes.

As described in *Appendix II*, most meditators continue with 'ordinary lives'. There have, however, been negative reports in the media about the dependency that some people are said to develop on either the techniques or the movement itself. Other reports have questioned some of the claims that scientists have made about the efficacy of the techniques.[263]

TRANSPERSONAL PSYCHOLOGY See HUMAN POTENTIAL MOVEMENT

UNIFICATION CHURCH[264]

The Holy Spirit Association for the Unification of World Christianity . . . was founded . . . to end the suffering of God and humanity.

262. See, for example, Jim Anderson and Bill Stevens *Feel Great with TM! An Introduction to Transcendental Meditation*, Mentmore: Golden Arrow Publications, 1988; David W. Orme-Johnson and John T. Farrow (eds) *Scientific Research on the Transcendental Meditation Program: Collected Papers*, West Germany: Maharishi European Research University Press, 1977, 2nd edition; *Scientific Research on The Maharishi Technology of the Unified Field: The Transcendental Meditation and TM-Sidhi Program*, Fairfield IA: Maharishi International University, 1987.

263. R. D. Scott *Transcendental Misconceptions*, San Diego: Beta Books, 1978; *Des Moines Sunday Register*, 14 December 1986; *Religious Freedom Reporter* July/August 1987, pp. 577–8, Report of *Kropinski v. World Plan Executive Council, United States*, No. 85-2848 (D.D.C., Jan 13, 1987.)

264. *Unification Church of Great Britain*: 43/44 Lancaster Gate, London W2 3NA, UK. *Holy Spirit Association for the Unification of World Christianity*: 4 West 43rd Street, New York, NY 10036.
Further Reading: Barker (1984); David Bromley and Anson D. Shupe *"Moonies" in America: Cult, Church, and Crusade*, Beverly Hills & London: Sage, 1979; John Lofland *Doomsday Cult: A Study of Conversion, Proselytization, and Maintenance of Faith*, New York: Irvington, enlarged edition, 1977; Williams, 1987.

Rev. Sun Myung Moon has said there are three great headaches for God in this age. First is the attack on moral virtue in our younger generation and growing individual and national self-centeredness evident in the world. Second is the decline of Christianity and the lack of unity and understanding among the world's religions. Third is the growth of God-denying and materialistic ideologies. . .

Unification Church members worldwide work tirelessly to comfort the suffering heart of God by striving to end the enduring pain of humanity. . . . The original goal of uniting Christianity, and eventually all people under God as the Heavenly Parent of humankind, is still the fundamental purpose of the Unification Church.[265]

In 1954 the Holy Spirit Association for the Unification of World Christianity was founded in Korea by the Reverend Sun Myung Moon (1920–). The first missionaries were sent out in the late 1950s, but it was not until Moon moved to the United States in the early 1970s that the movement started to become visible in the West.

The main tenets of Unification theology are to be found in the *Divine Principle*,[266] which offers a special interpretation of the Old and New Testaments with further revelations from Moon, believed by his followers to be the Messiah who can lead the way in establishing the Kingdom of Heaven on earth. It is believed that God's victory over Satan requires the defeat of atheistic communism.

Members, popularly known as 'Moonies', have typically joined the movement in their twenties and are disproportionately from middle-class backgrounds. Full-time members have usually spent some years 'fundraising' and 'witnessing' (that is, collecting money and introducing new members to the movement). In recent years it has become increasingly common for members to work in one of the movement's businesses, or in a non-Unification job, especially after they have been 'Blessed' in a mass wedding ceremony to a partner suggested to them by Moon. Sexual relationships are forbidden before, and for some time after, marriage.

Among the businesses and the activities associated with the movement are various publishing enterprises (including *Paragon Press* and *The Washington Times*), fishing, machine tool and ginseng businesses. The movement has a Theological Seminary in New York State, where it owns a considerable amount of real estate, including the New Yorker Hotel in Manhattan. The movement sponsors a large number of conferences for journalists, theologians, clergy, academics, politicians, military personnel and others who it believes can contribute to the task of

---

265. *New Vision for World Peace: Reverend Sun Myung Moon*, Holy Spirit Association for the Unification of World Christianity, 1988, p. 3.

266. Chung Hwan Kwak *Outline of The Principle: Level 4*, New York: Holy Spirit Association for the Unification of World Christianity, 1980.

establishing a God-centred world. There have been several fierce disputes over the propriety of attendance at such conferences.[267]

The Unification Church is one of the most controversial of the NRMs in the West. In Britain it lost a suit for libel against the *Daily Mail*, which had published an article accusing it of brainwashing its members and breaking up families. The jury asked that the movement's charitable status should be removed, but after several years' investigation by the Attorney General, this proposal was dropped. In the United States, the Unification Church has been involved in numerous court cases both as defendant and as plaintiff (mainly in deprogramming cases). Moon himself has been in prison on a number of occasions, most recently in the United States for a conviction of tax evasion.

Despite the frequent allegations of its powers of control over its members, the movement has a high turn-over rate and it has never succeeded in having more than about 10,000 full-time members in the West.

WITCHCRAFT See OCCULTISM, NEO-PAGANISM, WITCHCRAFT, SHAMANISM and SATANISM

---

267. See, for example, the special issue of *Sociological Analysis*, vol. 44, no. 3, Fall 1983.

Annotated Bibliography

I T IS DIFFICULT to select a satisfactory bibliography on this controversial subject. This list is confined to books and official Reports. Articles in journals and newspaper reports that are relevant to the text appear in the notes. Books that are written primarily to promote the views and teachings of NRMs are not included. A few of the books are manifestly anti-cult in nature. Although several of the books refer specifically to American society, the scholarship is of value in understanding the movements in Britain and other Western cultures.

★ Books marked with an asterisk have been selected as possible introductions to the subject, but it should not be assumed that the inclusion of these or of any of the other books in this bibliography implies agreement with views expressed in the books.

Annett, Stephen (1976) *The Many Ways of Being: A Guide to Spiritual Groups and Growth Centres in Britain*, London: Abacus. [Out of print, but still in some libraries; useful descriptions of about 150 assorted groups, provided mainly by the groups themselves.]

Bainbridge, William Sims (1978) *Satan's Power: Ethnography of a Deviant Psychotherapy Cult*, Berkeley: University of California Press. [Analysis of a satanic movement, The Process Church of the Final Judgment (which Bainbridge calls The Power), that was founded by two defectors from Scientology in London in 1963.]

Barker, Eileen (ed.) (1982) *New Religious Movements: A Perspective for Understanding Society*, New York & Toronto: Edwin Mellen Press. [Collection of papers by international group of scholars on society and the NRMs; 25-page glossary giving details of NRMs and older sects.]

Barker, Eileen (ed.) (1983) *Of Gods and Men: New Religious Movements in the West*, Macon GA: Mercer University Press. [Collection of 18 papers on NRMs, the Religious Right in the US and the 'anti-cult movement'.]

*Barker, Eileen (1984) *The Making of a Moonie: Brainwashing or Choice?* Oxford, Blackwell. [Investigation of the 'brainwashing' thesis; description of Unification recruitment methods, their basic beliefs and history.]

*Beckford, James (1985) *Cult Controversies: The Societal Response to the New Religious Movements*, London & New York: Tavistock. [Scholarly analysis of the NRMs and 'anti-cult movement', concentrating mainly, but not exclusively, on the UK]

Bowen, David (1988) *The Sathya Sai Baba Community in Bradford: Its Origin and Development, Religious Beliefs and Practices*, Department of Theology and Religious Studies, University of Leeds: Community Religions Project. [Monograph based on a Ph.D. involving intensive field work concerning followers in Britain of the popular Indian guru who performs 'miracles'.]

*Brockway, Allan R. and J. Paul Rajashekar (eds) (1987) *New Religious Movements and the Churches*, Geneva: World Council of Churches Publications. [Papers (and responses) given by theologians, academics and anti-cultists at a 1986 WCC consultation. Also included are some questions and recommendations concerning the pastoral challenge of the NRMs.]

Bromley, David G. (ed.) (1988) *Falling from the Faith: Causes and consequences of Religious Apostasy*, Beverly Hills and London: Sage. [Collection of essays about people who leave both mainstream religions and NRMs.].

*Bromley, David G. and Anson D. Shupe (1981) *Strange Gods: The Great American Cult Scare*, Boston: Beacon. [General introduction by academics writing in a popular style.]

Bromley, David G. and James T. Richardson (eds) (1983) *The Brainwashing/ Deprogramming Controversy: Sociological, Psychological, Legal and Historical Perspectives*, New York and Toronto: Edwin Mellen Press. [Collection of essays by scholars covering the controversy from a number of different perspectives.]

Burrell, Maurice C. (1981) *The Challenge of the Cults*, Leicester: Inter-Varsity Press. [An Anglican Canon compares the beliefs of seven NRMs with evangelical Christian beliefs.]

Cashmore, Ernest Ellis (1983) *Rastaman: The Rastafarian Movement in England*, London: Unwin. [Updated edition of a detailed study, originally carried out in the late 1970s.]

Choquette, Diane (1985) *New Religious Movements in the United States and Canada: A Critical Assessment and Annotated Bibliography*, Westport CT & London: Greenwood. [Useful information about reference works, historical, sociological, anthropological, psychological, psychiatric, theological, religious and legal studies as well as personal accounts and popular studies of NRMs.]

Clarke, Peter (ed.) (1987) *The New Evangelists: Recruitment, Methods and Aims of New Religious Movements*, London: Ethnographica. [Essays on evangelism by e.g. Friends of the Western Buddhist Order, *est*, Exegesis, Sai Baba, Sekai Kyusei Kyo, and the Unification Church.]

Conway, Flo and Jim Siegelman (1978) *Snapping: America's Epidemic of Sudden Personality Change*, Philadelphia & New York: J. B. Lippincott. [Book that argues that "Everyone, without exception, is susceptible to snapping" – that is, "sudden, drastic alteration of personality in all its many forms".]

Davis, Deborah (1984) *The Children of God*, Basingstoke: Marshalls. [Unsavoury account of this off-shoot of the Jesus movement in America, written by the daughter of its leader, David 'Moses' Berg.]

Donovan, Peter (ed.) (1985) *Beliefs and Practices in New Zealand: A Directory*, 2nd edition, Palmerston North NZ: Religious Studies Department of Massey University (1st edition 1980). [Brief details provided by well over 100 different religions (including many NRMs) about their beliefs, moral rules, rituals, organisation etc. The usefulness of this 283-page collection extends well beyond the shores of New Zealand.]

Downton, James V. (1979) *Sacred Journies: The Conversion of Young Americans to Divine Light Mission*, New York: Columbia University Press. [Analysis of the Divine Light Mission by a sociologist who interviewed 20 'premies', then did a follow-up study with further interviews or questionnaire.]

Dyson, Anthony and Eileen Barker (eds) (1988) *Sects and New Religious Movements*, Manchester: The Bulletin of the John Rylands University Library of Manchester. [Collection of 36 essays on contemporary NRMs and 'old' NRMs.]

Enroth, Ronald (1977) *Youth, Brainwashing, and the Extremist Cults*, Grand Rapids: Zondervan. [Seven case histories are recorded by a Christian sociologist who sees the cults as perversions of Satan, and concludes that they practise brainwashing and that skilled deprogramming can be justified.]

Fitzgerald, Frances (1986) *Cities on a Hill*, New York & London: Simon & Schuster. [The chapter on Rajneeshpuram gives a journalist's detailed account of the happenings in Oregon, leading up to Bhagwan's hasty departure from the U.S. and Sheela's eventual imprisonment.]

★Galanter, Marc (1989) *Cults: Faith, Healing and Coercion*, Oxford University Press. [Useful analysis of NRMs by an American psychiatrist.]

Glock, Charles Y. and Robert N. Bellah (eds) (1976) *The New Religious Consciousness*, Berkeley, Los Angeles & London: University of California Press. [Reports resulting from a research project to gather information about the 'new religious consciousness' in the San Francisco Area in the early 1970s. Includes a general survey, ethnographic studies, and theoretical chapters.]

Hall, John H. (1987) *Gone from the Promised Land: Jonestown in American Cultural History*, New Brunswick, NJ: Transaction. [Monograph describing and analysing the history, ideology, organisation and final tragedy of the People's Temple.]

Hassan, Steven (1990) *Combatting Cult Mind Control*, Wellingborough: Aquarian Press. [Ex-Moonie describes his work as an 'exit counsellor'.]

Hill, Daniel G. (1980) *Study of Mind Development Groups, Sects and Cults in Ontario*, Toronto, Ontario. [Study for the Ontario Government which concluded that "no public inquiry be held regarding the issues arising out of the activities of cults, sects, mind development groups, new religions or deprogrammers". (p. 596)].

Hounam, Peter and Andrew Hogg (1984) *Secret Cult*, Tring: Albatross. [Investigative journalists from London's evening newspaper, *The Standard*, carry out an exposé of the School of Economic Science.]

Kakar, Sudhir (1984) *Shamans, Mystics and Doctors: A Psychological Inquiry into India and Its Healing Traditions*, London: Unwin. [Nine different approaches to healing, including Sahaja Yoga, described and analysed so that their 'Easternness' is made understandable to the Westerner.]

*Levine, Saul (1984) *Radical Departures: Desperate Detours to Growing Up*, San Diego: Harcourt Brace Jovanovich. [Set of case studies written by a medical doctor who has specialised in families with a member in an NRM.]

Lewis, James R. (n.d.) *Apostates and the Legitimation of Repression: Some Historical and Empirical Perspectives on the 'Cult' Controversy*, Santa Barbara: The Institute for the Study of American Religion. [Analysis of a circular practice in which anti-cultists instil negative attitudes towards their movements into ex-members and then use the ex-members' testimonies as proof of the movements' malevolence.]

Lifton, Robert J. (1961) *Thought Reform: A Psychiatric Study of "Brainwashing" in China*, London: Gollancz. [Study of both Westerners and Chinese intellectuals who had been subjected to 'thought reform' in China. Chapter 22 is frequently referred to by those who believe that NRMs use brainwashing techniques.]

Martin, Bernice (1981) *A Sociology of Contemporary Cultural Change*, Oxford: Blackwell. [A perceptive account of the British youth culture within which NRMs have emerged.]

Martin, Walter (1985) *The Kingdom of the Cults* [Revised edition], Minneapolis: Bethany House. [The cults that the author (an American, known as 'The Bible Answer Man') examines, from his Biblical perspective, include other traditional faiths and some older sects.]

McGuire, Meredith B. and Debra Kantor (1989) *Ritual Healing in Suburban America*, New Brunswick: Rutgers University Press. [Detailed research into healing groups and analysis of how these function to provide meaning for the individual and to provide a holistic response to the fragmentary lives of contemporary middle-class Americans.]

*Melton, J. Gordon (1986) *Encyclopedic Handbook of Cults in America*, New York & London: Garland. [Useful reference book with about five pages per NRM, including bibliography.]

*Melton, J. Gordon and Robert Moore (1982) *The Cult Experience: Responding to the New Religious Pluralism*, New York: Pilgrim Press. [Overview of the movements with a section on how to react to a child becoming a member of an NRM.]

Melton, J. Gordon (1989) *The Encyclopedia of American Religions*, 3rd edition, Detroit: Gale. [The most comprehensive collection of information available about religious groups in North America, including over 750 'nonconventional' groups.]

Milne, Hugh (1986) *Bhagwan: The God that Failed*, London: Caliban. [Bhagwan Rajneesh's former bodyguard gives a lurid account of the goings on in Poona and Oregon.]

Mosatche, Harriet (1983) *Searching: Practices and Beliefs of the Religious Cults and Human Potential Groups*, New York: Straven Educational Press. [Accounts giving introductory flavour of nine NRMs, including the Unification Church, Hare Krishna, Scientology and *est*.]

Naipaul, Shiva (1980) *Black and White*, London: Hamish Hamilton. [The prize-winning novelist's disturbing account of the People's Temple.]

Patrick, Ted (with Tom Dulack) (1976) *Let Our Children Go!* New York: Dutton; page numbers in text refer to Ballantine Books 1977 edition. [The 'Father of Deprogramming' writes about the unpleasant methods he has employed to 'save people from the cults'.]

Rhinehart, Luke (1976) *The Book of est*, New York: Holt, Rinehart and Winston. [Gives details of the *est* seminar which are helpful for understanding the genre of several 'self-religions'.]

Richardson, James T. (ed.) (1988) *Money and Power in the New Religions*, Lewiston, Queenston & Lampeter: Edwin Mellen Press. [Collection of essays about how a number of different NRMs collect and use money.]

Richardson, James T., Joel Best and David Bromley (eds) (1991) *The Satanism Scare*, New York: Aldine de Gruyter. [Collection of essays, mainly by American scholars who explore and find little factual evidence for the growth of Satanism.]

Robbins, Thomas and Dick Anthony (eds) (1990) *In Gods We Trust: New Patterns of Religious Pluralism in America*, 2nd edition, New Brunswick & London: Transaction. [Wide-ranging collection of essays by American scholars, including a section on mainstream traditions.]

*Robbins, Thomas (1988) *Cults, Converts and Charisma: The Sociology of New Religious Movements*, Special edition of *Current Sociology*, vol. 36, no. 1, London and Beverly Hills: Sage. [Detailed and perceptive analysis, commentary and review of the literature by an American scholar who has specialised in the sociology of NRMs for over twenty years.]

Rochford, E. Burke (1985) *Hare Krishna in America*, New Brunswick: Rutgers. [Informative analysis of an NRM resulting from research for a Ph.D.]

Rosen, Richard D. (1975) *Psychobabble: Fast Talk and Quick Cure in the Era of Feeling*, London: Wildwood House. [A scathing analysis of the concepts employed by New Age therapies and their potentially harmful effects.]

★Ross, Joan Carol and Michael D. Langone (1988) *Cults: What Parents Should Know, A practical guide to help parents with children in destructive groups*, Weston MA: The American Family Foundation. [While some of its generalisations might be questioned, *Cults* contains much sound advice that could help parents to encourage their child to re-evaluate his or her involvement in an NRM.]

Roszak, Theodore (1976) *Unfinished Animal: The Aquarian Frontier and the Evolution of Consciousness*, London: Faber. [An early account, with a decidedly Californian flavour, of movements searching for a new consciousness.]

Saliba, John A. (1987) *Psychiatry and the Cults: An Annotated Bibliography*, New York: Garland.

Saliba, John A. (1990) *Social Science and the Cults: An Annotated Bibliography*, New York and London: Garland. [Invaluable resource with 2219 entries.]

Savage, Peter (Chairman) (1980) *Christian Witness to New Religious Movements*, Thailand Report No. 11, Wheaton IL: Lausanne Committee for World Evangelization. [Evangelical Christians' "Mini-Consultation on Reaching Mystics and Cultists" grapples with the problem of distinguishing between "that which is truly of the Spirit of God and that which is satanic".]

Shupe, Anson D. and David G. Bromley (1980) *The New Vigilantes: Anti-Cultists and the New Religions*, Beverly Hills: Sage. [Two sociologists describe the anti-cult network in America.]

Stark, Rodney and William Sims Bainbridge (1985) *The Future of Religion: Secularization, Revival and Cult Formation*, Berkeley: University of California Press. [Essays containing original data and theories about sects and cults, which the authors carefully distinguish.]

Streiker, Lowell D. (1978) *The Cults are Coming!* Nashville: Abingdon. [General introduction, critique and advice from executive director of a Mental Health Association in California.]

Tipton, Steven M. (1984) *Getting Saved from the Sixties: Moral Meaning in Conversion and Cultural Change*, Berkeley, Los Angeles & London: University of California Press. [Analysing some changes that young people who were part of the counterculture have undergone, an American sociologist looks at a Pentecostal Christian Fellowship, a Zen Buddhist meditation centre and *est*.]

Van Zandt, David (1991) *Living in the Children of God*, Princeton, N.J:
   Princeton University Press. [First-hand account of a Ph.D. student
   who lived with the Children of God/Family of Love in England and
   the Netherlands in the 1970s.]

Vivien, Alain (1985) *Les Sectes en France: Expression de la Liberté morale ou
   Facteurs de Manipulations?* Paris: La Documentation Française. [Report
   commissioned in 1982 by Pierre Mauroy, the then Prime Minister
   of France. The report's proposals include the appointment of a top
   civil servant to oversee matters connected with the NRMs and that
   the law as it stands should be enforced when necessary by the proper
   authorities.]

Walker, Andrew (1988) *Restoring the Kingdom: The Radical Christianity of
   the House Church Movement* London, Sydney, Auckland & Toronto:
   Hodder and Stoughton. [Updated 2nd edition of informative analysis,
   by a Christian academic, of 'Restorationism' – the House Church
   Movement in Britain.]

Wallis, Roy (1976) *The Road to Total Freedom: A Sociological Analysis of
   Scientology*, London: Heinemann. [Now somewhat out of date, but
   still worth reading, scholarly analysis of Dianetics and its transformation into the Church of Scientology.]

*Wallis, Roy (1983) *The Elementary Forms of the New Religious Life*, London:
   Routledge & Kegan Paul. [Analytical comparison of types of NRMs
   by a British academic.]

Westley, Frances (1983) *The Complex Forms of the Religious Life*, Chico,
   CA: Scholars. [Perceptive study of the 'cult of man' groups (including
   Arica, *est*, Psychosynthesis, Scientology and Silva Mind Control) and
   other NRMs in Canada.]

Williams, Jacqui (with David Porter) (1987) *The Locust Years: Four Years
   with the Moonies*, London: Hodder and Stoughton. [A readable account
   of a British girl's joining the Unification Church in California, and
   her life in the movement until she returned to England and decided
   that the local Baptist church could offer her something more.]

Wilson, Bryan (1970) *Religious Sects: A Sociological Study*, London: Weiden-
   feld and Nicolson. [Classic work on the different types of sects that
   developed before the present wave of NRMs. Worth reading for a
   comparative perspective.]

Wilson, Bryan (ed.) (1981) *The Social Impact of New Religious Movements*,
   New York: Rose of Sharon Press. [Collection of papers, most of
   which were written for a Unification conference, by sociologists of
   religion covering various social aspects concerning NRMs.]

*Wilson, Bryan (1982) *Religion in Sociological Perspective*, Oxford University
   Press. [Chapters 4 & 5 describe many of the characteristics of sects
   and NRMs, and compare them to more traditional religions.]

Witteveen, T. (1984) "Epilogue and Summary" *Overheid en nieuwe religeuze
   bewegingen* The Hague: Tweede Kamer, vergaderjaar 1983–1984,

16635, nr. 4. pp. 314–318. [Study commissioned by the Dutch Government into NRMs, which concluded that no action should be taken to restrain the activities of the NRMs *per se.*]

Wright, Stuart A. (1987) *Leaving Cults: The Dynamics of Defection*, Washington DC: Society for the Scientific Study of Religion Monograph Series, No. 7. [Report of detailed research into voluntary defection from NRMs and 'relocation' into society.]

Zaretsky, Irving I. and Mark P. Leone (eds) (1974) *Religious Movements in Contemporary America*, Princeton: Princeton University Press. [One of the earlier, but still useful, collections including essays on movements such as ISKCON, Meher Baba, Satanism, Scientology and modern Witchcraft.]

Index

Printed in the United Kingdom for HMSO
Dd295758 5/92 C15 G531 10170